(*continued from front flap*)

here of the 1,000 *most used* popular songs from the 1890's into the 1950's.

Deac's father died in 1892. The boy's childhood was spent on a remote back-woods farm in Oakdale, Shelby County, Missouri where he attended a one-room school. He was already playing guitar in the railroad town of Shelbina where he worked at a boarding house while attending high school, graduating in 1908. Though he attended Iowa State University briefly (and got his nickname there) he says that most of his education came "from omniverous reading, observation and association with better educated persons".

After marriage to Helen Cramer in 1915 he joined a Chicago advertising agency, then was in New England for about ten years. In Cleveland in 1934 he opened Deac Martin Unique Services, doing editorial, trade and public relations work.

In 1938 he joined the Society for the Preservation and Encouragement of Barber Shop Quartet Singing in America (SPEBSQSA) in its first year, and has been active in almost all phases internationally. He founded the Cleveland Chapter January 31, 1940.

He has written many articles about music in *Music Journal, Esquire,* and elsewhere, has had a column, "Way I See It" in the Harmonizer since 1943 and is the author of several books including HANDBOOK FOR ADELINE ADDICTS, KEEP AMERICA SINGING, and FROM SCHOOL TO INSTITUTE. He has played piano, guitar and mandolin for about 60 years.

He still delights in singing bass harmony.

Deac Martin's

Book of Musical Americana

Deac Martin's Book of Musical Americana

By

Deac (C. T.) Martin

Prentice-Hall, Inc., Englewood Cliffs, New Jersey

Design by Janet Anderson

Deac Martin's Book of Musical Americana
by Deac (C. T.) Martin

ISBN 0-13-197392-4

Library of Congress Catalog Card Number: 70-111052
Printed in the United States of America • T
Prentice-Hall International, Inc., London
Prentice-Hall of Australia, Pty. Ltd., Sydney
Prentice-Hall of Canada, Ltd., Toronto
Prentice-Hall of India Private Ltd., New Delhi
Prentice-Hall of Japan, Inc., Tokyo

To Helen (Cramer) Martin who,

for more than fifty years,

never protested—

well, hardly ever

before three o'clock

in the morning

Contents

Deac Martin's

Book of Musical Americana

PART ONE

Country Music Old-Style

Websterian Confusions

A musical amateur is one whose interest and participation in music is prompted primarily by his love for music and by no other ulterior consideration.

Amateurs have little by little been discouraged and cowed into a condition of substantial passivity. An eminent musician, for whose musical judgment I have otherwise the most profound respect, expressed in public the opinion that the only proper role for amateurs in music is that of listeners.

A beautiful voice or elaborate voice culture is no more necessary for the most intense pleasure and satisfaction from group singing than is the eloquence and training of an orator essential for delightful conversation.

Why cannot amateurs regard and enjoy their music in the same simple and straightforward way that they do golf, or bridge, or interesting books, or looking for birds, or the thousand and one other things which we do every day with no thought at all of attempting to show off or to compete with the expert? *

The notes on music here stem from an avocation. They are set down by a minimal musician who functions a bit above the level of "Chopsticks" but who shies away from Chopin, a musician who has participated in music's variety by "ear" so often that both ears should be worn down to nubbins. They are the notes of an undistinguished member of the midnight crew who makes music for his own enjoyment and the pleasure of such others as enjoy group participation. Not surprisingly, therefore, these pages will not aspire to affording nutrition for those who take serious music seriously.

The jottings here include speculations as well as conclusions about phenomena observed and lore absorbed in a lifetime of homemade and other musical experiences. The experiences have ranged from Maine's towering Mt. Katahdin to peaks high in the residential owe-zone of the San Francisco Bay Area with stopovers at the countless way stations between.

Though great musical satisfactions have colored my life, it has been so far removed from vocational music that I am seldom sure whether to write C sharp or D flat when setting down simple harmony the way I want to hear it. That, I hope, clears the commentator from any pretense of musicianship beyond the minimal. However, it does not indicate a lack of ambition. Before circus parades

* From an address to the Music Educators' Conference, 1935, by the late Henry S. Drinker, Jr. (1880–1965).

were frowned upon by city traffic departments, there were times when I aspired to doing big things in music on a steam calliope. But housing and firing that mammoth instrument presented problems that I have not been able to resolve.

Nowadays there is much disagreement as to what is music. To some no sound is music unless the volume control on the record player or a combo's sound system is turned up to the limits. To others, a composition isn't music unless it lies within the sphere of the classics. Branded as "classical," a piece is music whether the auditor likes the sound of it or not, and to those of that persuasion, the festering slums of "popular" music stretch outside that boundary. Happily, not all professional musicians, teachers, and music critics have arrived at that conclusion.

The term "popular," as applied to music written with the hope of widespread popularity, has never been the right term, but change is unlikely after generations of Popular and Classical. The late composer-conductor Kurt Weil said that there is no light (popular) or serious (classical) music, just good and bad. Without introducing supporting evidence, it is safe to surmise that not more than one "popular" composition among a thousand published has attained even modest popularity, and only one out of thousands has stood the true test of musical worth and popularity, has gained acceptance and been requested over generations, as, for instance, Stephen Foster's songs have been accepted and requested. Much of our allegedly popular music is rubbish, but that judgment applies equally to much serious music, notwithstanding the composer's reputation or a music critic's approval voiced with the authority of a Moses receiving the Ten Commandments firsthand from Above, or its proclivity for "in" conversation over cocktails.

Though it may appear that we the people feel that last month's hit song is as expendable as a five-year-old car, this country has produced songs in every generation that endure because of a tune or words or a lucky combination of both. (As when we order a hot dog and include the bun, unspoken, we expect most of our "popular" music to include lyrics.) Mere words have carried songs to quick and lasting popularity, particularly words expressing romantic sentiments ("I Love You Truly") or words related to an upsurge of national feeling ("Over There," written on the three-note theme of a military bugle call, rode the crest of the emotional wave that washed us into World War I).

Lyrically, a few songs have attained short-lived popularity because of tricky words. Among them: "C-o-n-s-t-a-n-t-i-n-o-p-l-e," "Yaddie Kaddie Kiddie Kaddie Koo," "The Music Goes 'Round and 'Round," "Zizzie Ze Zum Zum," "Mairzy Doats," "Ja Da," "Rose O'Day," "A-tisket, A-tasket," "Zip-a-dee-doo-dah," "Two to Duluth," "Rum-tum Tiddle," and "The Hutsut Song." On the other hand, simple run-of-the-mine words can so aptly express a popular sentiment that a song may live through generations because of them. The melody to which it is wed need be no more than pleasing to the ear of the multitude and within the compass of the average voice.

It is comforting to have those old reliables when, at times, it seems that the nation has dropped its balancing pole and teeters like a blindfolded slack-wire walker above a cataract. No need to be too perturbed or to go haywire when we still have "Up a Lazy River" and "White Christmas," and hundreds more just as good, to reassure while restoring our national balance.

5

Websterian Confusions

Perhaps that statement immediately brands the writer as shallow, specious, and insensitive to the branding iron's sear of present-day realities. Nonetheless, those songs and the many that will present themselves are among the few constants in American life during an era of unprecedented change. They are stout bollards to tie to, anchors to windward, or, if you don't like old-style metaphors unfiltered, you may roll your own. The popular songs of any period touch American lives in so many ways that the associations alone make them important Americana. "Please, Oh, Please, Little Suffragette, Don't Take Away My Cigarette" recalls the terminus of the long trek toward woman suffrage (1920) and also male apprehensions before cigarettes became common to both genders.

Some of the Americana in our music was not written into it by its composers. It is there by tradition according to the manner in which it was presented (a tortured clarinet solo, a gravel-voiced singer, or even handclaps such as those punctuating "Deep in the Heart of Texas") and by whom (Paul Whiteman, "Wang Wang Blues," or Eva Tanguay, "I Don't Care," or Sophie Tucker, "Some of These Days"). That refers to public performance. It's the American way to play or sing music as we feel it, and no two persons can feel exactly alike about it. With or without an audience, musical self-expression, among those to whom it is important avocationally, also leans toward individualism. When a Dixieland band of businessmen lugs its instruments into a member's living room and gives out with staid old "Liebestraum," a keen ear may detect an occasional clue to what's being played. When they're well warmed up, the ear must be unusually perceptive to distinguish that classic from "Hornets in the Henhouse," a confection stirred up by the band's percussion man and never played the same way twice.

To the professional musician, music is a job as is proved by flare-ups, even in symphony circles, over wages, hours, and working conditions. Too, because he is a professional, a musician may be called upon to give his best to a composition that he doesn't like. Nonprofessionals are free to choose what they like. Their Bill of Rights protects bathtub singing as well as assembling for the purpose of performing in their own way the music they like.

Association with my own kind in dubious duos, tremulous trios, and foursomes (in which a baritone volunteers to sing tenor if you'll pitch it low enough) exposes one to phenomena probably unknown to formal musicians. Those who sing or play in informal harmony need no audience. At times, they resent one. Give them the right place, free from interruptions, enough time to feel each other out as to ability and tastes before getting down to business, include a rememberer who may not sing or play but who can suggest a series of "good ones," and they're Paid in Full. Any written music used is merely for reference to clear up misunderstandings, to avoid arguments about melody or words, or to revive a memory that went blank in the last two bars of "My Wild Irish Rose."

No census figures identify the number and locations of these American primitives, but the tribe is vast. Its members absorb musical sequences as a blotter sucks up ink. Their awareness and retentiveness of musical sounds is in a sort of built-in echo chamber; when echoes start to bounce around, the desire to reproduce them becomes compulsive.

To comment upon these phenomena necessitates herding words into line. There a main difficulty raises its ugly head: words. To avoid stumbling into a

Country Music Old-Style

verbal morass, it must be stated now that "country" in "Country Music Old-Style" does not refer to the output of guitar-plunking vocalists or bands since they became self-conscious about "hillbilly" in recent years and coined the less exact term.

As to old-style or new-style, that depends upon one's birth year. Today's high-school student recalls "Davy Crockett," if at all, as an ancient song of the distant 1950's, somehow associated with a synthetic fur cap made from coonskins "captured" in a Brooklyn factory. To another person, a pre-World War I song may be approaching maturity, though it is still too young to be called old. Such a person remembers "Summertime" as Harry Von Tilzer's lilting national hit and George Gershwin's lullaby in a minor key—also called "Summertime"—from *Porgy and Bess* about thirty years later. Whether Gershwin's seems old or new to you, Junior and his gang would date it in the Chester A. Arthur era. The variations of opinion within his group are minor as compared with the opinions of his parents and grandparents as to what is old-style or new-style.

Now that we're well muddled into a state of Websterian confusion as words become involved with meanings, I may add that the "country" as used herein will clarify itself along the way. This commentary will go beyond music and words into other phases of our popular songs and the folkways associated with them. Some of these excursions are in territory as ancient as the singing in a Shakespearean barber's shop. More recent references touch upon American phenomena: vaudeville and musical shows, the road companies that played small towns along the railroads, the medicine shows that hauled their tents by wagon through the mud to the hamlets of the hinterlands. Folk songs, old and new, and the resurgence of barbershop quartets are also discussed. In the main, these notes are *about,* rather than *of,* music. The view of our popular songs is ex-cathedra, which is to say from the musical fringe where more than fringe benefits have accrued during a lifetime of listening, observation, and participation. Since songs can activate a memory to unusual recall because of their associations with persons and incidents, the lingering nostalgic echoes may evoke either gay memories or old aches.

Beyond misunderstandings due to different ages and terminologies, our reactions to what is pure corn or pure gold in our songs are affected by the individual's temperament and preferences, ear for music, and musical experience (which may be casual or may include intimate exposure to limited types of music or to wide-ranging miscellany). Located between music that is branded as classical and the simple traditional folk music, most music is called popular because, if it is good music, it sticks in the memory to be played, sung, hummed, or whistled—often subconsciously. It is the music that everybody knows—almost—or knew or recognizes by a few bars of melody or words, what they say as well as how they play: "Some enchanted evening you will/may see/meet a stranger across" a—ah—what are the words? * Other comparable lapses will crop up later in "Memory Lame." These and related phenomena are amplified in a recall of that which has enveloped much of this commentator's life in a pleasant pink haze.

In Part One, some autobiographical basting threads show through. As biography, they are unimportant, but they serve several useful purposes. They show how circumstance (Lady Luck) may expand a confined horizon, and the

* From *South Pacific.* Copyright 1949 by Richard Rodgers and Oscar Hammerstein II. Copyright owned by Williamson Music Co., Inc., New York, N. Y. Used by permission.

threads are useful too in stitching backgrounds of Americana, in the main musical, to the present. Excess threads twist into a sort of line on which to hang the rest of this musical hamper's variety. It includes excerpts from a few of my older published pieces. All of them have been cut, then some have been pieced out for patching and fitting into the new unworn materials. They are here with the approval of the publishers for whom they were originally fabricated.

1932 A Handbook for Adeline Addicts (*out of print*)
1934 *"How Popular Songs Mirror America," NEA Syndicate*
1935 *"Ewer 16, My Villidchkween,"* Esquire
1948 Keep America Singing (*out of print*)
1955 *"Songs We Ought to Like—Ought Ain't Is,"* Music Journal
1957 *"Folk Songs or Populars,"* Music Journal
1957 *"Our Songs Reflect America's Moods,"* Music Journal
1958 *"The Negro in Our Popular Songs,"* Music Journal
1960 *"Parodies Are Compliments,"* Music Journal
1961 *"They Don't Write Good Songs Any More—or Do They,"* Sunday Magazine
1961 *"From the Old Piano Bench,"* Harvest Years
1964 *"The Old Fashioned Singing Commercial,"* Music Journal
1964 *"Music That Lasts,"* Harvest Years
1965 *"The Evolution of Barbershop Harmony,"* Music Journal, *anthology issue (July)*
1942–68 *"The Way I See It," column in* The Harmonizer

My thanks to all of those book and music publishers who have permitted the use of excerpts from their copyrighted material. I am grateful to Carol Bridgman of ASCAP's index department and to all whose writings on popular music have made joyous reading over the years. Several books suitable for reference use are described in some detail in Appendix F for those who might enjoy them as much as I have.

And now a bow of gratitude to Florette (Mrs. George M.) Vaughn for manuscript and proof reading and to Earl J. Stutzman, teacher of music in the Cleveland, Ohio, public-school system, for checking and correcting the signs and the time in several melodies and harmonizations unwritten until now. Without his supervision, they might have been written in daylight saving time.

As American As Route 30

For panoramas or candid snaps of life in these states, our popular songs are as revealingly American as Route 30 can be when we travel it leisurely enough to get acquainted with its twists, straightaways, and the scenery and people along the way. It provides opportunity to know the open country, historic cities and places, undistinguished towns, and a host of surburban villages as new as their ranch houses and crops of babies. When we stop by necessity or whim, it becomes apparent that the local speech, thought, and attitudes of people in certain sections stem from the land, while at another stop they are geared into urban production and the mores of city life.

A thoughtful tour through our songs can reveal equal variety and also glimpses that are more intimate than is possible on an actual cross-country trip. There is hardly a state, navigable river, mountain chain, or principal lake without a song in praise of its charms, or an area without lyrical panegyrics, from the sidewalks of New York to the top of Old Smoky, to way down yonder in New Orleans to San Francisco Bay or a tumbledown shack in Athlone. This is exemplified by a little more than one hundred songs selected from the much larger number that touch geography by title or in the words.*

Great numbers of them reveal the writer's longing to return to a designated area, most frequently to a section of Dixie where the fields of cotton are not forgotten. Wherever she may be on land or sea or foam, which rhymes nicely with home, mother has also exerted a powerful magnetic attraction to songwriters. Most frequently, however, a younger female waiting beneath a June moon while the doves croon love's old sweet tune was the magnet. Twin magnets show in a song such as "California and You" and in many songs related to Ireland where the shamrocks so green supplement an Irish colleen as the double-feature attraction.

Though songs in praise of places usually followed that well-marked route, exceptions are exemplified by George M. Cohan's "Forty-five Minutes from Broadway" (1905), in which he derided country and village life in places now populated heavily by urbanites in search of suburbia's releases.

* See Appendix A.

If you want to see the real delegation
The place where the real rubens dwell,
Just hop on a train at the Grand Central Station
Get off when they shout "New Rochelle."

FIRST CHORUS:

Oh what a fine bunch of rubens
Oh what a jay atmosphere
They have whiskers like hay,
And imagine Broadway
Only forty-five minutes from here.

Parodies of popular songs were caricatures designed, of course, to twist what may have been a solemn or sad theme into a laugh for an audience at a burlesque performance and in subsequent repetitions at sing-outs. An excellent example is the parody of Paul Dresser's "On the Banks of the Wabash," now Indiana's official state song. The parody is quoted in part in the chapter "Parodies Prove Popularity."

Most of our popular songs are storehouses of Americana of high order because of the musical patterns preserved from different eras and because the words are a record of people, actions, events, developments, and much of the dominant thought and American attitudes toward life during various periods. Words such as "ruben," "jay," and "bird" as used by Cohan preserve American slang that is now obsolete.*

"Popular" music implies words carried along by a melody, and mere words are in back of the popularity of some of our songs. Over many generations "Auld Lang Syne" has won no medals musically. It has a simple unpretentious melody known to nearly every adult. The words and their associations in special-occasion use make it a number that can still evoke tears. Let us jump from that ancient song to one that was heard dozens of times daily in the early 1950's. During the frenzied part of her short life, "Dearie" (not to be confused with a 1905 song of the same name) was hummed nationally. She provides a test of one's age, memory, and, among young persons, general information. "Dearie" includes names, incidents, and customs set to an easily sung gay tune that sticks in memory. So much is packed into the song that several theses could be written about the Americana in the lyrics. Some items of reference have vanished from public knowledge so long ago that, to some, they might need explanation:

Sousa's band	*for many years America's most famous*
The waltz	*essence of the dance of the early century*
Chowder parties	*paired with the Fourth of July, pure Americana*
Henry Ford	*pioneer in low-cost personal transportation integral with our life and economy*
Chandler six	*three speeds forward, self-starter, 'n' everything*
Keystone movies	*Sennett, Arbuckle, Normand grotesqueries that flickered—and often snapped*
Crystal set	*"Can you get KDKA on yours?"*
Coogan-Chaplin	*early movies again, funny with a heartbreak*
Spats and wing collars	*only dudes wore them west of Pittsburgh, and not on dude ranches*

* The comparison of nationwide travel with a trip through our songs is more than coincidental. In each case we can merely touch upon a minimal number of places and songs as examples of what we'd find in infinite details if we were to spend the rest of our lives in exploration of all that is on the map and on the song record. Even then, we'd end with a feeling of frustration and regret that hundreds, even thousands, of interesting spots would remain unexplored travel-wise, musically and lyrically.

Derby hats	*connecting the era of Roman gladiators' helmets with the steel ones worn today for safety*
Bustles	*they bustled in, rather than muscled in*
John L. Sullivan	*pride of Boston and the sporting world*
Caruso	*many still acclaim him as the greatest tenor*
Diamond Jim Brady	*symbol of lavish spending*
Gilda Gray	*introduced the "shimmy" dance in the 1920's*
San Francisco earthquake	*referred to in the Bay Area as "the fire" of 1906*
Harry Lauder	*purveyor of Scottish songs and bur-r-red jokes*
Jenny Lind	*'way back in 1850, press agents introduced her as P. T. Barnum's "Swedish nightingale"*
Man O'War	*famous racehorse*
Rin Tin Tin	*with FDR's Fala, was among America's best-known dogs since Beautiful Joe, probably even more so than the current Lassie*
Babe Ruth	*until they heard "Dearie," many didn't know that he had pitched (lefty) for the Red Sox* *

Where else is so much variety from more than a century of America compressed into such small space? Of course, the song is an exception that is cited here for a quick demonstration of how songs preserve Americana. Most of them do so incidentally rather than deliberately. Like others that record our backgrounds, this one has an occasional anachronism such as holding Gilda Gray's shimmy-shake of the 1920's responsible for the San Francisco earthquake of 1906. But only a peck-sniffish critic would enlarge upon that minor and natural error. Contemporary writers are inclined toward dumping everything back of the Depression (1929–35) into the Gay Nineties.

The words in our songs record popular thought and desires, environments and aspirations. Evolutions in our speech are written into the lyrical record. "They're sweet and fair and on the square/The maids of Manhattan for mine" (from "In Old New York," *The Red Mill,* 1906) praises feminine integrity along with charm. "When a Fellow's on the Level with a Girl That's on the Square" carried quite different implications than did "A Square in the Social Circle" half a century later.

As to attitudes and conventions, before the Volstead Act brought national prohibition that didn't prohibit (1920–33), the attitude of great numbers of women was "Lips That Touch Liquor Shall Never Touch Mine." But when drinking became smart in the twenties, many women let down the bars and patronized them in speakeasies. After the repeal of Prohibition, "Cocktails for Two" was an immediate hit with its "No longer slinking, respectably drinking like civilized ladies and men . . . as we enjoy a cigarette." †

Cigarettes! Ugh! As described in at least one section of these states, "Tobacco is a filthy weed. It was the devil sowed the seed. It drains your pockets, soils your clothes. And makes a chimney of your nose." That was before women started to dally with lung cancer as they learned to smoke wetly, during the twenties. Before that, "Two Cigarettes in the Dark" would have been scandalous.

Our songs are usually in tune with public acceptance of customs and conventions. Those that are composed in an attempt to sway public opinion are usually as widely popular as a tariff section in the *Congressional Record.* In *The Drag-*

on's Seed, 1959, R. S. Elegant told how China's millions were being urged to write song lyrics to aid the communistic programs. One of the snappier titles was "Mamma Wants to Go to the Country to Assist in Building Up the Nation's Agricultural Production." Swallow that one with your trombone!

Of course there are exceptions to the rule that songs written to influence public thought are usually duds. We'll meet some of those exceptions when we linger on tour to inspect old-time singing commercials and other oddities. Composers who write songs that become truly popular can exert a powerful influence upon the nation's thought. But a song's association with a publicly-held sentiment can lead us astray. Some of us think that "God Bless America" is our national anthem.

A principal reward for traveling unhurriedly across the country or through our songs is the immediate enjoyment of what we see and hear for the first time. That is repeated later as we recall scenes and relive incidents of travel. There is also probability of a third reward from touring and in songs. Even on a short trip over familiar territory nearly everyone has heard "I never noticed that before," whether "that" was a structure or a natural object passed on previous trips. When we retravel our songs and heed the speed zones, as traffic departments label our *slow* zones, we add new appreciations of songs that were passed unheedingly before.

As an example of that, consider "Just Break the News to Mother," a sad ballad of 1897. If heard today, it is usually a travesty on the old tearjerkers, though on rare occasions men whose hair and chests have slipped render it in what they optimistically call "close" harmony. Look twice at merely the two opening lines of the verse:

While the shot and shell were screaming upon the battlefield
The boys in blue were fighting, their noble flag to shield.

Shot and shell scream today in many parts of the world, but what about the boys in blue? Blue uniforms in field operations were obsolete even before World War I when doughboys went to France in khaki in 1917. By that time a flag in the front lines would have been shot to shreds, and a bearer of such an obvious target would have been disgraced for setting it up for bracketing by the enemy's artillery. So much for that second look which reveals the American hiding in just two lines of an old song. Later, we'll examine others for further insights.

Our song styles have changed as often as skirt lengths and hairdos. (Many have been as temporary as a permanent.) When we take time to look at them, they become more than songs. Lyrically and musically, they are mirrors that reflect much of America in each generation. Often, a lyric line is condensed American history and sociology with a beat. Musically, sad ballads in waltz time, swing, boogie, hillbilly (now country), calypso, and tango rhythms dot the panorama of our musical modes. To go no farther back than ragtime, each of them was here to stay and would bulldoze out of existence all previously popular styles, according to each new crop of enthusiasts.

Songs have soared swiftly into national popularity. Then, because of shifting musical styles or popular thought and attitudes, they become as inconspicuous as a red bud tree which in early spring inserts its exclusive feathery red-purples into the gray-brown tail of winter. Having cheered us as a harbinger as well as a colorful splash of immediate beauty, it fades into summer's verdancy, unnoticed except by the few who recognize it. Some of our songs burst into bloom perennially, then disappear until another revival.

Radio, television, and other electronic devices present such variety that a delver into musical artifacts ponders where to start, which course to follow, and how far in the era before nervous breakdowns and tête-à-têtes with psychiatrists became status symbols. To present a sampling of songs since Colonial days would require encyclopedic space, and in the main the chronological tracings would appeal only to those few whose interests are antiquarian. To present merely the types and groups (Indian titles "Arawana," "Red Wing," "Hiawatha," and such as example of others) would be comparable with an attempt to condense the nation's record into an evening's reading. ("Hiawatha," 1903, started a flood of Indian songs that continued until 1909. Every publisher was promoting "his" Indian song that—so the ads all claimed—surpassed all others.)

So, the songs of the earlier 1900's will predominate. They are new enough to be recalled by many adults. Some will be unknown to younger people. Thus we have a review for those "strolling again memory lane" * blended into discovery for others. Any comparisons of a few songs of the 1850's with those of the 1950's or others between those dates are to show demonstrable differences, not to appraise the musical merits of an era or of one song over another. Of critics, H. L. Mencken wrote that they can smite without being smitten. Musical values are opinions in "an art where tastes rather than facts are paramount" wrote musicologist Ernest Bacon. We all have opinions about music. Only music critics are paid to disagree among themselves.

Music off-the-cuff in personal participation continues to produce the joyous thrills of new discoveries while I learn progressively how much of the older worthwhile was missed by speeding through the Americana in our songs, as on Route 30. There is hardly any limit to the diversity—country and urban, original jazz and its variants that are so important to aficionados, Dixieland—musical modes that preceded rock 'n' roll and today's throwback to folk music. Its recrudescence in original forms was a musical phenomenon of the 1950's. A decade later, the fabrics of our "folk" songs are in the main newly woven from synthetic fibers, many of them of excellent quality. Folk music will come up for inspection later.

Let's go back now to the beginnings of this trip through country music oldstyle and related Americana. We shall pull off the road frequently to observe things and persons and neighboring vistas. The tour started in a kind of country and under conditions that no longer exist and can never be repeated in America.

Far, Far Away

They said she wasn't land poor or money poor, just "tollable" in the second instance. The widowed mother of the little boy owned the forty-acre hill farm and four-room one-story house with a dividing hallway from front to rear. Much of the time she sang or hummed at the tasks which the women of the neighborhood liked to rhyme in apothegm: "A man's work is from sun to sun/ But a woman's work is never done." When they said that to their men folks, the echo came back, usually smilingly gruff: "Women's work! Huh!"

At night in the bedroom across the hall the boy heard familiar sounds and listened for others. On quiet nights, winter or summer, a hoot owl's whoo-whoo carried from the deep woods, and the wind hummed softly in the chimney, sometimes three or four notes of a recognizable tune, but it never repeated. When it was windy, particularly in winter, the chimney shrieked dissonances like a chorus of tone-deaf demons. He could imagine them squatting on the roof. Then it was a comfort to hear his sheep dog stir under the floor directly below his bed. A melodious humming from across the hall was the most comforting sound as his mother sewed or darned by coal-oil lamplight. At other times she'd iron clothes in the kitchen where she could reach from the creaky off-key ironing board to the top of the wood-burning stove for another hot iron. Sometimes she baked bread while ironing musically. It smelled so good that the boy would go to sleep hungry. Not really, his stomach just felt that way.

The house stood on low limestone blocks as the principal in a farm complex that included a summer kitchen connected with the house by a door-to-door platform, a smokehouse, a buggy shed open at one end, a barn, a log sheep pen and a hog pen partly roofed over, and a log chicken house chinked with clay originally, though most of the chinking had weathered out. All were framed or built entirely of oak and walnut (all sawed on the farm), with whitewood clapboards where customary. The main buildings were rainproofed by rived oak shingles split by her father's froe.

Rusting deeper each year, it hung on a square nail in the dark, greasy, musty dampness of the smokehouse. Candle molds that had become scabby with green verdigris dangled nearby. A worn flax hackle, a handmade spinning wheel's bobbin to which a few strands of linsey-woolsey still clung, a hand-forged adze, several discarded hickory withe chairs, and a miscellany of other outmoded holdovers gave evidence of the artisanship of the boy's grandfather. Each year when it was time for the boy to carry baskets of hickory chips into the smokehouse to cure the hams, shoulders, bacon, and sausage, his mother threatened to throw out all that clutter-muss. Then she'd say she didn't have the heart—"maybe next year."

She wasn't money poor. After the war she'd married a Yankee soldier she met while visiting below the rapids at Keokuk where the palatial Diamond Joe steamboats churned past while the dingy little packet boats from Quincy and Hannibal stopped at the levee for freight and local passengers. When she met him, he was building wooden trestle bridges for the new railroad lines along the river. After a timber fell on him, when the boy was about two years old, she received ten-dollars-a-month pension from the government, not the railroad.

Her thirty-dollar check came every three months as regularly as a team of mules could pull the mail wagon through the mud or snow from the railroad to the Jeff Davis store where the post office was back of the hardware side. Jeff (you know which side *his* parents were on) always whistled a few bars of "Buffalo Girls" dubiously, accepted the government's blue slip suspiciously, inspected it several times on both sides, then cashed it as if he were doing her a favor in allowing her to settle her bill for the past three months. Sometimes there was a smidgen left over when her other sources of income had been high.

That depended upon factors as unrelated as well digging and Bob Gaines' craving for store whiskey. The woods were thick on both sides of the limestone-ledged branch on the farm. (Mrs. DeHaven called it a brook, the time she visited from the East.) When a neighbor needed rock to wall up a dug well, he'd pay her twenty-five cents for as big a load of limestone as his horses could pull up the hill from the branch, in short pulls between chocking the wagon wheels so the horses could have a breather. Gaines lived on ten poor acres back of the woods. When his urge for store liquor couldn't be put off again, he'd cut a twenty-foot walnut saw log in her woods and pay her a dollar for it. He paid if she saw him drive his scrawny horses through her barnyard to the road that went to the railroad town where under-the-counter whiskey was fifty cents a pint at the drugstore in that dry territory. She collected then or never. He'd return after dark, swaying on the reach of his log wagon, broke, and singin' drunk. "Dunderbeck's Machine" was his favorite song. Mrs. DeHaven called it "Johnny Rebeck."

Chickens and eggs traded at the store were the same as cash money, as much as six cents a dozen when eggs were up. In winter the store paid a nickel each for rabbits shot in her woods. Three of them bought a box of .22 shorts for the boy's single-shot Flobert. He couldn't afford many misses. When the white cornmeal was low, they'd select several sackfuls of corn at the barn crib and take them to 'Rasmus Parker's mill over on Black Creek for grinding. Sometimes he kept a little for miller's toll, not always.

No, they weren't money poor. They just couldn't afford some things. Of course every family saved its cooking grease to make brown lye soft soap in the big iron kettles that stood in the backyards. Some families still leached the lye from wood ashes poured into outdoor troughlike lye hoppers. A Granger Twist wooden bucket caught the drip after a rain. Clothes, boiled outdoors in the big kettle over a wood fire and punched down by a wooden paddle, always smelled smoky, soft-soapy, and "brownish," she said. The boy scoured their kettle with sand when it was time to try out lard at hog-killin' time.

Most of the cream that rose in the pans in the cool cellar was skimmed for churning butter. Usually she saved a little for cornmeal mush, often sweetened with sorghum molasses that the old folks called long sweetnin', just for fun. Then they'd talk about the war when sorghum was the only kind of sweetening. In that neighborhood, molasses was a plural word, like "Pass them molasses."

They picked buttery blackhaws and smoky-tasting persimmons after the frost got to them and the pawpaws along Black Creek. Hazelnuts and walnuts and hickory nuts were close by in the woods, and in June big black mulberries and sarvis berries. Mrs. DeHaven called them serviceberries or shadbush. After that, the striped wild gooseberries and shiny blackberries hung so thickly that their vines, with the fish-hook thorns, bent almost to the ground. That was the time when the yellow transparent apples ripened on the branches that the boy's grandfather had budded into a red June apple tree. In midsummer a trotline, pulled from the creek while the night fog still hung low over the bottom lands, might have hooked a fat lazy yellow catfish or, less often, a squirming two-pound channel cat.

On sunny days they spread a clean old sheet on the gently sloped back roof of the house to hold layers of drying okra, which the old folks called gumbo, sweet corn, and thin-sliced apples for winter. Then the boy would sing what he'd heard: "I loathe, abhor, detest, despise, a-*bom*-inate dried apple pies." Actually, he liked them in fried apple turnovers, but he really loathed the black-eyed peas spread on the roof for a final drying in late summer.

In hot weather the thermometer with the Black Draught ad on it sometimes stayed near 100° in the little one-story house. However, on a pallet of quilts spread on the floor they slept toward morning, better than if sunk into a smothering feather bed. In winter the dipper in the kitchen water bucket had to be broken out of the ice that quite often froze there overnight. The boy's mother made a joke of that by singing "From Greenland's Icy Mountains," the first bars of a hymn they sang at church on foreign mission Sunday. With fine-split wood it didn't take too long to have a fire sputter cracking in the kitchen stove and in the big box stove that had been crammed with four-foot chunks at bedtime. In the morning a bed of coals still glowed under the white ashes.

A stove like that one heated the one-room schoolhouse. When they'd waded through soggy snowdrifts for a mile or more, the pupils draped their heavy brown duck coats and mittens and mufflers around the stove. Sometimes the boys added wet leather or felt boots. When moisture started to trickle in streams down the steamy windowpanes, the teacher would crinkle her nose and ask a boy to open a window. The felt boots were the worst, but they were apple blossoms compared with fetid asafetida bags that a few children had to wear on strings around their necks to ward off smallpox. Those unfortunates expected to be called stinkpot and polecat, and they were.

On Friday afternoons about three o'clock, if somebody hadn't riled Teacher since noon, she'd stand by her desk. Slate pencils stopped their clicket-clacks.

Everything quieted down in an excited sort of way. Everybody hoped for a spell-down or a cipher-down on the blackboard. From the little A-B-abs in the front seats to the biggest boys and girls in the rear, each was chosen into two lines. Teacher started by giving out "cat" or "one plus one" to the smallest, then moved into hard words or blackboard problems in compound interest for the oldest. When only two spellers or cipherers were left standing, the tensions left the rest of them breathless.

It could be exciting at home, too. Almost every day, when the road wasn't a loblolly of clay and water, a boy might hear the cluckle-clockle and crickety squeaks of a loaded wagon coming, or the rhythmic thud-a-thud of a pair of trotters pulling a buggy across the wooden culvert at the foot of the hill. Maybe whoever it was would stop at the horse block and tie to the front fence. The horse block was two segments of log, one higher than the other when stood on end. That made a step for women in their riding skirts to reach their side saddles.

When some of the older folks stopped in while one of the boy's aunts was there on a visit, they'd ask for the songs that the sisters had sung before the war when, as girls, they'd lived in the stone house that their father had built when he came out from Kentucky. Without instruments, they sang "Joys That We've Tasted" and "Widow Malone—who lived in the town of Athlone, alone" and "Beautiful Rose—pride of the prairie bow-er" and more that the old friends called for.

There never was enough music at school because the older boys were bashful about singing, so they made fun of any smaller soprano boy who did sing. The Kincheloe girl cousins sang the best. Usually, they were called up front at any neighborhood get-together. They sang the new songs: "In the Baggage Coach Ahead," "White Wings—that never grow weary," and "She Was Bred in Old Kentucky." That always got a sneaky snicker from the older boys. The girls learned their newest songs from the Will Rossiter song pamphlets that could be ordered by mail.

When some man brought a French harp (Mrs. DeHaven called it a harmonica), he'd blow out the loose tobacco crumbs and play "Over the Waves" and "Creole Belle" and other new ones such as "There'll Be a Hot Time in the Old Town Tonight." Always some of the older folks asked for a hoedown tune such as "Turkey in the Straw":

Tie a little string around the turkey's hind paw
And he'll jerk a little tune called Turkey in the Straw.

On special occasions such as a birthday party or anniversary there might be a fiddle and guitar.

In the whole neighborhood, four or five miles across, and between there and the railroad town far, far away, there wasn't even one musician, and instruments were few. But there was music.

People, Place, and Kind

Music for art's sake rather than the listener's, music of the symphony, opera, concert, musical comedy, vaudeville and minstrel stages, and the many in-betweens of professional performance are written into America's voluminous musical record. It includes those who composed, arranged, performed, presented, and published many sorts of music. Even so, a few gaps remain. Among them is a missing section of country music old-style. Earlier, I stated that this does not refer to the so-called country music of recent years.

It is called old-style because no one, regardless of age, is likely to refer to music carried over from the 1890's into World War I as new-style. Musically, there is no line of demarcation between the two centuries. In the early 1900's some of the most sung songs had attained adulthood. Some are still heard. The gap to which I refer is largely that of people and place.

The people were not engaged in nor associated with the musical arts. They were rural and small-town people whose musical centers were country towns where the music performed sporadically for the public was often presented in the musty dusty opera house reached by creaking wooden stairs above JONES DRUGS—*Cigars and Toiletries.*

It was the music of farm and village folks before radio and television brought us news while it happens and today's variety of live and transcribed music. The automobile had not arrived to carry with it a demand for hard roads that now give country dwellers easy access to towns, jukeboxes, and movies with music on their sound tracks. Though the place of reference here is Oakdale, Missouri, the kind of people and the types of music were common to a host of crossroads hamlets too small to be dotted on the nation's map, and to a vast number of villages along the sprangling railroad lines. Oakdale was in Shelby County, about thirty miles, two days when the roads were dry, from Mark Twain's Hannibal. It "was" because it isn't.

The tiny community, clustered 'round the Jeff Davis store, is less than Goldsmith's "Deserted Village," even less than a ghost town of the old West where some of the buildings remain. At the center, only a crumbling chimney of my great-grandfather's home pierces the mat of thistles, mullein, and goldenrod on which red haw, wild crab, and thorn trees add to the evidence of abandoned land. In four directions, six houses within a quarter mile of the Davis store–post office and the blacksmith shop, left ample room for fields, orchards, and pastures. On the periphery, the church, school, and cemetery were on land given to the community from Grandfather's farm.

Nearly everyone stemmed directly or circuitously from Virginia or Kentucky. Names of Scottish origin, Blackford, Broughton, Douglas, Craigmyle, and Crawford alternated along the rutted roads with Baker, Perry, Elliott, Evans, Franklin, Jordan (Jerden to the old folks), Parker, and Gooch. Grandfather Gooch was about two generations removed, via Kentucky, from the Goochlands section of Virginia. Some families had come west more recently, after their idol had surrendered at Appomatox Courthouse. Several of the old-timers talked as if they'd been on a first-name basis with him.

By tradition they were Confederates only thirty-odd years removed from the war. They were Democrats and members of the Methodist Episcopal Church South, with accent upon the ultimate. The older families had been slaveholders. Many had been hit hard when Confederate money became usable only for fire kindlin', and when slaves such as Ann and her baby Charlotte, who cost my grandparents one thousand pre-inflation dollars, were freed.

No telephone lines paralleled the roads, nor power lines to provide news and music by radio which hadn't been invented. That section was as remote from the rest of the nation, when McKinley was President, as a Libyan oasis may be today. The mail came by horse or mule-drawn spring wagon from the railroad to the store, which was also the post office. Sometimes in late winter, a team of seventeen-hand mules couldn't pull a wagon's bare running gear through the gluey mud. When Black Creek was in flood, its ford was impassable. At other times the mail came through from Shelbina, pronounced with an "eye," on the C. B. & Q. railroad, now the Burlington. Even though a farmer knew that mail arrival would be canceled by mud or snowdrifts, mail time in late afternoon gave him an excuse for saddlin'. At the store he'd tie to the hitching rails, swap news, criticize the administration, squirt tobacco juice with bulletlike accuracy, and among the older men refight Shiloh.

Travel distances were calculated in terms of what a team could cover in a day, depending upon the vehicle and the load, with time out for breathers on the hills, watering at the fords, and feeding time at noon. Shelbina was about twelve miles, four hours or so with a loaded wagon, by roads that in general right-angled along section lines. In winter and spring there were times when the only transportation to town was on horseback, well splashed. Hoofs could fit like pistons into an earlier hoofprint filled with liquid mud that could squirt above a rider's head. So the women, riding sidesaddle to the store or church, wore long protective riding skirts which they shed at the end of the trip. In summer the skirts doubled as dust protectors when each hoof fall squirted dust.

Because there were no electric lines along the roads, the four bluish arc lights, which Shelbina hung at its principal intersections, were worth staying till after dark to see. They were truly marvels, chronicled in the song "The New Electric Lights." News traveled by word of mouth as the old folk tunes had been transmitted—and garbled—from voice to ear. Just as singers substitute notes or words that fit the tune or meter when they can't recall the original, some local news bearers with creative instincts often improved upon the facts, while impressing themselves.

The character of the area had changed little since the war, except in deforestation which was noticeable to my mother who'd been born there in the California gold rush year of '49. Local personalities were as varied as would be found today among a comparable number, rural or urban. Only the candidates running for county office at Shelbyville talked about independence. The people lived it. Under all circumstances each family took care of its own from birth till death, while retaining a strong sense of community responsibility, expressed usually in physical aid.

When women gathered in someone's home for a quilting, it was a contest of skills. Endurance also entered into it when the men flocked 'round at a wood choppin' to help a neighbor wrest another acre of stumpy cornfield from the woods. Later, the owner would split the logs into rails to be laid zigzag, ten rails high, as protection against questing cows. Too often the rail fences were practice hurdles for athletic mules. At a community affair held in the evening, a loose term to indicate any hour between midafternoon and lamp-lighting time, there was music.

In such a setting folk tunes and hymns were held over from the pioneers' influx which began soon after the War of 1812. At Oakdale, some of the very old songs of England or Scotland had survived the overseas trip, life for a few generations along the Atlantic seaboard, and transplantation to an inland terrain. Passed along from person to person, all such songs undergo changes in melody and words as the singers forget and substitute. Typically, the ancient "Twa Corbies," or crows, was sung thiswise and to the tune of "Bonnie Doon," note for note:

There were two cro-ows sat on a tree-ee
And they were bl-ack as cro-ows could be
Said one old cro-ow unto his ma-ate
"What sh-all we do-o for meat to ate?"
"I see a ho-orse on yonder pla-ain
Whose bo-ody has been three days slain
We'll perch our selves on hi-is backbo-one
And plu-uck his ey-eyes out one by one."

But the old folk music was secondary to the music heard most often in Oakdale and thousands of comparable communities. That was the music of Thornton, Dresser, Harris, Marks, Stern, Luders, Williams (Rossiter), Lamb, Jerome and Schwartz, Van Alstyne, the Von Tilzer brothers (Harry and Albert), Whiting, Cobb, Edwards, and Ball, to name a few who wrote the music most popular in the early 1900's. These were the composers of my own generation, the third in that sparsely settled rural section. Some of their music is recognized by our children, and even by theirs, as it filters in varying arrangements, sometimes disagreements, from a record player or a PA system, as durable music that lasts.

There were no musicians or music teachers at Oakdale. When my mother took me there to live at age eight, I carried quite a collection of melodies and lyrics in my memory file where an odd assortment had already accumulated subconsciously. Some of the file's content included the old first-generation pioneer music which my mother sang or hummed while doing her homework. To those she added the songs of her own times, the 1850's, 1860's, and postwar. About the house she sang both kinds. Among those of her girlhood and womanhood: "The Hazel Dell," Longfellow's "Bridge at Midnight," "Rosalie the Prairie Flower," "Darling Nellie Gray." Others were somber in character. The heroine often expired of some unidentified malady in the second or third verse. But the "Singing Skule Beautifule," "Jim Along Josie," "Kingdom Comin'," and "Little Brown Jug" had bounce.

The memory file also included songs of a newer generation, my older sister's, of the 1880's and 1890's. I remembered them, though she had not joined us in Oakdale. She had sung, and I knew in consequence, "White Wings," "In Old Madrid," Tosti's "Beauty's Eyes" and "Goodbye Forever," "Her Golden Hair Was Hanging Down Her Back," "Twickenham Ferry," "Sailing—over the bounding main," and "Afterward," which exemplify her repertoire, a melange of semiclassical parlor songs for young ladies and the populars of her teens and twenties.

These and hymns were grown-ups' music, far more interesting than that of my own age group had been before coming to Oakdale. Then, we had sung: "This is the way we wash our clothes so ear-r-rly in the morning," and, at Sunday school, a song about pennies dropping, "Every one for Jesus/He will get them all." Just how the monetary exchange would be accomplished was the puzzler.

The rural relatives and neighbors were eager for new music from the outside. I had the temperament of a participant but not that of a solo artist. (Quartetting is still the most fun.) A great-uncle warned my mother grimly: "A bird that can sing and won't sing ought to be *made* to sing." That was an era of "spare the rod and spoil the child" when permissiveness hadn't come into common use. Arbitration by mother resulted in my placement behind the door where, shy as a catbird, I sang in seclusion to their hearts' content, *a capella* since we had no instrument to accompany vapid Victorian songs such as "I Don't Want to Play in Your Yard," "Won't You Come to My Tea Party?" and "Kiss and Let's Make Up" as alternates to sprightly "Anne Rooney" and sad ballads typified by Gray's old weeper, "The Church Across the Way."

Some of the farm families owned ornate parlor organs that were triumphs of jigsaw design. The girls struggled self-consciously through "The Gondolier," "Hiawatha," and "Narcissus" under the guidance of a young woman who'd taken music lessons in Shelbyville. Dr. Owen's family had a piano. One neighbor could play intricate compositions, "The Whistler and His Dog" and "Mosquitos' Parade" on his French harp-harmonica. 'Rasmus Parker and his son Chet were usually available for special occasions, though not for pay. 'Rasmus, a friend of my mother since childhood, owned the grist saw mill on Black Creek. He had lost two fingers to his circular saw, but the accident seemed to have doubled the agility of those remaining as they danced over his fiddle's strings.

Chet needed only three major chords and a minor to accompany on his guitar his father's joyous "Sourwood Mountain," "Old Dan Tucker," "Skip to M' Lou," and the other traditional square-dancing favorites. They also played old unwritten tunes: one that 'Rasmus called "Tater Soup," and "Little Old Man":

Little old man goes ridin' by
Says I, "Old man your horse will die."
"Well if he dies I'll tan his skin
"An' if he lives, I'll ride him agin."

In recent years I wrote them down for a summer playhouse that asked for little-known folk tunes. Here's "Git Along Home, Sally Gal":

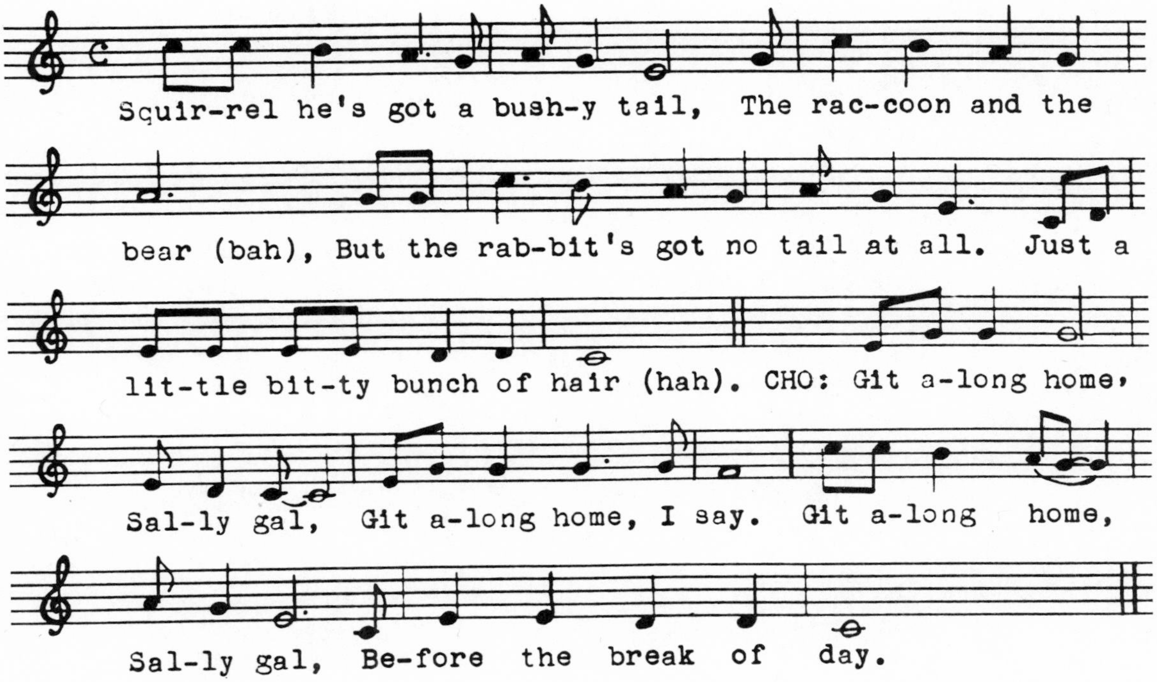
Squir-rel he's got a bush-y tail, The rac-coon and the
bear (bah), But the rab-bit's got no tail at all. Just a
lit-tle bit-ty bunch of hair (hah). CHO: Git a-long home,
Sal-ly gal, Git a-long home, I say. Git a-long home,
Sal-ly gal, Be-fore the break of day.

'Rasmus and Chet also played modern numbers such as "My Sweetheart's the Man in the Moon" (1892), "After the Ball," and that new ragtime piece "At a Georgia Camp Meeting" (1897), which was re-created as recently as 1966 at the international contest of the men's quartet society, the Society for the Preservation and Encouragement of Barber Shop Quartet Singing in America (SPEBSQSA). Though these tunes were played by Missourians, "The Missouri Waltz" wouldn't be written until about 1911.* Radio had not been invented when 'Rasmus and Chet played, so we were spared the dolefully whinnied duets of later hillbilly music years.

* See Appendix B.

About 1900–1902, a composite inventory of the shelves in the neighbors' ornate organ cabinets would have looked something like this:

"The Battle of Waterloo"	*Colorful huzzars charging into cannons' mouths on the sheet-music cover—"Realistic effects," it said.*
"Sweet Bunch of Daisies"	*Usually confused with Anita Owen's later opus "Daisies Won't Tell."*
"Will Rossiter's Songster"	*Ten-cent pamphlet with original words, parodies, some music, jokes, conundrums, and ads. (Comment later—here.)*
"The Fatal Rose of Red"	*The plot got sticky when "instead of the white she wore that night the fatal rose of red." He had hoped it would be a white one.*
"Talmadge's Sermons"	*Deluxe binding. Pages uncut beyond page 12.*
Moody & Sankey's Gospel Hymns	*Forerunners of the Billy Sunday–Rhodeheaver variety*
"The Pardon Came Too Late"	*Sad ballad, typical of the many then popular such as "Just Behind the Times" and "Those Wedding Bells Shall Not Ring Out."*
The re-ceet for strawberry-pieplant cobbler	*It had disappeared that time when Grandma lost her specs. (She found them later in the salt barrel in the smokehouse.)*

On some organs there might be a copy of "Good Old Songs," dog-eared and in poor condition. Its index included favorites of my mother's era:

Annie Laurie
Billy Boy
Birdies' Ball
Blue Juniata
Darling Nellie Gray
Down the Shadowed Lane She Goes
Heart Bowed Down
Her Bright Eyes Haunt Me Still
Little Brown Church in the Vale
Life on the Ocean Wave
Loch Lomond
My Old Kentucky Home
Nelly Was a Lady
Old Folks at Home (Swanee River) *
Rock Me to Sleep, Mother
Rocked in the Cradle of the Deep
Tenting on the Old Camp Ground
Twinkle, Twinkle, Little Star

* Stephen C. Foster, the composer, sold the song to E. P. Christy of Christy's Minstrels for fifteen dollars. At that time, Foster didn't want his name connected with the current "Ethiopian" trend in song popularity. Later, he wrote Christy a request that his name appear as composer. The request was granted. Sigmund Spaeth did much research in getting the full story for his *History of Popular Music in America,* 1948. It includes Foster's request.

Now that samples of the content of the memory and neighborhood files have been poured out for inspection, it is evident that the country music at that time was in part as new as the 1890's and early 1900's, while some of it was already old when the century turned. Many of the numbers were so well built that they have survived the musical rat race for popularity which goes on perennially. "Old Folks at Home" (Swanee River) and "Little Brown Church" as examples must be pretty good music to have outlived competitions of the last hundred years. That applies also to hymns.

The Ay-Men Corner

A choir director, Richard Lindroth, once wrote (*Saturday Review*), "A hymn is not a work of art in the sense that a stained glass window is. You don't stand and admire a hymn, you enter into it." No stained glass decorated the little white box of a Methodist church at Oakdale, heated by two wood-burning box stoves and lighted by kerosene lamps. Two matriarchal rivals entered into the hymns so vigorously that "Mary Lou outsung Aunt Molly this morning" needed no explanation to the locals.

Hymns were a part of a boy's education, extracurricular like his practical dendrology. You didn't call an elm a maple tree or an ash tree a hickory or whitewood. If you did, a bigger boy would poke fun at you, as he would if you called a jimson weed a pokeberry, or a bloodroot a hepatica. No, sir! He might knucklerub some sense into your wooden head, and that hurt.

There was plenty of study time in church for hymn education while you tried to keep awake during two hours, at least, of the circuit preacher's sermon, unless it was Baptism Sunday or the Sunday for his dramatic temperance sermon. The way he'd act it out and yell, the drunkard's doom was terrible. If you looked upon the wine when it was red, "At the last it biteth like a serpent and stingeth like an adder," which meant you'd die of delirium tremens while seeing pink snakes. On one Temperance Sunday three little boys, shaking in their shoes instead of weekday leather boots, walked a long mile to the pulpit platform, glanced gulpingly at the preacher for their starting cue, and gasped:

A pledge we make no wine to take, nor brandy red to turn the head. To quench our thirst we'll always bring cold water from the well or spring . . . And so we pledge perpetual hate to all that can intoxicate.

On Foreign Missions Sunday or just a regular Sunday, you had to do something to keep awake, and it helped to read the hymn book. It became a matter of pride to memorize words so you could sing them with no more than an occasional pickup glance at three or more verses in "All Hail the Power" or "From Greenland's Icy Mountains" on foreign missions day. "Leaning on the

Everlasting Arms" had a thumping antiphonal bass from the men's side of the church.

Because of pioneer customs held over, the women sat on the right facing the pulpit. Only a young man who was courting a girl ever sat on the women's side, in a declarative sort of way, though not with her mother or sisters. At the front of the men's side, in the corner beside the pulpit, white-hearded patriarchs held down the Amen Corner, pronounced Ay-men. I never knew whether they were there by succession or election to that exclusive club. Over the years while I knew the Amen Corner, the personnel changed only when one of the oldsters was laid away in the adjoining cemetery. One ancient had been in the Mexican War. He could still spot a squirrel in a tree while riding to the store, and shoot it from the saddle. When the preacher made a point that pleased him, he'd boom, "A-a-aymen, brother." Sometimes his aymen was so powerful that it made a sensitive chain jingle on one of the pulldown coal-oil lamps. Usually another veteran would chime in with an echo effect: "God be praised, a-a-aymen."

All the old men in the Corner were called "Uncle," a traditional courtesy in those parts to all gray beards. Since then I have participated in much music of great variety and have heard more that was truly grand music. Little of it has affected me in grandeur as did some of the old hymns at Oakdale, sung *a cappella* until Uncle Solomon Evans capitulated to the Young Progressives' plea for a reed organ. He'd maintained that it wasn't fittin' because the Book didn't mention organs. The way they sang those old hymns gave evidence of beliefs that centuries had not eroded. Their faith and their hopes came out majestically when the men's side boomed a bass that sent shivers up your back. "There Is a Land of Pure Delight," "On Jordan's Stormy Banks I Stand," "Yield Not to Temptation," "Guide Me, O Thou Great Jehovah," "How Firm a Foundation," "There Is a Happy Land," and others were sung to the old tunes that had come out from Virginia and Kentucky with the pioneers.

At that time and place several members of the congregation sang in a manner that is familiar to all who have attended Protestant church services in small towns of the South or who have tuned in to the Sunday morning programs aired, usually early, by many radio stations direct from the source. It is a style that is reminiscent of what you may call country or hillbilly or western in which the melody carrier sometimes anticipates the next melody note.

Judged only as verse without the music, many hymns, including traditional ones, often limp badly. Their forced rhymes and assonance set them apart from other lasting published verse. Frequently, the end rhymes provide proof of the lyric writer's eye-mindedness ("prove" matched with "love," "Lord" with "word," "will do" with "will go," and such), though in some instances the evidence may indicate archaic English pronunciations held over or sectional phonetics that have become obsolete. Without good melodies, harmonies, and churchly backgrounds some hymn lyrics would have deserved the sudden death that overtakes poetic effusions that don't measure up. But hymns are not entered into critically, as one would contemplate and perhaps criticize Lindroth's stained glass.

The hymns that follow constituted an important part of country music old-style at Oakdale, as they did in thousands of other rural areas where English was the predominant language. Some are universal while others have fervor in their music or words that would exclude them from a conservative's collection. An Episcopalian's teeth would be set on edge by some of them. The nuances of others must be explained to Catholic or Jewish friends. That is because they have no recall of the brand of gospel preached by a mud-splashed circuit rider, his admonitions, or the responses from the Amen Corner of that country church. So, I confess, sentiment triumphs over critical judgment.

ALL SORTS OF HYMNS

Abide with Me
Am I a Soldier of the Cross?
Angels from the Realms of Glory
At the Cross
Away in a Manger
Beneath the Cross of Jesus
Beulah Land
Blessed Assurance
Bringing in the Sheaves
Calm on the Listening Ear of Night
Come Thou Almighty King
Day Is Dying in the West
Dear Lord and Father of Mankind
Faith of Our Fathers
Glory to His Name
Greenfields
Hark, the Herald Angels Sing
He Leadeth Me
Holy Night
I Am Thine, O Lord
I'm Going Home
I Need Thee Every Hour
In the Cross of Christ I Glory
Is My Name Written There?
It Came upon the Midnight Clear
Jerusalem the Golden
Jesus, Keep Me Near the Cross
Jesus Loves Me
Jesus, Saviour, Pilot Me
Jesus Wants Me for a Sunbeam
Joy to the World
Let the Lower Lights Be Burning
Love Divine All Love Excelling
Majestic Sweetness
Must Jesus Bear the Cross Alone
Now the Day Is Over
O God Our Help in Ages Past
O Little Town of Bethlehem
Oh, Come All Ye Faithful
Oh, Think of the Home Over There
Oh, Worship the King
Precious Jewels

Rock of Ages
Shall We Gather at the River?
Softly Now the Light of Day
Stand Up for Jesus
Sweet Hour of Prayer
There Is a Green Hill Far Away
Throw Out the Life Line
Watchman, Tell Us of the Night
We Praise Thee, O God (Hallelujah thine the glory)
We're Marching to Zion
When I Survey the Wondrous Cross
When the Roll Is Called up Yonder
Whiter Than Snow
Will There Be Any Stars in My Crown?
Yield Not to Temptation

Hymns such as "Just As I Am [without one plea]" and "Lord, I'm Coming Home" were sung at the end of the sermon when converts were invited to come to the altar. Revival meetings were big events at Oakdale. They bordered upon the theatrical on the part of visiting revivalists and were definitely so when an individual would "get religion" and parade the aisles, shouting his conversion. At those meetings the songs often became quite secular in their musical moods. "Are You Ready for the Judgment Day?" and "Washed in the Blood of the Lamb" and "There's a Great Day Coming" had stuff that a Dixieland combo could send.

All, including those that shouted "The Old Time Religion—it's good enough for me," are magic touchstones of recall.

Music From Heaven

For reasons related to music, the period around 1902 was a most exciting one. My older brother returned from the gold diggings of Cripple Creek, Colorado, with a mandolin. Then he ordered a Harwood guitar from Jenkins in Kansas City. Though I had never before heard a mandolin, I knew the instrument by hearsay. Mother enjoyed telling of the occasion when a young man came by the new railroad to visit her family at Oakdale when she was a girl there. The final stage of his journey was on a horse, rented at Ben Dobyn's Livery Stable in Shelbina. In the saddlebags he carried a small gourd-shaped musical instrument.

They had no instrument in their home, and in consequence she and her sisters went into ecstasies over his exotic mandolin. After he'd gone back to the railroad, the girls were still twittering. Then Grandpa ha-rumped and spoke: "Hm! It sounded to me like an old sow scratchin' her tail against a splinter." That was more than a century ago. My personal participations on the mandolin cover at least half that time. Based upon intimate acquaintance with it, I declare that Grandpa's ringside statement is the outstanding blow-by-blow description of all contests between man and mandolin.

To show how important musical self-expression can be to some, my brother Clarence played his mandolin in reverse. A shotgun wound had crooked the fingers on his left hand used normally in fingering strings. He restrung it backward. By determination and application, such as few of us have, he taught himself to finger with his right hand. Every thought and motion was reversed, as in mirror writing. He did not develop a split personality.

In the mail-order book of *Arrangements for Mandolin and Guitar* (fifty cents), I was introduced to foreign-looking names such as Mascagni, Chaminade, Czibulka, Verdi, De Koven, and Schumann. The introductions led to some fraternization, but only after discouraging struggles to relate the strings and frets with the little black dots and symbols in the book. My brother said that the staff lines signified Every Good Boy Does Fine, but I didn't care to after the first five minutes of practice. Nonetheless, he was determined to make up my mind for me. Conscientiously, he tried with minimal success to bend the twig so that the tree would incline in the right direction. Sullenly, I learned "Stephanie Gavotte," selections from "Martha," "La Czarina," "Evening Star," "Cavalleria Rusticana," the meditation from *Thaïs,* Mendelssohn's "Spring Song," and other standards. He also taught me to tinkle the "Spanish Fandango" and to pluck four chords in C on the guitar. They were adequate, according to local standards, when applied to "Bedelia," "In a Cozy Corner," "Goodbye, Dolly Gray," "Ain't Dat a Shame?" "Bill Bailey, Won't You Please Come Home?" and "Just Because She Made Them Goo-Goo Eyes."

In addition to the mandolin and guitar, other great experiences were in store. There were no telephones, so the unannounced arrival of a traveling medicine show shook the community to its boot tops. Four wagons and their exhausted teams were red with mud when the show slogged to the blacksmith shop and pitched tents back of it. By nightfall the grapevine telegraph had spread the news throughout the immediate community, as much as two miles away. A brilliant gasoline lantern made the ticket booth (ten-cent tickets) as light as day, we thought, and attendance was good.

While an instrumentalist pedaled his tiny portable reed organ, the entire company, seven including two wives and one mule driver who filled in but didn't sing, did the grand opening chorus of "Dixie" in a walk-around on the diminutive stage, in keeping with composer Dan Emmett's intent when he wrote "I Wish I Was in Dixie's Land" for Christy's Minstrels in 1860. The organist sang "I Got Mine," "Under the Bamboo Tree," "My Hanna Lady," and other Latest Hits from Broadway it said on the song pamphlets which he sold for only the tenth paht of a dollah—get 'em while they last.

He was also the company's cook. Naturally, the medicine-show tents were powerful magnets for the neighborhood's children by day as well as night. The cook-organist basked in the admiration of small fry whose round eyes followed his every move in the open cook tent as he plied his part-time trade. His dexterity with flapjacks on his gasoline stove, a marvel in itself, drew audible applause from his admirers. Flipjacks, he called them while flipping with dextrous wrist motions. That was *very* funny. He was the favorite.

The medicine show's doctor was less approachable. He was a learned man of immense dignity. He wore a white sombrero above his white hair that hung in curls to his shoulders, like pictures of Buffalo Bill. He must have attended most of the great colleges to be able to expound so eruditely upon human ills and to use words like "superabundantly." That referred to the energy his Nerve Elixir would give if we took only three bottles. Between the acts of the show, which included daring trapeze work in the top of the tent by the mule driver who couldn't sing, the doctor extolled the merits of the elixir from the stage while others in the company roved through the audience with baskets of it. It was *"magnetized"* to draw out super-a-bund-dant-ly the re-sid-u-al im-pur-i-ties in-here-ent to the hu-man sys-tem, but it cost only a dollar a bottle. When an excited "All sold out, Doctor" came from his assistants traveling through the tent, the radiance of the smile on the good doctor's face dazzled even those in the top rows of the knockdown wooden board seats.

The perennially popular medicine sold at the Davis store, also for a dollar, was Peruna, but it wasn't magnetized. Even so, it remained on the store's best-seller list after the medicine show. Some adults would have been hard put to live without it when sporadic drives by W.C.T.U. women and church groups dried, temporarily, the flow from the bourbon barrel in the back room of the drugstore at the railroad town. Several neighbors needed their Peruna regularly for coughs, lack of appetite, and general debility—an ounce or two before meals. It was medicine, like rock and rye. Rye on the rocks would have been intoxicating liquor.*

The show closed with "Over the River, Charley," as fine a dramatic bit as had been seen in those parts. On the last night the doctor broke his rule of years, he said. He cut the price of the remaining bottles of elixir to only fifty cents. Experienced older citizens, who had been waiting cannily, invested heavily at that bargain price. Later, Dr. Owen said that the elixir bottles held Broughton Branch water with a dash of sugar and licorice. He said that the stuff floating in the elixir was pulverized senna with a few crushed pennyroyal leaves that the medicine-show doctor had picked back of the tents.

That epochal event and the musical legacy of instruments, song sheets, and music books from my brother, added to the well-remembered songs held over, made that little box of a house a music box, Mother said. Among the newer numbers demanding attention were:

Ain't Dat a Shame?
Alexander
Any Rags?
Beautiful Isle of Somewhere
Bill Bailey, Won't You Please Come Home?
Bird in a Gilded Cage
By the Watermelon Vine
Daisy Bell (Bicycle Built for Two)
Doan You Cry, Mah Honey
Down Where the Cotton Blossoms Grow
Drowsy Babe
Forgotten
Good Morning, Carrie
Hiawatha (it introduced an Indian song cycle)
Honeysuckle and the Bee
If I Only Had a Dollar of My Own
I Got Mine
I Guess I'll Have to Telegraph My Baby
I'm Wearing My Heart Away for You
In the Shadow of the Pines
I Want Dem Presents Back
Just Because She Made Them Goo-Goo Eyes
Kentucky Babe
Learning McFadden to Waltz
My Coal Black Lady
My Dusky Rose
My Gal Is a High Born Lady
My Old New Hampshire Home
Mid the Green Fields of Virginia
Mr. Dooley
Picnic for Two
Put Me Off at Buffalo
Rastus on Parade
Rosary (The), by Nevin (there are others)
She Was Bred in Old Kentucky
Sing Me to Sleep
Tell Me, Pretty Maiden (Florodora)
That Bully
When the Bees Are in the Hive
When the Harvest Days Are Over, Jessie Dear
When You Were Sweet Sixteen
Where the Silvery Colorado Wends Its Way

Since songs lasted long, some were carried over from the nineties. Others were remembered from the medicine show. Still others were memorized from a magic machine heard in Shelbina. The man put a little cylinder into it, a grinding sound came out, then a voice that introduced Ada Jones and Billy Murray in "Kiss Kiss Kiss"—"Edi-son Reco-o-rd."

Suddenly the glories of the medicine show dimmed by comparison when the

* See Appendix C.

Shelbina *Torchlight* announced special excursion rates to the St. Louis World's Fair. It marked, a year late, the 100th anniversary of the Louisiana Purchase which had given the young nation Lebensraum.* Though anticipations are so often beyond actualities, in this case the event topped anything hoped for, in part (you guessed it) because of music. This was not because of the hit song of 1904, "Meet Me in St. Louis, Louis—meet me at the Fair," to which the nation was waltzing. The reason was quite different.

To go to St. Louis necessitated taking a train on the "Q" to Macon where the Wabash railroad's excursion train from the north would stop in the early morning. Mother's letter requesting that I be allowed to stay overnight with some fourth cousins brought an immediate cordial invitation. It included a warning about pickpockets and suggested that my cash, life savings of eighteen dollars, be pinned into my underwear. Late on a Sunday afternoon I arrived in Macon firmly pinned. That evening, the cousins took me to their church. When we entered, the place was filled with music that must be coming right from heaven. They said it was from a pipe organ. A theme recurred again and again. It became so firmly fixed in my music memory that it outlasted the marvels of the fair, where I heard Guilmant play another greater organ.

Returning to Oakdale by a neighbor's farm wagon, I could hardly wait to tune the mandolin and start scratching at that Sunday night theme, still so vivid. It was a long time before I learned that "Traumerei" had entered my life on a pipe organ and had survived as That Tune on the mandolin.

"Hearts and Flowers" was among other instrumental numbers in our country music. Played on a parlor organ with the tremolo stop pulled out, reactions to it were invariable: "So sweet." About that one and the earlier "Flower Song" in my sister's repertoire, it wouldn't have seemed possible then that in 1948 my old friend Sigmund Spaeth would refer to both of them in his *History of Popular Music in America* (Random House) as "sentimental tunes that Americans of the naive '90s simply adored." They were and they did.

Played today by an organist capitalizing upon the beautiful agonies inherent to his electronic instrument, either of those sentimental tunes could make a lonely listener cry as copiously into his beer as if the newer "Sweet summer breeze, murmuring trees..." were dripping in syrupy sadness. Fritzi Scheff popularized, then made a career, of that one, "Kiss Me Again," long before PA systems.

* See Appendix D.

Music Opens Doors

The desire and intention to go beyond the one-room school at Oakdale was not approved by all the elders consulted. Some felt that the boy was gettin' uppity. At age fourteen he could hire out on a farm and earn ten dollars a month and board and room for the rest of his life. Why take a chance? In town he might drift from bad to worse and end up in some wicked city. Tales were told of the vices of Hannibal and Quincy.

Luck rode with me and a load of hogs hauled by a neighbor to Shelbina. There I became the companion and chambermaid to a leading citizen's temperamental horse, a cow that kicked viciously while being milked, an enormous hungry furnace, a garden, and a quarter acre of lawn. That in exchange for a folding bed and meals. What a bargain! No wonder that I snapped it up. The livestock is explained by the lack of zoning or health restrictions as we know them now. Horses, cows, poultry, and flies in stable yards behind fine homes in small towns were natural to the civic scene.

Schedules in winter started at 5:30 A.M., just after a growing boy had gone to sleep, it seemed. That furnace! Between it and the domestic duties, school hours and study, the days left little time for the Devil to find mischief for idle hands to do. But there was time for music. A high-school music teacher who was broad-minded for that community and era encouraged the formation of a boy's quartet. Its first appearance, singing "Good Night, Ladies" at 8:30 in the morning before a captive audience of tolerant teen-agers, was a success. They asked for more, so Miss Blanche Simpson taught us other standard quartet numbers and went even beyond that. She coached us in songs that were currently popular. The peak performance came at a gathering of pre-PTA parents when we sang that new 1906 hit "I Picked a Lemon in the Garden of Love—where they say only peaches grow" and were made.

A gifted young amateur violinist lived across the street from my town house. He played with the windows open. Sometimes it was music that I'd never heard—concertos, he told me later. His musical meanderings always picked up a trail to numbers that I recognized. With patrician deliberation he began to recognize the presence of the boy in the funny six-dollar suit who milked the neighbor's cow. One day the boy managed to mumble something about owning a guitar. Eventually, that led to an invitation to come over and bring it.

Social lines in a very small town are hardly definable. Economic status has the most frequent bearing, though length and place of residence may enter into it too. One who lived in the older part of town, even before they built the new courthouse, is inclined to look down the nose at a newcomer who converted the old Blue Front Restaurant into Jim's Dog 'n' Suds, and is now in the country club. To an outlander from the backwoods the social lines seemed etched on steel. Yet the guitar as background harmony for the violin became a key to doors behind which the socially elite retired after a hard day in the furniture or feed store (livestock not a supermarket). The fiddle-guitar duo became a trio, then a singing quartet that alternated on strings. It performed regularly for its own enjoyment and the town barber's.

Since that reference to the barber may be incomprehensible to some, let's halt the tour for a minute to inspect the duality of the small town barber's shop in that era. Villages had no Ping-Pong tables at a Y.M.C.A. building, nor swimming pools or lounges for local youth. There were no recreation or rehabilitation centers. In countless small towns and in some urban neighborhoods the barber's shop often did double duty as a men's club of a sort. That included an option for the musically inclined to frequent his place by permission of the barber. Later, we shall delve deeply into this condition which eventually led to the American musical phenomenon now called "barbershop" harmony.

The string-sing foursome which developed from our violin-guitar twosome experienced special enjoyments on the soft May nights before graduation from high school in 1908—experience unknown to a later motorized generation. The quartet drifted aimlessly in a surrey (with a "fringe on top," of course), singing and playing to the gentle clop-clop of a fat mare's hoofs as she plodded unguided, reins hooked over the dashboard, through the dust of the unpaved streets. What did the four play and sing? Here are a few more in the repertoire of country village musicians of those days:

Anona (from Arizona, of course)
Best I Get Is Much Obliged to You
Blue and the Gray (The)
Cousin of Mine (A)
Dreaming
Everybody Works But Father
Honey Boy
I Can't Tell You Why I Love You (but I do-oo-oo)
I'd Leave My Happy Home for You
I Don't Know Where I'm Going (but I'm on my way)
In the Good Old Summertime
It Looks Like a Big Night Tonight
Love Me, and the World Is Mine
Mighty Lak a Rose
Message of the Violet
Navajo
Picnic for Two (A)
Please Go 'Way and Let Me Sleep
Sing Me to Sleep
Tale of the Bumblebee
Tale of the Kangaroo
That's What the Daisy Said
There's Class to a Girl Like You
Toyland
When You Know You're Not Forgotten (by the girl you can't forget)

They are from the many that included "Cuddle Up a Little Closer—lovey mine" and others built of such durable goods that they have survived the abrasions of the jazz era and rock 'n' roll. Even then we called some of them oldies, a term which when heard today may suggest a song written 'way back in 1960. Farther along, we'll inspect the factors that make a song an oldie or newie, and arrive at a formula to gauge them.

Music continued to open doors when I went to teach in a one-room school near Shelbyville. It might well have been designed as a duplicate of the one at Oakdale. No teaching certificate was necessary, and there were no queries about my knowledge, aptitude, or experience. They wanted a man teacher who could handle the big boys attending school between corn cuttin' time in the fall and spring plowin' time. The $30-a-month salary was quite a boost from $10 a month for fifteen or more hours of hard labor as a farmhand, with Sunday afternoons off until milking time. Higher education was paying off fast. But I had to disburse $2.50 each week for a room in a nearby farm home and twenty-one meals invariably bountiful and excellent.

One Saturday morning in Shelbyville I picked up a guitar from the window ledge in the barber's shop window. As in many other such shops, the barber supplied it for customers who might care to strum while waiting their turns. Glenn Hayward, second in command, was busy cutting hair, but he took notice of the stranger's modulations. As he finished his shearing, there was a lag in business. He produced a mandolin from a locker, but just then the first in a procession of farmers, in town for Saturday tradin', entered. So we had time for only one tentative string duet, "Alice, Where Art Thou Going?" currently popular, and zippy as compared with the staid old Claribel opus "Alice, Where Art Thou?" on whose name the new song capitalized. That introduced a winter of joyous musical participations.

By now, the reason for the earlier differentiation between country music old-style and the commercial "country" music of later years, into which hillbilly was graduated, must be as evident as a beechnut in a boot. The music of Shelbyville and such villages throughout the country was broader in variety and in instrumentation than that at remote Oakdale. Current hits arrived earlier than at the farm. Yet, isolated as it was by flood, mud, and snow, Oakdale's music was in its limited way the popular music of America when the nineties peered 'round the corner into the 1900's and after the old century became the new. It took longer for new music to arrive in the backwoods than in the country villages. A chief difference between the Oakdales of the nation and more urban communities was in the retention of traditional folk-type tunes after they'd worn out their welcome among city folks. Particularly Negroes in our section kept many of the old tunes alive.

Negroes and Our Popular Songs

In the tiny town where I attended high school the white attitude toward Negroes was one of friendliness "as long as they keep their place." That was in rundown houses on the north (wrong) side of the C. B. & Q. tracks. Socially their place was about the same as when the state was admitted to the Union, March 3, 1820—the period when Congress approved Henry Clay's "Missouri Compromise" bill which made Missouri a slave state, the last one admitted west of the Mississippi and north of the state's southern line, 36′30″ latitude.

The majority of the white people in this country town stemmed from the same Virginia-Kentucky roots as those in rural Oakdale. Everyone took segregation for granted. The colored children attended school in a dreary frame building on the North Side. Many of the older Negroes had known slavery and its traditions. The northerly flood from the South had hardly begun to trickle. Local friendships with the Negroes came out clearly on election day, a day of holidaylike celebration comparable with Christmas when the old Negroes still used the greeting "Christmas gift," a holdover from the era when "massa" was duty bound to give largess to those who beat him to the greeting.

Election day was a men's day. (Women would not be enfranchised until 1920.) It was expected that certain characters, white, would get drunk on drugstore whiskey and bask in the spotlight as they passed through their traditional evolutions from jollity to a stage where any remark could be twisted by them into an insult and the inevitable election day fight. But even fighting men were tolerant of their Negro friends. Amicably, they were allowed to vote before eight o'clock in the morning. After that, "Black boy, keep off the streets." During the morning the town marshal helped to enforce apartheid. After that, he was carried home to sleep off his election day drowsiness, but white supremacy continued until the polls closed.

At other times, the Negroes contributed to local music in a way peculiar to that community and era. A tiny strip of park opposite the "Q" depot and its tracks, the dividing line, was a favorite gathering place for certain of the colored men on summer nights. In the darkness under the park's trees a voice would lead out a melody. The deep bass of Bud, shoeshiner by vocation in the barber's shop, a voice recognized throughout the community, would chime in foundation harmony, and the other parts would slide into their grooves. Whether only four were at a sing-out or a dozen were joining in, nobody other than Bud sang bass. He had volume and depth to hold his own against the field. Their harmonies spread throughout the little town on a quiet night.

SLOWLY
Melody
Night shades are fall-ing, Fast gath-er round me.
The bright moon is beam-ing When the day has past a-way.
(SLOWER)
Life's long dream is o'er. Life's long dream- is o'er.

Many of the songs were held over from long-forgotten originals into which they pieced scraps of their own melody, harmony, and lyrics, as did the white barbershop quartets. A favorite among the Negroes was called "Night Shades Are Falling." Charley Dimmit, man of all work for the Dimmit family, usually led it—that is, he sang melody. As nearly as it is possible to reduce their singing to notations, they follow. But notes cannot reproduce the effects of their rubato when a note was shortened in order to sustain another note. Nor is it possible to indicate their shadings when Bud, as example of others, would hold back to let the others dominate, then let go with a bass note on the first "dream *is* o'er" that almost twisted the nearby railroad tracks. However, there were none of the dissonant ululations that present-day Negroes, and whites trying to copy them, throw into the hymns and spirituals heard on radio and TV. Referring again to Bud, if he felt just right, he might choose to sing a low F on the next to the last note (*is*). When he did that, seconds of awed, respectful, almost worshipful silence followed. The others knew that they'd heard the impossible. (Of course they may have been singing in a higher key than the above.)

When Charley Dimmit sang with us (he wasn't choosy), it was inevitable that someone would suggest "Night Shades," which was always acceptable. It was also inevitable that someone would ask him the meaning of "x-a-bee," though he'd stated it many times before. Bandy-legged Charley would wriggle with embarrassment for folks who asked such foolish questions. "Them's the *words,*" he'd reply. Like many of his color, he could neither read nor write. I've never been able to connect the tune or lyrics with any song of any era, including authentic folk. Musically, the first two bars are reminiscent of "Alice, Where Art Thou?" of 1861. I am quite sure that Charley's "x-a-bee" was written originally as "one moment's ec-sta-sy."

Changes like that had precedent among off-the-cuff white singers. Even today, a favorite among the chapters, coast to coast in the states and Canada, of SPEBSQSA, is one called "Bright Was the Night." As written by H. R. Williams to Egbert Van Alstyne's music in 1907, the song was "There Never Was a Girl Like You." The verse opened with "Bright was the day..." As sung now, it follows Van Alstyne's melody at the beginning, then branches off. There are many such.

Many of the songs sung by the Negroes in the darkness of the little park were the populars of the day, and that included many "coon" songs that are never heard publicly nowadays, though some of them were composed by Negroes who rated high in musicianship. Here should be the place to comment upon the national contributions made directly by Negroes or in the songs about them. It will demonstrate a changed and still changing status. To do so necessitates the use of words and allusions that are offensive to most Negroes and equally so to many white people. But without them the song story of Negro progress cannot be told. A skeptic might construe "progress" as a predetermined conclusion. Actually it is the result of the findings that will be obvious as the songs present their own evidence. As we peruse songs by and about Negroes since slavery days, remember that great numbers of our popular songs constitute records of our national thought and attitudes in their eras, in this case several eras, of change.

To be "popular" in fact, songs must be tuned to the thought of great numbers of people, whose thinking yesterday isn't necessarily what they think today or will think tomorrow. (This does *not* introduce a thesis on our foreign relations policies.) There is no clearer proof of changing thought than what has been written into songs in Negro themes. To show the changes in attitude it is necessary to flash back, as in the movies.

During more than half of the 1800's most Negroes were chattels, and the songs about them took that ownership for granted. In the main the early songs about Negroes were in humorous vein, though a few composers, including Stephen Foster and James A. Bland, a Negro, wrote about Negroes as humans rather than creatures with little more sensibilities than the family houn' dog. Benjamin Russel Hanby's "Darling Nellie Gray," written before Lincoln's

Emancipation Proclamation, typifies the understanding expressed by a few of that era's songwriters:

Oh, my poor Nellie Gray
They have taken her away
And I'll never see my darling any more.
I am sitting by the river
And I'm weeping all the day
For you've gone from the old Kentucky shore.

J. P. Webster's "Zula Zong" (1860), which my mother sang, was another lament by a slave. (Three years before, he composed "Lorena," the song that was so popular on both sides of the lines during the Civil War.)

In those days Negro stage characters spoke Uncle Remus American and most songs with Negro themes followed the pattern set by the jocular endmen of the touring blackface minstrel troupes. Dan Emmett's "I Wish I Was in Dixie's Land" (our "Dixie") was written for Christy's Minstrels:

Den I wish I was in Dixie, Hooray! Hooray!
In Dixie land I'll take my stand
To lib or die in Dixie.

It is reasonable to believe that New England abolitionist H. C. Work, who wrote "Kingdom Comin'" in 1862, copied his exaggerated dialect from the Sambos and Topsies of fiction and the stage:

Say, darkeys, hab you seen the massa
Wid de mufstas on his face
Go long de road some time dis mornin'
Like he gwine to leab de place?

The attitudes of the great majority of the nation had been stated more than a decade earlier by Harriet Beecher Stowe in her preface to *Uncle Tom's Cabin, or Life Among the Lowly.* She wrote: "The scenes of this story, as its title indicates, lie among a race hitherto ignored by the association of polite and refined society...." Few today have read *Uncle Tom* or the lines with which the book closed: "A day of grace is yet held out to us. Both North and South have been guilty before God; and the Christian church has a heavy account to answer...not surer is the eternal law by which the millstone sinks in the ocean, than that stronger law by which injustice and cruelty shall bring on nations the wrath of Almighty God."

Because her book rocketed to the best-seller list, it became a subject for songs immediately. To those few who have read *Uncle Tom,* the origin of several 1852–53 song titles are obvious: "Eliza's Flight," "Eva to Her Papa," "The Death of Little Eva," and more. Long before that, the feelings of polite and refined society had been clear in the songs of the earlier 1800's such as "Jim Along, Josy," "Zip Coon" ("Turkey in the Straw"), "Jump, Jim Crow," "Old Dan Tucker," which was another Emmett song hit, and in the rollicking lyrics of Foster's "Camptown Races" and "Oh, Susanna." Usually he wrote about the somber sides of Negro life. Here is a lesser known verse of his classic "My Old Kentucky Home":

The head must bow and the back will have to bend
Wherever the darkey may go.
A few more days and the troubles all will end
In the field where the sugar canes grow.

Lines such as these and the thoughts expressed in comparable songs were sung by millions of Americans. Since relatively few of them could, or would, read *Uncle Tom,* the songs may have had as great an influence in bringing slavery's issue to a head as is credited to the book itself.

In the majority of the Civil War era's songs about Negroes they were unschooled and illiterate "darkeys," a word which might express scorn, tolerance, or affection, depending upon the user. Since national attitudes cannot change overnight and may shift only slightly over a century or more, the songs of the emancipation period (1863) and the later Reconstruction years were, in general, cut from the earlier patterns, with an exception. In addition to freedom, emancipation changed the nation's thought about the Negro's status in a most important respect, which became evident musically. Freed, the Negro had the new privilege of travel, of seeking a livelihood, of congregating, and in other ways placing himself more conspicuously against a broader background of white people than during slavery days. Before emancipation a Hanby song "Old Shady" (1861) had depicted the longings of the runaway "contraband" slave.

Goodbye, hard work wid never any pay
Ise a gwine up North where the good folks say
Dat white wheat bread and a dollar a day
Am coming, coming, Hail! Mighty day.

A verse of Work's "Kingdom Comin' " refers to contraband, the term for runaway slave, often described in handbills which offered a reward for his apprehension as the "Wanted" bills for criminals are posted today in post offices. In Work's song, old massa had seen the smoke of the Yankee gunboats 'way up de riber and had taken off like a rocket:

He six foot one way, two foot tudder
An' he weigh three hundred pound.
His coat so big he couldn't pay de tailor
An' it won't go half-way round.
He drill so much they call him Cap'an
An' he get so drefful tann'd,
I spec he try to fool dem Yankees
For to tink he's contraband.
De massa run? ha, ha!
De darkey say? ho, ho!
It mus be now de kingdom comin'
An' de year ob Jubilo.

Two years after the proclamation and while the war still raged, he wrote "Babylon Is Fallen" in quite different vein.

Don't you see de black clouds
Risin' ober yonder
Whar de massa's plantation am.
Neber you be frightened
Dem is only darkeys
Come to jine an' fight for Uncle Sam.
Babylon is fallen, Babylon is fallen
An' we's gwine to occupy de land.

Some continued to occupy the land under about the same conditions as when they had lived in slavery. Many others started the northerly migration that continues into the troubled 1960's.

In the North "the character so essentially unlike the hard and dominant Anglo-Saxon race," according to Mrs. Stowe's preface, became a natural subject for songwriters and others. The humor magazines, jokebooks, the stage, and particularly the minstrels shaped the older conventional plantation darkey into a new caricature exemplified by countless stories and references to "dinges," "smokes," and "shines," among others as examples of the national attitude. Since songs mirror public sentiment and speech, quite naturally the songs of the seventies, eighties, nineties, and early 1900's followed the pattern.

The popular concept was that the Negro was illiterate and maintained a jester's attitude toward life. His interests centered upon eating chicken, pork chops, and watermelon whether acquired honestly or not, rolling dice, drinking gin and then carving someone with his ever-present old-style razor, dancing at night on the levee or elsewhere, sleeping all day, loving in an amoral sort of way, and playing the banjo as exemplified by the 1877 "De Banjo Am de Instrument for Me."

"The Whistling Coon" of 1888 included:

He's a knock-kneed, double jointed hunky-plunky moke
And he's happy when he whistles this tune.

Also there was "Whistling Rufus" (1899).

Near the century's end a few songwriters wrote with understanding: Noll's "Doan You Cry, Mah Honey," Geible's "Kentucky Babe," and Nevin's "Mighty Lak a Rose." Such songs referred to the tiny ones rather than to the adults whose parental problems as free people crept gradually into such songs as "Little Black Me," "Why Don't They Play with Me?" "Stay in Your Own Backyard," and much later, "Mammy's Little Coal Black Rose."

A few of the songs about the adults were as straightforwardly sentimental as "Mandy Lee," perennial favorite of old-time barbershop quartets. But usually the adult Negro was considered to be lazy, carefree, irresponsible, one whose "troubles, sorrows and care" ("My Gal Sal") were laughable to whites and of only slight concern to the Negro stereotypes who, in song lyrics, lived only for the day. Many Negro songwriters and entertainers helped to carry and prolong that myth through the era when coon songs and ragtime were dominant, until about 1914. Vaudeville artist Bert Williams was the most famous of them. "All Coons Look Alike to Me" was written by a Negro, Ernest Hogan. "Some of These Days," always identified with Sophie Tucker by those who'd heard her, was written by Canadian-born Shelton Brooks, the Negro who also wrote the perennially popular "Darktown Strutters' Ball."

"You're in the Right Church But in the Wrong Pew" and "Down Among the Sugar Cane" were written by dark-skinned Cecil Mack and Chris Smith. Two Negro writers Cole and Johnson, among others, contributed to the flood of coon songs, which by the early 1900's had swept much of the older sheet music off the nation's parlor organs and the new pianos. The inundation was loaded with references to the characteristics that have been noted and with words objectionable to Negroes.

Cole and Johnson's "Wedding of the Chinee and the Coon" introduced other songs with an integration theme, of which "Navajo" was typical. The verse introduced an Indian maiden who lived on a reservation "down in the sand-hills of New Mexico":

And every evening there was a coon
Who came his love to plead
There by the silv'ry light of the moon
He'd help her string her beads
And when they were all alone
To her he would softly crone.

Williams, who wrote the lyrics for Van Alstyne's music, coined a nice verb in "crone." Those days, he couldn't "phone" the Indian reservation, and "drone" and "groan" or "moan" were out.

In 1902 Cole and Johnson's "Under the Bamboo Tree" introduced a jungle-type song: "Down in the jungle lived a maid of royal blood though dusky shade." In Tin Pan Alley's language, it was colossal. ("Supercolossal" did not arrive until Hollywood's ascendance.) As always, when a song landed with national impact, other songwriters tumbled aboard this hot jungle train. Soon Zulu girls, lady Hottentots, and lassies from other dark-skinned nationalities adorned the nation's sheet-music racks. (For any who might be using these pages for research in a high-school music project, in the quaint folkways of the earlier century, music in the home was produced by hand, not by audio tubes.)

The Negro's innate laziness, according to the conventions of the times, was characterized in "I Hates to Get Up Early in the Morning" and "Please Go 'Way and Let Me Sleep," his shiftlessness by "What You Goin' to Do When the Rent Comes 'Round? (Rufus Rastus Johnson Brown)," and his lack of trustworthiness by "Who Picked the Lock on the Chicken House Door?" His propensity for gambling was the theme in many songs. One that was sung by Charley Dimmit went:

Come on, se-ven, Where are you, 'le-ven?
Nigger, won't you close that door?
I can't keep a- throw-in', When the wind am a- blow-in',
I'll be Jon-ah if I did-n't throw a four.
Go a-way, sis-ter Kate, I don't want your lit-tle eight,
Mis-ter Sev-en, I am on to your traps. So I've
throwed my Lit-tle Joe, And I guess I'll take the dough.
I'm a win-ner in the game of craps.

Best known in that theme is the perennial quartet favorite "Roll Them Bones—when the cops are out of sight." None is more illustrative of that phase of caricature than "I Got Mine" (1901):

I went out to a nigger crap game
It was against my will
The coons took all my money
Except one green-back dollar bill
There was a hundred dollar bet on the table
The nigger's point was nine
Just then the cops stepped through the door
But I got mine.

CHORUS:

I got mine, boys, I got mine
I grabbed that hundred dollar bill
Through the window I did climb
Ever since then I've worn good clothes
Living on chicken and wine
I'm the leader of society since I got mine.

Watermelon, credited with being irresistible, came into mention in many songs, of which one of the best is "By the Watermelon Vine," better known as "Lindy—sweet as the sugar cane." Its composer, Thomas S. Allen, wrote the beautiful harmonies of "My Dusky Rose" and the nostalgic Americana in "Any Rags?—any bones any bottles today?" Later, "He's a Rag Picker" referred to ragtime music rather than gathering discarded fabrics.

"Dats' the Way to Spell Chicken" and "Every Morn I Bring Her Chicken" illustrate the alleged craving for fowl. That second one played on the words of the polite and refined art song "Every Morn I Bring Thee Violets." To further the understanding of the coon song era, here is a small list in which several titles speak for themselves. Many of the covers shout the tenets of these times:

Ain't Dat a Shame?
Ambolena Snow
Bullfrog and the Coon
Good Morning, Carrie
Hello, My Baby
Hot Time in the Old Town Tonight
I Don't Know Where I'm Going (but I'm on my way)
I Guess I'll Have to Telegraph My Baby
Just Kiss Yourself Goodbye
Ma Ebony Belle
Ma Lady Lu
Mammy's Shufflin' Dance
Mandy, How Do You Do?
Mandy Lane
Moving Day
My Coal Black Lady
My Gal Is a High Born Lady
My Hanna Lady
Rastus on Parade
Shame on You
When Uncle Joe Plays a Rag on His Old Banjo

The nation laughed about the Negro's domestic woes in "Ain't Dat a Shame?" In it "Bill Bailey told his lady friend 'our dream of love is o'er.' He said no more; just slammed the door" as he walked out. But he regretted his walkout later:

He wandered 'round the town but he didn't have a cent
He thought about his pork chops, then back to the house he went

and begged in the chorus: "Will you open dat door and let me in/I stand yere freezin' wet to the skin." The song's successor, "Bill Bailey, Won't You Please Come Home?" a year later, which crowded the original Bill out of popularity, accomplished a nice switch by presenting Bill's lady love as "hanging clothes in her back yard and weeping hard" for his return. The song was so successful that other Bailey songs followed, all of them pale imitations. "I Wonder Why Bill Bailey Don't Come Home" and "Since Bill Bailey Came Back Home" are examples that carried even into 1915 "When Old Bill Bailey Plays the Ukulele." That one showed a good sense of publicity by combining the still-cogent Bailey name with a stringed instrument then coming into popularity.

Listeners laughed at Bill's wife's woes, but no more than at the grief in "Have You Seen My Henry Brown?" and "Alexander" (1904) which chronicled another lockout: "While I took in washin' you just played the races." Nonetheless, home wasn't home without her man:

Can't you see the rain and hail am fastly fallin'
Alexander, Oh Alexander
Can't you hear your lady love a softly callin'
Alexander, Oh Alexander
Take me to your heart again and call me "honey"
All I want is lovin' I don't want your money
Alexander, tell me, don't you love your baby no more?

Lesser frustrations were amusing, too, as in "I Am a Jonah Man" and "Thursday Always Was My Jonah Day." Jonah was early-century slang for unlucky, or for one who brought bad luck, as in the "whammy" of baseball. In "Best I Get Is Much Obliged to You" (1907), Sylvester Johnson Lee went to New York from Tennessee to make his fortune in the big town. He "worked around in swell hotels, a-shinin' shoes and hoppin' bells," but invariably a block was thrown in his progress toward the goal of financial success:

It's mighty strange, it's mighty strange
No one ever says "Sylvester, you keep the change"
I try to do as folks tell me to
But they all get absent-minded when my work is through.

"If I Only Had a Dollar of My Own" also dealt with economics. Still in that field of personal finance, "That's Where My Money Goes" might be heard today. In it a man "ran a barber shop, the swellest one in town/And shaved the aristocracy for many miles around" but still had money troubles:

Why boys, my money goes
To buy my baby clothes

I buy her everything to keep her in style
She's worth her weight in gold
My coal black baby
Say, boys, that's where my money goes.

"I Guess I'll Have to Telegraph My Baby so I won't have to walk back home" portrayed the troubles of a minstrel man, stranded when his road company closed. "Back to Baltimore" was another in that theme. The most popular song of the type portrayed the troubles of a minstrel man in a different way in "Just Because She Made Dem Goo-Goo Eyes." Here "A nice black gal in the very front row with heaps of dough to spend looked up at him with a silly smile/He started singing his end song, forgot most every line/The manager hurried back and said 'You've got to stand a fine'/He lost his job for quite a while—/Just because she made dem goo-goo eyes."

"Never Raise a Razor Less You Want to Raise a Row" and "The New Bully," the one made famous by the early "shouter" May Irvin, presented in a jocular way how grim life could be in a city's darker areas:

Have you heard about that bully dat's just come to town
He's 'round among the niggers a-layin' their bodies down
I'm a lookin' for that bully and he must be found
I'm a Tennessee nigger and I don't allow
No red-eyed river roustabout with me to make a row
I'm lookin' for that bully and I'll make him bow.

To one who has not had the opportunity to sense the flavor of an era, it might seem that "Every Race Has a Flag But the Coon" and "Coon Coon Coon —I wish my color would fade" and others that have been sampled here were written by sadists. But there was no deliberate cruelty in the thinking of verse writers of the coon song era. They were in tune with the sociological standards. They reproduced in song the common attitudes expressed in countless other ways toward a "race ignored by the association of polite and refined society," as Mrs. Stowe had written. National thinking among white people still retained the attitudes of the chattel era with the early northern influx of the race "unlike the predominant people." Dressed alike, Mike Zychowski and Augustus Tremaine III, descendant of a *Mayflower* family, might be mistaken for twin brothers. But a different color is so obvious.

There is no counterpart of the coon songs today. The nearest approximation is the amusing dialect story based upon the fast-dimming stereotypes of the older Jewish, Scandinavian, German, Irish, Italian, and other peoples. By about 1910, the songs in Negro theme were fast losing their Afro-American verbiage and connotations. In unadorned English "Play That Barber Shop Chord—Mr. Jefferson Lord" told the story of a "soothing melody." It was followed a year later by one of the great song hits of all time, "Alexander's Rag Time Band." In it Berlin made slight use of conventional Negro dialect as he wrote straightforwardly about the best band anywhere.

A host of mammy, Dixie, down-south, and comparable songs dotted the teens and twenties. Nearly all of them were in a theme of longing to return to a southern environment. Great numbers of them pictured cotton fields on the covers. Frequently Negroes danced on the levee down where I want to be or where someone cries for me. Often the cover showed a steamboat bound for the old hometown down Dixie way. Usually, the artwork and the lyrics were done by "southerners" who'd never been south of Jersey City. But ambiguity had set in. They went down the river, not the ribber where the Lincum gunboats lay in composer Work's Civil War era. In most of the lyrics of the twenties the words could apply to either colored or white. It might be Old Black Joe, or mammy, or a white sweetheart waiting there for me in the southland. In the main, they were songs of nostalgia rather than about a particular type or race. A few of those I'm-going-back-to titles in praise of life in the South might be useful as reminders in a jam session:

I'M GOING BACK TO

All Aboard for Dixieland
Are You from Dixie?
Carolina Moon
Carolina in the Morning
Carolina Sunshine
Down in Dear Old New Orleans
Down Among the Sugar Cane
Everything Is Peaches Down in Georgia
Floating Down the River
Georgia
I'm All Bound 'Round with the Mason-Dixon Line
I'm Going Back to Carolina
In Dear Old Tennessee
In Dear Ole Georgia
Is It True What They Say About Dixie?
I Want to Be in Dixie
Mammy's Shufflin' Dance
Mid the Green Fields of Virginia
On the Mississippi
Sailing Down the Chesapeake Bay
Swanee
Swanee River Moon
Take Me to That Swanee Shore
Tuck Me to Sleep in My Old Tucky Home
Underneath the Cotton Moon
Waiting for the Robert E. Lee
We'll Have a Jubilee in My Old Kentucky Home
When It's Night Time in Dixie Land

Most of their themes were wrapped in packages comparable with "They made it twice as nice as Paradise and they called it 'Dixie Land.'" The ambiguity that is in most of them continues today when a song about the South can be about Negro or white and is thought of racially only in terms of the entertainer who presents it.

"Blues" songs were associated with Negroes because they evolved from unwritten Negro themes characterized by sad-and-blue words and musical slurrings, particularly of the third and seventh tone flatted. W. C. Handy's "St. Louis Blues" swept the country in 1914. It was the apotheosis of blue-type themes up to that time, and many will agree that it still is. It was followed by his "Memphis Blues," "Beale Street Blues," and others. Handy's blues ushered in a long succession, such as "Livery Stable Blues," "Yellow Dog Blues," "Jackass Blues," "Wildman Blues," and ludicrous attempts to capitalize upon the blues' popularity by hitching the blues to a current theme, such as "Inflation Blues."

More and more they followed the trend patterns of other popular music concerning Negroes, without application to any race. As example, "Bye Bye Blues," one of the best, and "Wang Wang Blues" and "Wabash Blues" are no more Negroid than George Gershwin's "Swanee," written five years before his famous "Rhapsody in Blue."

A few songs of the 1920's and 1930's left no doubt as to racial intent, "River, Stay 'Way from My Door" and "Am I Blue?" as examples. Along with others, such as "Old Man River," both of them were lyricized in what might be called modern-Negro dialect which, to most northerners, is practically synonymous with that of the white in the South. But no attempt was made by the lyric writers, or seldom by singers, whether Negro or white, to re-create Little Black Sambo or the Uncle Remus and Tom-Topsy dialects of the early era. The subject theme in "Am I Blue?" is reminiscent of the domestic clashes and crashes of coon songs, such as "Bill Bailey" and "Alexander." But what a difference! There's no implication or inference of humor as in the old ones. A broken heart may be hidden under any color. As Ethel Waters sang it, the song was universal.

A few songs in more recent years have re-created the old dialect:

Go 'long, mule, there's a steamer at the landin'
Waitin' for the cotton to load
Go 'long, mule, the boss is understandin'
*There's a pasture at the end of the road.**

Everyone who recognizes the words of "Wagon Wheels" (1934) knows also that they are quaint throwbacks to a departed era rather than an attempt to chronicle modern Negro speech.

By the 1930's, vaudeville was fading, and moving pictures and radio were replacing it. Concurrently, a shift in popular music became apparent, most notably due to a change from personal participation to listening and watching. In public performance the singer and the melody of his or her song was often less important than the name of the band or an individual in it whose virtuosity on an instrument provided the principal audience attraction. "I *saw* Benny Goodman last night." By the 1940's, Negro bandleaders such as Duke Ellington and featured Negro instrumentalists and singers were holding their own against white competition. It was about that time too when changing attitudes became evident, apart from music, as Negroes came into prominence in sports to mention only one other sector of Americana.

Most songwriters have been white. In their trade they had to be and must continue to be alert to the majority's sentiments, because a song must be in tune with its times to attain popularity. So, our song archives reveal the national attitudes of white people before and since Lincoln's proclamation. They show an evolution in thinking that in the main reflects the growing respect that great numbers of Negroes have earned, not received as largess from the white majority.

Many of our songs in Negro theme are among our greatest. In consequence I am bothered and resentful when a magnificent song is so cleaned of words and allusions objectionable to some Negroes that it is an emasculated imitation of the original. As a whitey, I feel no sense of embarrassment that my grand-parents and theirs experienced "Flies in the sugar bowl, shoo, fly, shoo" and "Rats in the dough pan, what'll I do?" and "Fly in the buttermilk, shoo, shoo,

shoo," leading into "Skip to M' Lou, My Darling." Songs by and about Negroes—from slavery days to "We Shall Overcome"—are among our important treasures of Americana.

To present the evidence from our popular songs about the Negro's creeping glacierlike advancement toward citizenship it has been necessary to use references that are often objectionable. The slow motion of a glacier can't be gauged by the eye, but its advance is measurable, and in this case the songs are the gauge. There just aren't any songs being written in the 1960's that show the old patronizing attitudes toward chattels, or the later stereotypes of the Negro that were so common to songs from the 1870's into World War I. Our songs mirror America and they demonstrate that the race has been integrated at least into a borderland that is far removed from the old South and the North of the earlier century. The limits of that border state become less apparent each year. Our songs and their mirrorlike reflection of national thought provide the evidence.

Ushering in a New Era

Music, and particularly its harmony possibilities, continued to be an avocational compulsion and an open sesame after deserting the high pay from teaching country school. It just wasn't quite suited to training and temperament. The government was opening Indian reservations in South Dakota to settlement, mostly by Midwestern farmers who wanted larger acreage but couldn't afford more in the home vicinity. Too young to homestead on a 160-acre claim by fourteen months' residence and payment of $1.25 an acre, I did join my brother who was proving-up, as homesteaders called it, near the townsite of Faith, South Dakota, beyond the Missouri River.

About 1910, that metropolis, not far from the deep ruts of the old army post wagon trail from Bismark to Deadwood, was outlined slightly by two one-story wooden stores and about a dozen tents. They stood in a sagebrush flat that had been granted by the government to the railroad for opening the territory to settlers. A line of wooden stakes stretched to the eastern horizon as proof that the railroad's surveyors had been there, though the mule skinners and their hand-dumped dirt scrapers were still scratching away at the flinty prairie far to the east in the Cheyenne reservation.

Irritable rattlesnakes, sneaking coyotes, an occasional vicious badger, curious antelope, and home-loving prairie dogs, all resentful of human take-over far outnumbered the settlers. In one of the tents on Faith's embryonic main street, gambling at Mexican monte, faro, and blackjack ran at all hours, lighted by kerosene farm lanterns at night. It was common gossip that a Meade County deputy sheriff had staked out his exclusive claim to the beer concession in this dry territory and that he cracked down on all competition.

In the gambling tent I hit a jackpot, though not in the blackjack game. A cowman from the nearby 7D ranch mentioned his guitar. Later he taught me a piece full of intricate pizzicatos which he called the "Mexican Fandango." Nowadays, a grandson, Ted Pattison, plucks it when he's not beating out amplified rock 'n' roll. Music does get around.

Western South Dakota had fresh air and views unlimited but only a dribble of rainfall. It was so dry that the wells squirted dust. The Midwest settlers' hopes of raising corn were choked off. For needed cash we hauled lumber from Sturgis in the Black Hills to Faith's townsite—four horses at about three miles an hour for a hundred miles over unfenced and bridgeless trail. Perhaps it was the painful monotony of hearing a million prairie dogs squeaking off-key or finding that an anticipated water hole held only a few gallons of alkali water, spurned even by the thirsty horses, but whatever the cause, I returned eastward to the little town of Red Oak, Iowa, adjacent to the state corners of Missouri and Nebraska.

After lining up a job in a printing house, it didn't take long to form a barbershop quartet whose *pièce de résistance* was "Summertime," Harry Von Tilzer's not Gershwin's. A brief excerpt from our topical chorus fixes the date. It asked: "Nine-teen ten, nine-teen ten, what in the world will we do then?" The answer: "All will be sunny, Edelweiss, and money in the nine-teen ten." Edelweiss here was not an alpine flower, but a brand of beer shipped, legally, from Omaha into that dry territory in Iowa. Today's mishmash of legislation which makes it legal, or illegal, to buy drinks standing, or sitting, or with or without food, publicly or privately, and the rest of the rulings has a heritage. Red Oak was close to the great city of Omaha. There high-heeled cowmen were common sights on Farnum Street, and blanket Indians caused no commotion. For a five-dollar bill we could take the Saturday noon train, have a city dinner, see Ethel Barrymore in *The Twelve Pound Look* at the Orpheum or a road company in *The Girl Question,* and be home shortly after midnight.

Red Oak's own theater, the Beardsley, booked the road shows which played along the transcontinental railroad lines and even in smaller towns on branch spurs. Some of those weary traveling thespians had been very good before age or alcohol or both had reduced them to third-company status. As an usher at the Beardsley, I earned fifty cents a night. Mr. Beardsley didn't know that I'd have paid for the privilege of absorbing the music of *The Prince of Pilsen, The Red Mill, Three Twins* ("Cuddle Up a Little Closer"), and other touring musical comedy successes. Each company carried its own orchestra, and most of them were excellent.

During nonmusical attractions playing the Beardsley, an actor might step out of character between acts. The villain in *Uncle Josh Spruceby,* foiled in his attempt to saw the heroine in two during the Great Sawmill Scene (heralded weeks in advance by three-sheet posters), might step before the curtain between acts to sing comical parodies on popular songs such as "In the Shade of the Old Apple Tree," accompanied by Mr. Beardsley's daughter on the theater pit's tinny piano. It was not uncommon for the heavily made-up heroine, blonde wig and all, to sell candy between acts. One box was supposed to contain a gen-u-wine sol-i-itary diamond ring. "Who'll be the lucky winner?" chanted Little Eva (*Uncle Tom's Cabin*) or Isabelle (*St. Elmo*) hawking stale sweets in the aisles.

Between the appearances of the "legitimate" road companies, Mr. Beardsley experimented with the new silent hand-cranked moving pictures. One week, while Ben Hur's famous chariot race danced about the screen, I made a professional appearance singing "The Holy City." This ancient holdover from the nineties is still popular as a semiclassical "sacred" song. No talent scouts appeared at the end of the week, but I had earned a dollar a night on stage, compared with half that for ushering.

In a different musical atmosphere I met a girl in the Congregational Church choir to which I had been attracted by the best choral singing I'd ever heard. Dudley Buck's "Te Deum" was a special favorite. Later in her home she played "My Beautiful Lady" from *The Pink Lady* as the first among the current hits, including "The Glow Worm," with which I began to load her music rack. For years we played them as duets on piano and organ. About this time, the printing-house boss reached into the factory for a billing clerk in the office. At double the former salary, the college campus on which I'd set my sights seemed almost within view. At eighteen dollars a week it took several weeks to arrive there, even though there were no salary deductions then. At the State College math was king and chem was queen, and one bowed to them or else. My head remained bloody but unbowed.

Since then, Des Moines, Chicago, Boston, New York, and Cleveland have made their contributions to the memory file. More importantly in a practical way, they provided daily bread, also some cake, added to the opportunity of travel and knowledge of the states and Canada. A friend who retains a box at Symphony Hall and for Metropolitan Opera Week often gloats at me about his latest Fats Waller or Whiteman 78 that he picked up in practically mint condition. Musically, we agree upon much—for example, that Al Jolson as a singer was a good actor. We sometimes disagree as to whether we get the most from symphony, barbershop quartets, or from conductors' interpretations of deathless *La Bohème* and other Italian or French operas. The principal difference between us musically seems to be that on his early excursions into musical circles he didn't ride a Missouri mule or a mandolin.

In the 1920's Olin Downes, my co-worker who was the music critic of the Boston *Post,* used to invite me to join him at concerts by Boston Symphony and others equally famous at Symphony Hall on Massachusetts Avenue. To this country lad who'd left his country home to go to the city to seek employment,* and who had just growed musically, Olin's comments upon what we heard and upon some of the famous names back of it were as worthwhile as the glorious music. Some of his spoken criticisms were as caustic as the stuff we used to rub on a calf's tiny button horns, at the farm, to keep them from developing.

That locale, era, and environment are so distant that at times they seem to be the experience of someone else, researched rather than experienced. Then "Sourwood Mountain" or "Captain Jinks of the Horse Marines" comes over a radio or TV set, and I'm back, listening to 'Rasmus Parker's square dance music in the Oakdale that was. This love affair and lingering liaison with music of almost every sort, but particularly the populars, continues as if it were only the beginning.

* A line from a song by the famous Charley Case, the first comedian with the courage to lampoon the sad ballads of the early 1900's. See Sigmund Spaeth's *Read 'Em and Weep* (Doubleday, 1926).

PART TWO

I Never Thought of That

More Than Fringe Benefits

Commenting upon a meeting of sheet-music collectors in April 1959, the Philadelphia *Bulletin* said: "Practically everything of importance in this country's history is commemorated in some sort of song. Songs of the American frontier, half myth, half history, tell its story more movingly than dates and facts and figures." Whoever wrote that added: "A disquieting thought is that this generation too may be judged someday by the songs it writes and sings."

Most adults with an ear for music will agree, at least in part. As self-protection, I believe that we should tell those future generations, who will judge the music of the 1960's, a few facts so that they will have an inkling of why it is what it is. The turbulence in our musical atmosphere has steadily increased since the 1930's. After World War II it reached tornadic velocities in the late 1940's and the 1950's. This demonstrates that *popular* music reflects an era just as painting reveals something of the period in which its artist worked. In the 1960's we have heard disturbed music. So are we. Among many, particularly juniors, jazz and its variants that are so important to a few have been largely supplanted by atomic music.

Because songs mirror people, activities, beliefs, and cultures, the comparatively restrained songs of the earlier 1900's reflect freedom from tensions that grind and abrade today. The horse set the ambling pace of life before its acceleration into the rush and roar of snarling cars, earthshaking trucks, and sustained speeds and hums of the domestic laborsaving devices that keep us so busy. Two words, participation and listening, highlight much of the difference between older songs and today's trends, excepting rock 'n' roll and the folk song revival. In general, the older songs of the 1900's lend themselves more readily to musical self-expression by those who are not musicians but who know what they like than do the songs composed since World War II, particularly in the rock 'n' rollin' 1950's and early 1960's.

This does not imply that older means better nor that parents are more musical than today's juniors playing rock 'n' roll and singing the folk-type songs that will come up for comment shortly. American life is different. It bears only slight resemblance to American living before the Depression of the 1930's. Health education, transportation and communication, dogmas, social and socialistic trends, the tools of teaching, as examples, are different. Songs swing in that changing cycle because they reflect how we live and what we live with.

Musicologist Sigmund Spaeth said that many of our songs may be lacking in the refinements of expression, but they express thoughts and emotions common to most people. He believed that such popular songs will go on and on because the experiences they reflect are common to mankind.

Since sound tracks were perfected, much of our music is visual music. Some of it is captivating on stage or on the screen where it is supplemented by lavish stage sets and orchestral backgrounds. Nonvisually, great numbers of today's songs have no more character than the mood music of a soap opera. They are not difficult to forget, as Heywood Broun once said. "Alexander's Rag Time Band," "Mammy's Little Coal Black Rose," "Let Me Call You Sweetheart," and "Swanee" stood on their own feet. They were repetitive music, easy to live with. Their melodies and harmonies followed you around. They had the after-tang of old tawny port. They recur in hums and whistlings.

Much of the newer music depends upon grandiose orchestrations. Frequently they sink the singer in a sea of sounds. Sometimes, it's better that way when personalities back of the microphone present personal interpretations of what the song's composer should have written, they think. When such a notable sings "Stars Fell on Alabama," the words in the fallout are needed to keep us informed that it isn't "Stardust." Much of the time, we hear and see tremendous musical efforts that vanish like sun-struck fog immediately after the hearing and seeing, because the themes are too elusive to capture and remember. That makes recall and participation difficult. It also accounts for colossal expenditure of effort by those who present opuses written for such occasions as a television special. "That was great," we say. Next day we remember what we saw, but not an echo of the music remains in memory, sunk without a trace. Of course, that may be good for the economy since it keeps composers, arrangers, and professional band men off relief. So much for future archaeologists about our current popular music as it may be judged, according to the *Bulletin* editorial.

Interest and participation in music of many sorts have opened doors for me to lasting friendships which could not exist without the original introduction supplied by musical associations. That alone is a reward beyond price out here on the musical fringe. There are more rewards, such as the fascinating views of our land and its people as revealed in popular songs.

Participating in the words of songs is comparable with reading a record of our national interests, fads, foibles, hopes, manners, language and slanguage, and modes of dress. "She don't have to wear rats in her hair nor a straight-front XYZ" was a play on words in the advertising of "ABC straight-front" corsets in 1910. The trade name was paraphrased in "Any Little Girl That's a Nice Little Girl Is the Right Little Girl for Me." * On cue, more history from our song lyrics will appear later.

The artwork on the covers of older sheet music is rewarding pictorially. A collection of old songs becomes a reference work of clothing sketched as worn in succeeding eras. Hoopskirts and pantalettes show on many Civil War song covers. The effect of bustles as big as buckets are evident later. Ascot ties, peg-

* Copyright 1910 by Maurice Shapiro. Copyright renewed and assigned to Shapiro, Bernstein & Co., Inc., New York, N. Y. Used by permission.

top trousers, "The Bird on Nellie's Hat" when women went in for ornithology, low waistlines, bathing suits by eras, and more participate in the music covers' style parade. Many of the pictures include touches of the environment of a period, sketches of the things lived with in succeeding generations.

Our attitudes show, too. As only one example written into music's sociological record, "I Didn't Raise My Boy to Be a Soldier" was the song hit of 1915 when World War I had devastated Europe for a year, while our national attitude was still isolationist. Audiences *stood* to cheer the song at the Empire Theater in Des Moines on a bill which included zany Ed Wynn in his classic skit, "The Perfect Fool." The reaction to the song was typical of audiences throughout the country. Then the harassment of American shipping, the necessity to arm merchant ships, and the sinking of the *Lusitania* drew us into war in 1917. (The *Lusitania* is in the song record "As the Lusitania Went Down," with unbelievably ghastly artwork on the cover.) Immediately, the national attitude changed, and George M. Cohan's "Over There," based on the bugle's notes, seemed to be the national anthem. "America, Here's My Boy" and others that showed complete commitment to the war effort came later. That war brought out well over a hundred songs, of which "The Rose of No Man's Land," "Till We Meet Again," "Pack Up Your Troubles," "Roses of Picardy," "Long, Long Trail," "Keep the Home Fires Burning," and a few others are still heard.

Earlier here, "Just Break the News to Mother" was touched upon. It rocketed into popularity at the time of the Spanish-American War and was still sung widely during World War I. As an example of the Americana tucked away in a thousand others, here are its two verses and the chorus.

"JUST BREAK THE NEWS TO MOTHER"

While the shot and shell were screaming upon the battle field
The boys in blue were fighting, their noble flag to shield

[As pointed out earlier, the discerning eye sees a record of blue field dress for the infantry, long obsolete, and a reference to combat troops following a flag.]

Came a cry from a brave captain "See, boys, our flag is down
Who'll volunteer to save it from disgrace?"

[The traditions of the flag as well as its presence in combat.]

"I will," a young boy shouted, "I'll bring it back or die"
Then sprang into the thickest of the fray

[That dramatic statement was in the literary tradition of the period. Therefore, it constitutes a literary record within the song's record of front-line action.]

Saved the flag but gave his young life all for his country's sake
They brought him back and softly heard him say

[Another tradition. The first verse of a ballad introduced the principals in their locale, and projected them into action or speech. Usually one of them said what became the song's chorus.]

"Just break the news to mother
She knows how dear I love her
And tell her not to wait for me
For I'm not coming home
Just say there is no other
Can take the place of mother
And kiss her dear sweet lips for me
And break the news to her."

The second verse is included because it exemplifies a device utilized by writers of ballads that told stories, particularly the sad ballads of the early century. Frequently they used, and abused, the long arm of coincidence until it had to be carried in a sling:

From afar a noted general had witnessed this brave deed
"Who saved our flag? Speak up, lad, 'twas noble brave indeed."
"There he lies, sir," said the captain, "He's sinking very fast"
Then slowly turned away to hide a tear
The general in a moment knelt down beside the boy
Then gave a cry that touch'd all hearts that day
"It's my son, my brave young hero; I thought you safe at home"
"Forgive me, father, for I ran away."
(Repeat chorus.)

That clarifies the statement that the long arm of coincidence was abused by songwriters, particularly in the weepers. Before we pull away from this vista of coincidence, let's examine another which, in happier vein, challenges all laws of probability and stretches the imagination until it fractures.

"If Jack Were Only Here" ("My Mother Was a Lady") may be heard occasionally nowadays as a travesty upon the songs of the so-called Gay Nineties. The characters introduced in the first verse in true ballad style were two drummers who "sat at dinner in a grand hotel one day." A young person reading that might have a mental picture of two percussionists dining before filling a date with their band, so let's understand immediately that in the earlier 1900's a drummer was a traveling salesman. They amused themselves by making personal remarks, then as now, to their pretty waitress. In fact when she brought them a tray of food, "they spoke to her familiarly in a manner very rude." This went on until in tears she spoke the chorus:

My mother was a lady like yours, you will allow
Perhaps you have a sister who needs protection now
I've come to this great city to find a brother dear
And you wouldn't dare insult me, sir, if Jack were only here.

At heart, the two drummers were gentlemen. Distressed at what he'd done, "one man cried in shame/'Forgive me, miss, I meant no harm/Pray tell me, what's your name?' "

She told him, and he cried again "I know your brother too
Why we've been friends for many years and he often speaks of you
He'll be so glad to see you, and if you'll only wed
I'll take you to him as my bride, for I've loved you since you said."
(Chorus)

This not only records extraordinary coincidence, when trustingly she gave her right name to a stranger who claimed to know her brother, but more importantly it chronicles the shortest courtship leading up to a proposal of marriage in all popular-music history. It took less than the time between soup or tomato juice and pie or ice cream. Now we leave that long arm of coincidence to a deserved rest and recuperation.

Our songs can also provide a systemless system for the recall of places, dates, incidents, faces without names, persons met, and others seen though not met. Personally, they are cross-indexed in the memory file with certain musical compositions or incidents. As example, the female baritone who in August 1946 at about 12:30 A.M. left her party at Buffalo's Statler to add a fourth part to "Back Home in Indiana" and "If You Were the Only Girl in the World" as they were being harmonized (sung anyway) by a male trio whose members had met for the first time within the hour. I don't recall their names nor hers, but it was good while it lasted until her friends flashed the time-to-go signals.

Conversely, among the musical rejects in the memory file is an unseen ukulele player in the shelter next to ours on Maine's Mt. Katahdin. He had been introduced to three chords in G, but friendships had not developed. He played the three in different sequences from bedtime-for-climbers until 3 A.M. By that strategy he was able to harmonize twice, both times in "Clementine," with the songs uttered in unvarying crescendo by his party. Other comparable rejects fill quite a large section of the memory file.

Ernest R. Ball and Chauncey Olcott are there as examples of persons seen though not met. Ball came to Omaha's Orpheum Theatre near the end of his career which had started as a concert pianist. It detoured into the composition of some of our greatest song hits. The detour included road trips where he played and sang his live-forevers, "Love Me, and the World Is Mine," "Dear Little Boy of Mine," "Mother Machree," and the many which include one still popular when the beach fires glow, "Let the Rest of the World Go By."

He wrote for, and with, Olcott many of the songs, such as "When Irish Eyes Are Smiling," that were Chauncey's trademarks as he packed them in at musicomedy matinees for more than thirty years. He had passed his singing peak when I saw him uncharacteristically in Sheridan's *Rivals* with Mrs. Fiske. He played Sir Lucius O'Trigger to the hilt. In his last exit he trolled a stave of "My Wild Irish Rose" in the tenor that had carried him to popularity's peaks in the early 1900's.

He and others are compartmentalized with the music that calls them to mind. Maude Powell and her violin and Fritz Kreisler are there. And Paderewski on concert tour, Bert Williams singing "Nobody" at the Palace in New York, Montgomery and Stone in *Chin Chin* at Chicago's McVickers' theater, Chaliapin's *Faust,* and more recently the Mills Brothers' "Lazy River" at the Fairmount in San Francisco. These and many more stir about when joggled by the name of a song, a singer, or an incident in the memory file.

Another file, a physical one—the collection of sheet music—brings them to life even more vividly. In many cases their names are on the covers, often with pictures of singers or band leaders who introduced or popularized a song. A good example of that is on the cover of the 1894 tearjerker "While the Dance Goes On." It pictures a very young man with a butch haircut. The caption reads: "Sung by the Celebrated Descriptive Tenor Singer Joseph E. Howard." Characteristically, as he'd have wished, Howard died backstage in Chicago while participating in a TV spectacular. He was in his eighties. And look at this sheet-music cover with the picture of Al Jolson on "Swanee," 1919. That song was the first step toward the popularity heights for its composer, George Gershwin, whose "Rhapsody in Blue" shook the musical world when presented in 1924 at Aeolian Hall (New York) by Paul Whiteman.

In the "Y" section of the file is an unusual item of interest to those who enjoy Americana. Almost every adult, whether or not interested in music, recognizes "You're a Grand Old Flag" written by George M. Cohan in 1906. Without the slightest intent of disrespect, he said years later, he wrote it originally under the title of "You're a Grand Old Rag." The brash slangy youngster tossed off "rag" for "flag" as a sort of compliment to the old red, white, and blue that he worshiped and waved for years in his Yankee Doodle Dandyish songs and plays. When criticisms of "You're a Grand Old Rag" flooded in, they tried to recall the original, to be replaced by "Flag" copies with a new title and cover. Not all the originals came back, as is proved by the sheet-music file.

Tuneful, dainty, and winsome "Alice Blue Gown" of 1919 offers another example of Americana embedded in our popular songs. Alice Roosevelt (Longworth), independent daughter of President Theodore Roosevelt, made such impress upon the nation that women everywhere recognized the color and the origin of that particular shade named for her. The song preserved more than the current mode. Its lyrics caught the very essence of femininity as it was when this century was in its teens, referred to nowadays as the feminine mystique, which in many cases bears slight outward resemblances to that of World War I days. Our songs are almost cinematic in retaining detailed records of the passing show in any era.

These are some of the reasons why our popular songs capture the affections of one to whom they've introduced friendships; they've opened views of American history, sociology, and events; and have revealed activities, customs, beliefs, and attitudes, while providing a workable system of recall of persons, dates, and incidents.

More American Attitudes Revealed Musically

The nation's dispositions toward just about everything in our environment are written into songs as clearly as the record of changing thought about Negroes. The white immigrants to America had to hurdle barriers of language and national and local customs. Great numbers of songs proliferate from the immigrations that brought people whose ways of life were quite different from those of the earlier settlers and their offspring. Also, they brought non-English-language songs that have entered the national repertoire to become everyday music. A few examples:

Ah, Marie
Aloha Oe
Au Claire de la lune
Cieleto Lindo
Die Lorelei
Du, Du Liegst Mir Im Herzen
Funiculi Funicula
La Paloma
La Spagnola
O Solo Mio
O Tannenbaum
Otchi Tchorniya
Santa Lucia

All of them are familiar to the nation in translation.

In his colossal work *The American Language,* H. L. Mencken commented upon words other than English that infiltrated American speech so thoroughly that they are now part of it. Mencken believed that German was second only to Spanish in that respect. He added that the Irish immigrants exerted influence upon the language "vastly greater than that of the Germans . . . but their [Irish] contributions to the actual vocabulary were probably less." Be that fact or opinion, in the song record the Irish had more influence than any other nationality until recent years. During the 1930's and 1940's songs of Latin-American type grew in numbers. They were, and are, used largely by professional musicians for audiences and for dancing. Few are played or sung as spontaneously as "My Wild Irish Rose" or "Sweet Rosie O'Grady."

Some of our made-in-America songs of Irish flavor were written by those whose family trees had roots in the ould sod. But greater numbers have been written by Irishmen named Schwartz or the equivalent. Many of the songs have been in praise of the land itself, Olcott's "My Isle o' Dreams" as example. Others have declared the determination to return to a mother or a colleen waiting "Where the River Shannon Flows," or almost anywhere within the borders. But one of the most successful devices of our native songwriters has been to give an American girl in a U.S. locale a name that is Irish in origin, such as "Peggy O'Neil" or "Nellie Kelly" or "Peg o' My Heart."

It is understandable why in Boston a song that referred to Ireland or an American girl's Irish-origin name could make thousands cheer at Loew's or Keith's or Waldron's or The Old Howard as compared with a song about my Lithuanian lollipop. But audiences showed the same favoritism to the Irish in the German outposts of Sous Beslehem, Pennsylvania, and Milwaukee, and in heavily Scandinavian Minneapolis and Duluth, as old vaudeville troupers will testify. A song of Irish flavor was almost as effective as waving the American flag.

As in the songs about Negroes, many states-written songs were based upon traits attributed to the Irish stereotypes of stage and joke books, particularly drinking and fighting. "Did McSorley hit McFadden with his fist or with a brick/Is the question for the jury to decide" sang Lizzie Raymond as recalled by the late George E. Vaughn of Cleveland. He maintained that Maggie Cline's "Throw Him Down, McCloskey" was the loudest sound ever heard by man. Like others, that song was conventional in its use of dialects: "The rules were London Prize Ring, and McCloskey said he'd try/To bate the nagur to one punch or in the ring he'd die." That brogue followed the pattern long established in songs of Irish flavor. In "Finnigan's Wake":

First they laid in tay and cake
Then pipes and tobacco and whiskey punch
Miss Biddy O'Brien began to cry
"Such a purty corpse did ye ever see?
Arrah! Tim Avourneen, an' why did ye die?"

Not as old as that one, "The Party at Odd Fellows' Hall" expressed the spirit of its times (1891) in Boston. The verse told about Pat McKenna meeting Tim Doolan on Washington Street. Pat sold Tim a ticket to a party. It said "Admit a gent and lady." At the party his lady left Tim and waltzed away with ticket-seller McKenna:

I waited until they had finished
Then up to him boldly I goes
And says to him "Patsy McKenna
Say where did ye hire them clothes?"
"You're a liar" says Pat in a second
Says I "What's the word that ye call?"
And the next minute me and McKenna
Were cleaning up Odd Fellows' Hall.

Next morning the judge said, in the next verse, "Ten dollars or ten days." They spent the ten on Deer Island, the local Alcatraz. These were in an era when nationality and racial jokes were as crude as the songs cited earlier that caricatured Negroes. An example from a joke book of the period: "After a colored man was well beaten up in a fight, they asked him, 'Was it a white man?' He replied 'No, it was an Irishman.' "

Gradually, the jokes and songs about the Irish changed with a new generation. In addition to lace curtains,

> *There's an organ in the parlor to give the house a tone*
> *And you're welcome any evening at Maggie Murphy's home.*

More and more, the songs took on a nostalgic tinge, then added the device mentioned, using an American girl's Irish name: "Peggy Brady—she came from County Kerry" and "Eileen—from old Killarney." The little treasury that follows, songs of Irish origin or written in Yankee Doodle Irish, makes no pretense to completeness. With those already cited, they do represent every *type* of song related in any way to Erin:

IN IRISH THEME

A Little Bit of Heaven
All the Irish Do the Tango Now (you must tango to avoid a row)
Along the Rocky Road to Dublin
Arrah Go On (to Oregon—of all places)
Beautiful Irish Maid
Bendemere Stream
Biddy McHugh
Casey Jones (so named perhaps by a proud mother)
Colleen Bawn
Come Back to Erin
Did Your Mother Come from Ireland?
Foggy Dew (two of them—one imported, the other Produce of America)
Harrigan (That's me . . . It's name that no shame had ever been connected with)
Has Anybody Here Seen Kelly? (Kelly with the green necktie)
I Long to See the Girl I Left Behind
In Dublin's Fair City (the girls are so pretty)
In My Harem
Ireland Must Be Heaven (for my mother came from there)
Irish Washer Woman
It's a Great Day for the Irish (tonight)
Kathleen Mavourneen
Killarney and You
Londonderry Air (Would God I Were a Tender Apple Blossom; also, Danny Boy)
Machushla (popularized by Irish tenor John McCormack)
McNamara's Band
Mr. Dooley (the finest man the country ever knew)
Mother Machree
My Isle of Dreams (land where the shamrock grows)
My Wild Irish Rose
Nelly Kelly (officer Kelly's daughter)
On Dublin Day

Peggy Brady
Peggy O'Neil
Peg o' My Heart
Pretty Maid Milkin' the Cow (Genuine old sod Irish)
Rose of Tralee
Shanty in Old Shanty Town
She's Got Rings on Her Fingers (and elephants to ride upon, my wild Irish rose)
Sweet Rosie O'Grady
That Tumbledown Shack in Athlone
Too-ra-loo-ra-loo-ra (an Irish lullaby)
The Girl I Left Behind Me (genuine Irish import)
The Lass from the County Mayo (She's my Irish lass from . . .)
The Same Old Shillelah
The Widow Malone (who "lived in the town of Athlone—alone")—ancient
They're All Good American Names (see page 120)
Tipperary Daisy (by two Irish boys—Fulton and Helf)
Wearing of the Green (see page 101 for parody)
When Irish Eyes Are Smiling
Who Threw the Overalls in Mistress Murphy's Chowder?

The shamrock imprint is on all of them; if not in the title, it is in the lyrics. A few were written in the brogue but the great majority are in American English. They express American attitudes as definitely as if written about the Fountain in Indianapolis or Monument Square in Portland, Maine.

Songwriters who have used Italian dialect seem to have loved the sons and daughters of Italy. The writers laughed with them rather than at them, just as we can smile and chuckle with the sad ballads, the weepers of the early century, without deriding their quaint portrayals of customs and thought. The second-generation young folks of my acquaintance chuckled at the bombastic bragging about a lyrical blood relationship with the great Italian tenor, Caruso, in "My Cousin Carus" ("He mak' de all cry 'Brave Gratsi' when he sing Pagliacci. His voice so dream-a lak a-peaches and cream-a.") * Pride of relationship fairly bubbled out of "My Brudda Sylvest" ("he got a strong a grip/With a one punch a sink a da ship"), 1909.

"My Mariuccia" ("take a steamboat—back to Italy") was a lament. "She made a skidoo with tough Tony . . . She's gone back to the old-a-country," but Victor Herbert's "Italian Street Song" in *Naughty Marietta,* still heard, vibrated with joy of living and dancing. Two others from the same musical comedy, "Sweet Mystery of Life" and "I'm Falling in Love with Someone," are still heard regularly in supermarkets on Muzak. "Please No Squeeza da Banana, coconuts are better, they don't bruise," tells in its title its own plaintive story of an Italian fruit vendor's woes. And there was another "Mariutch" who did the "hootch-a-ma-kootch down at Coney Isle . . . never move-a de feet. That's a funny style." Perhaps it should be explained that the so-called hootchy-kootchy oriental dance originated in the Street of Cairo, a concession on the midway at Chicago's World's Fair (1893), and spread like Beatle virus.

The sheet-music cover of "Sweet Italian Love" shows a handsome youth with a mop of wavy hair, a fashionable dip-front, padded shoulder coat, and a de-

* Fred Fischer, 1913.

tachable collar (Arrow's Belmont *circa* 1910 if memory's right), and a caption "As sung by the author Irving Berlin." In show biz terminology, the song was terrific. In his early song-writing years Berlin also wrote several in Yiddish theme that portrayed the characteristics and attitudes of the urban second generation just as surely as he was able, later, to capture every range of human emotion in his songs.

Somehow, the fractured German dialects, so common to vaudeville, burlesque, and musical comedy, didn't overflow into our American songs as might have been expected. Everybody knew "Johnny Schmoker" as most adults today recognize "Ist das nicht eine schnitzel bank?" In both cases the words were translated into approximate English but the original tunes lived. "How Can I Leave Thee?" when Anglicized became the melody of college songs such as "Dear Old Reserve." Hardly any songs utilized the low-comedy German dialect heard on stage from a standardized comedian, blond wig, padded waistline, often with a saxophone-shaped china pipe. (I'll told you a yoke. Ha-ha-ha! It's a very funny yoke. You ask me, "Vy iss de fourth of Chuly?" The straight man groans and asks, "Why is the fourth of July?" "Well, I'll told you. Chay iss de fearst. Oo iss de second. L is de taird, and Vy iss de fourth of Chuly. Ha-ha-ha!") Perhaps it was because such material lent itself more readily to the spoken word than to song lyrics. However, one of the ancient vaudeville gags would have lent itself to a song title: "De hurrieder I go, de behinder I get."

A song of the 1920's expresses the changing attitude of most native Americans, whatever their nationality origins, toward the continuing influx of unassimilated immigrants seeking what the states had to offer. Acceptance and even admiration of their diligence and acumen had crept into native attitudes, as they were expressed in a song published as "the comedy hit" of the 1915 season. "The Argentines, the Portuguese and the Greeks" includes sociology.

Columbus discovered America in fourteen-ninety-two
Then came the English and the Dutch, the Frenchman and the Jew
Then came the Swede and the Irishman who helped the country grow
Still they keep on coming, and ev'rywhere you go

CHORUS:

There's the Argentines and the Portuguese, the Armenians and the Greeks
They don't know the language, they don't know the law
But they vote in the country of the free
And a funny thing, when we start to sing "My Country, 'Tis of Thee"
*None of us know the words but the Argentines, and the Portuguese, and the Greeks.**

Earlier mention was made of "I Didn't Raise My Boy to Be a Soldier," when in 1915 the feeling in the states was "it's none of our affair." But we were providing food and munitions to the Allies in Europe. "Don't Bite the Hand That's Feeding You" showed some asperity toward those Allies who complained that we should be in action with them.

In England they were singing "Keep the Home Fires Burning," "It's a Long Way to Tipperary," and "There's a Long Long Trail" which was American

* Jos. W. Stern & Co., New York, N. Y.

in origin though published first in England. "Tipperary" was a humorous song that had lain dormant since 1912 until its marching rhythm caught on with the Tommies in 1914 to make it a "war" song. By 1917 we had declared war on Germany, and "Over There," in tune with changed American attitudes, was the big hit. More songs of 1917 were:

Dixie Volunteers
Goodbye, Broadway, Hello, France
Good Morning, Mr. Zip Zip Zip
I May be Gone for a Long Long Time
It's a Long Way to Berlin
Joan of Arc (they are calling you)
Liberty Bell, It's Time to Ring Again
Oh, Johnny, Oh (with topical lyrics sung by Nora Bayes)
Pack Up Your Troubles
Sister Susie's Sewing Shirts for Soldiers
Somewhere in France Is Daddy

Then came "Just a Baby's Prayer at Twilight" (for Daddy overseas), "The Navy Took Them Over" (it will bring them home), "Oh, Frenchy," "Oh, How I Hate to Get Up in the Morning," "Roses of Picardy," "Rose of No Man's Land," "Till We Meet Again," "Three Wonderful Letters from Home," "Wee, Wee, Marie," "Long Boy," "Send Me Away with a Smile," "When You Come Back," and dozens of others, until Germany surrendered. Promptly, Americans started to sing "How You Gonna Keep 'Em Down on the Farm?" and "I've Got My Captain Working for Me Now."

World War II is within the ken of most adults, including its "White Cliffs of Dover," "I Left My Heart at the Stage Door Canteen," "This is the Army, Mr. Jones," "Any Bonds Today," and "White Christmas." Few, if any, World War II songs had the militance or confident cockiness of 1917, exemplified by "We'll Knock the Heligo—Into Heligo—Out of Heligoland." In their restraint they resembled the songs that stemmed from the brief Spanish-American War: "Blue Bell," "Goodbye, Dolly Gray," "Just As the Sun Went Down," "A Little Boy in Blue," and "The Blue and the Gray." That last one was a mother's lament for her three sons. Two of them had lost their lives in the Civil War ("One lies down near Appomatox many miles away/The other sleeps at Chickamauga and they both wore suits of gray/To the strains of 'Down in Dixie' the third was laid away in a trench at Santiago [Cuba]/The Blue and the Gray"). The Civil War ended in 1865 and the Spanish-American in 1898. It would seem that the bereaved mother had set some sort of record in prolonged fertility.

To illustrate another American attitude, this a peacetime one, when I was a boy on the farm the big event one winter was the organization of a marching drill team of farmers who belong to the Grand Order of Something or Other. It was very secret, with passwords, grips, and rituals. Their wives were in the Women's Auxiliary. In one movement of the mixed drill the men marched in company front, split somewhat by the box stove, toward the standing line of wives. The men sang topical words to "Reuben and Rachael." The women curtsied and responded:

Reuben, Reuben, don't be foolish
We are only women, *true*
But we hope to make our Order
Just as big someday as you.

The italics are mine to point up the fact that they were still "only" women. The nucleus of woman suffrage had hardly begun to squirm under the proddings of Susan B. Anthony, Carrie Chapman Cat, and other feminine protagonists of votes for women. The words project the national thought in the early 1900's. Imagine singing today that they were "only" women! As time went on they developed volubility that provided the theme for songs in the teens such as "No Suffragette for Mine" (1914), exemplifying the male disposition before women's enfranchisement in 1920. "Please, Little Suffragette" in 1921 recognized that in many respects men would beg for privileges in the future.

In those early 1920's twenty-five million women began to realize that they were citizens whose rights included smoking, drinking in public, dressing and doing largely as they liked. Many demonstrated that they could do men's work, better in some fields that weren't hayfields. The traditions of special respects and protections of the "weaker" sex became increasingly difficult to maintain toward those who were more interested in being heard than respected. Self-conscious in newly bobbed hair and in skirts above knees that in the main were unglamorous, great numbers bellied up to speakeasies, waggled Fatimas, and danced cheek to cheek.

Coupled with this phenomenon was the strange one of Prohibition which made it illegal to ferment, brew, distill, or transport alcoholic beverages, though it was legal to drink them. Our states plunged into the ugliest era this country has known until the troubles of the 1960's. Citizens who were law-abiding in other respects disregarded the Volstead Act. Many who'd been teetotalers took up drinking because it was socially smart. Many made deplorable spectacles of themselves. While not as lasting as our continued ignorant use of the automobile, Prohibition had almost as much influence in creating disrespect for law. Today's youngsters who see their parents drive forty in a school zone and disregard other traffic regulations receive primary and advanced education in law-breaking from the most effective teachers.

The songs written about Prohibition before its legal status in 1920, and afterward until 1933, show the national attitude of nonacceptance. This small sampling shows progressive reactions:

Everybody Wants the Key to My Cellar	*1919*	*the hoarding year*
Sahara	*1919*	*aridity to come*
What'll We Do on Saturday Night?	*1919*	*when the town goes dry*
Prohibition, You Have Lost Your Sting	*1919*	*see below*
The Moon Shines on the Moonshine	*1920*	*everywhere*
Show Me the Way to Go Home	*1925*	*effects of the "moon"*

The reason cited for Prohibition losing its sting, a year in advance of stinging time, was because kisses are intoxicating: "I should worry about the 'bone dry' law/I'll date up the gals from Maine to 'Frisco Bay . . . I'll never draw a sober breath the livelong day." *

It would seem that it has been demonstrated that our older songs are mirrors of customs, attitudes, and dispositions. But how old is "older"?

* Meyer Cohen Music Publishing Co., 1619 Broadway, New York, N. Y.

Memory Lame

or

How Old Is an "Old" Song?

Imagine that we have microphones hidden right across the country in the midst of several adult groups singing simultaneously the songs that everybody knows —almost. We have bugged beach parties, campfires, homes—wherever these singing groups can be found. Every group sings impromptu and undirected, doin' what comes natur'lly, like song sparrows at dusk or cardinals in late winter, for the joy of self-expression.

The general effect seems to be "Let Me Call You Sweetheart—I'm in love with you." We might have recognized it sooner if all those on the Oregon Beach had been in the same key. What we hear from New Hampshire's White Mountains is not a series of backfires. It's a Boston camper expressing himself in low bass. As the chorus swells, it brings increasing evidence that the tie that binds those widely separated singers into what might be loosely called a singing unit is not their ability to carry a tune. It is their inability to remember the words. Songs do consist of words riding a musical steed. But quite often memory lane is memory lame.

Of course it doesn't really matter whether we remember the actual words or just ta-ta along with some of the other guessers at our microphones; "Keep the love light glowing/burning/shining/gleaming in your eyes so blue/so true/of blue." When they forget, they substitute a word that might have been in the original or should have been there, someone thinks. A tenory menace of my acquaintance insists upon singing, "Meet me tonight in dreamland where the sweet lovers spoon," instead of the original, "where love's sweet roses bloom." He says it rhymes better his way, even though "spoon" dates him. That shows how a helpless song can be garbled until the one who wrote it might hardly recognize his offspring. When several such individualists raise their voices in a quartet, consisting of six baritones who've just been introduced to each other at a party, it can become quite confusing.

Even when we sing our national anthem to which we've been exposed since childhood, most of us emit embarrassed mumbles until we brighten with "the rocket's red glare" and end with a grand burst on the "la-and of the free and the home of the brave." If you could find enough takers, you'd soar into higher tax brackets by betting that everyone will falter in the words of "America," "My Old Kentucky Home," "Long Long Trail," or others as recognizable as your front door. An exception might be "She'll Be Comin' 'Round the Mountain," written by a man of few words, as Ring Lardner once commented upon the lyricist of "Honey, honey, bless your heart."

These lapses in memory of words are not new. Robert J. Burdett (1844–1914) once wrote a parody on Charlotte Barnard's much older "I Cannot Sing the Old Songs—I sang so long ago." One verse of Burdett's parody, which was titled "Song Without Words," should give us comfort when we forget lyrics:

For though I'm full of music as choirs of singing birds
I cannot sing the old songs—For I forget the words.

In more recent years, N. R. Howard, former editor and columnist of the Cleveland *News,* packed grim fact into tight space as only a skilled writer who has listened, enjoyed, and suffered could condense it. Writing about an outdoor stag party he reported upon a guest who "made ten appearances as a basso when he was supposed to be carrying melody" and who "hotly denied that he was singing whatever part he was singing." "You wouldn't believe," Howard wrote, "that so many men (a) could remember so many songs, and (b) *forget so many words.*"

He noted also that the host grinned and gritted his teeth while "planning the proper apology" to the neighbors. In such an outdoor song clinic much does depend upon the neighbors' milk of human kindness. If it is not well pasteurized, curds are likely to develop with the third repetition of "Sweet Adeline" at 12:50 A.M. on a lawn. The curds are identified here as the Concurrent Echo:

THIRD REPEAT	BUILT-IN ECHO	CONCURRENT ECHO
Sweet Ade-line	*Su-wheat Ad-o-line*	*Hey! You!*
My Yad-e-line	*My Had-o-li-i-ine*	*Hold that line!*
At night, deah hot	*At night dear-r hear-rt*	*Git off that cat's tail!*
For you I pi-i-ine	*For you-eye pi-ine*	*Bury it! Quick!*
In all my a-dreams	*Hin hall my dru-heams*	*Whisper it!*
Your fair face beams	*Your fair fay speams*	*Ah-oo-oo-oo!*
You're the flow-wer of my hear-rt,	*Sweet Ade-e-o-li-ine*	*Now shut* tup!

Here the retentiveness of words is unusually high, though purists might note slight variations in the phonetics of the choral interpretation.

When singers forget, they fill in from their vocabularies, experience, and musical and lyrical abilities. That is why very old songs that have been passed along unwritten took on local flavors. A song's words may have suffered such erosions that identification is possible only from a line or phrase that has survived—"He was her man an' he done her wrong" as example from the countless versions of "Frankie and Johnny." Even song titles suffer as in "The Story of the Rose," which most singers call "Heart of My Heart." Another is

"You Tell Me Your Dream," which is commonly called "I Had a Dream, Dear."

That being true of music, words, and titles in this century, let's look at a song that was as well known along the Scottish border in Shakespeare's time as "I Could Have Danced All Night" is to us. Its title is "Barbara Allen" and an early English version was printed thus:

In Scarlet town where I did dwell
There was a fair maid dwellin'
Made all the youths cry "well-a-day"
Her name was Barbara Allen.

As printed in the American Colonies, it went like this:

In Scarlet town where I was born
There was a fair maid dwellin'
Made ev'ry youth *cry "well-a-day"*
Her name was Barbara Allen.

Because it was a traditional ballad even then, it is possible that the American printer had heard a variation. Yet he might have set his type from memory of the words printed earlier in England. If that is true, memories were also slightly lame in the Colonies.

For generations that followed Barbara's arrival in the memories of those who came here from the old country, the song survived in the southern mountains where the offspring of the original immigrants lived remotely. Because they had limited outside contacts, those people in the mountain coves passed along the traditional songs from voice to ear. Here is a version of "Barbara Allen" that you too might hear today in the foothills of the Smokies after its abrasions over centuries:

Away down south where I was born
'Twas there I got my trainin'
I fell in love with a pretty gal
Her name was Barb'ry Ellen.

That shows how lame memories and substitutions of local color can convert an ancient ballad into one that is recognizable only by vestigial shreds. As to the tune nowadays, it's called "Barb'ry Ellen." It shore ain't "Barbara Allen" of old.

Hundreds of versions of "Frankie and Johnny" have been sung. Its original composer, original lyricist, place and date of composition remain unknown. Claims have been made that its origin antedated the Civil War.

One figment of its lore might place it among the songs that early immigrants brought from England. In the 1920's my guitaring companion Don Knowlton was in the foothills of the Great Smoky Mountains with a guide, an old mountain man who'd never been outside his county. Talking and singing by the campfire one night, the old settler came out with:

Frankie was in Spain When she heard Little Albert's name
Gave him a hundred dollars for to buy him a walkin' cane
He was her man An' he did her a wrong.

He said he had learned it from his granpappy, who was born in those hills.

"Did her a wrong" is perfectly good olde English. Did some remote ancestor of his granpappy troll the ditty to a lute looted from the Spaniards in England's wars with Spain? The lyrics would have gone through the same evolutions as those of "Barbara Allen," but the vestigial tag line, the song's trademark, "he done her wrong," differs only slightly from the Smoky Mountain version. If it was peculation, it leads to speculation, and that's part of the fun in delving into oldies.

There may be better examples of stand-ins for original words and music than in "Only Once in a Lifetime," perennial favorite of barbershop quartets the country over, but if so, I haven't seen the evidence. The following is the version published in the Harmony Heritage series of SPEBSQSA, the international men's quartet society which receives full treatment here in Section Three. The original melody and words, 1902, by Raymond A. Browne, were harmonized by Walter C. West.

Memory Lame

On the following page are the melody and words as written about 1942 by the bari of a quondam amateur foursome, exactly as his quartet sang it then and later and as it is sung widely today.

Comparison of the two melodies and two sets of words seems to indicate considerable mishandling by forgetful singers between 1902 and 1942 as they passed it down the line unwritten in person-to-person calls. The second version is a rarity since hardly any harmonizers under the gaslights in the park could read or write notes. Most didn't care to be restricted to a written version. That would be regimentation. Whether the original or the eroded version is better, deponent saith not.

Limping memories account for another phenomenon that is recognized by even casual observers who have seen nonprofessionals musicalize from memory. After the first few songs, they can't remember what to sing or play next. "What's another good one?" They don't need a leader or director. They need a prompter. If they're indoors, they stare hopefully at the ceiling; if outdoors at the stars. Another good one might pop across the plaster or the Milky Way.

That immediate feeling of frustration is bad enough, but later is when wishful singers usually plumb the black depths in one of life's major tragedies. On their separate ways home each recalls a dozen good ones, too late. "I'm going to write down a list." They don't. The next chapter will be for them, a starter for cold voices of frustrated would-be singers and itchy-fingered amateur instrumentalists whose memories have gone lame. But don't look now. There's one bit of unfinished business to be completed.

The groups that were singing into our microphones earlier were adults singing the "old" songs. Many other old ones have cropped up. The question is how old is an "old" song? In the 1960's a disc jockey may refer to a song as a re-e-al oldie. An acquaintance of mine sputters like frying fish, "That's not so old. Crosby sang it when Junior was a baby." Junior now plays end on the college football team.

During every hour of the twenty-four, not consecutively, in every season of the year clinical studies have been conducted utilizing human guinea pigs of both sexes and all ages, representing every economic, sectarian, political, national, cultural, and cigarette-preference level. To paraphrase slightly from a genuinely old song, Koko's duet with Katisha in *The Mikado,* "To the matter that I mention I have given much attention." Conclusions are now available. The results are consistent on the study graphs whether "Annie Laurie" or "America the Beautiful" or "Rudolph the Red-Nosed Reindeer" or "Yellow Bird" are on test. As a check, I fed several thousand old songs, along with their singers, into the computer.

Conclusion: Regardless of one's age beyond thirtyish, an old song is one that was at its popularity peak when you were of high school–college age. A song that you consider very old was popular when you were in grade school. A really ancient song is one that you heard as a child. Statistically, the findings may be expressed this way:

Old—*popular at your high school–college age*
Very old—*popular at your age eight to thirteen*
Ancient—*recalled from the years before age eight*

It may be necessary to let out a seam here or take up a bit there, give or take a year or two, to tailor it to an individual's exact age measurements. But for a hand-me-down it fits the majority remarkably well. Related to that, most often adults place the Golden Age of Music in their eager school-college years when memory retention centers were most receptive and not overcrowded.

So now the thousand Tops in Their Times that follow can be used as starters or as a test tube for age. In that second case, use discretion when revealing your findings.

Tops in Their Times

Curious persons, alert to the importance of the unimportant, have been known to speculate as to which songs are the most used? The most used songs must be those in which the populace participates. Frequent participation means that the song stands on its own. Its melody doesn't need the crutch of instrumentation to carry it along. It hums and whistles easily. All of us remember songs that rocketed into frequent use by entertainers on radio, sparkled briefly, and trailed away like a shooting star. We remember some words of the song, but "how did the music go?" It's been demonstrated time after time that the public won't play, sing, whistle, or hum—in a word, *use*—what doesn't sing easily.

Almost everyone known to have special interest in older popular music has heard, "What! You don't know *that* one! Why everybody in Cornucopia was singing *that* one when..." The note of surprise usually carries overtones of accusation: If you don't know *that* one, you don't know much. "When" could be three years ago or the winter of 1933 when the Perkins Block burned. If your music memory antedates that fire, you can be in double disgrace.

No one has heard them all or remembers melody and words of all that have been heard. Addicts are likely to discuss a note or note sequence or a word in the lyrics. "That's how *we* sang it." Memory is so fragile and there are so many words and notes to remember that I seldom take sides or bets as to who's wrong or right. We may remember a song almost as we learned it from one who almost recalls it as sung by someone else with a lame memory.

Certain songs have been used so often that we accept them as fixtures in our environment. They've always been there, it seems. "Happy Birthday to You" was written as "Good Morning to All" in 1893 by schoolteacher Mildred J. Hill as a greeting sung by her tiny pupils. Other songs of the 1800's, or older, are so timeless that almost everyone knew them when the 1900's were young, and now. "Drink to Me Only with Thine Eyes," "Believe Me If All Those Endearing Young Charms," "Oh, Susanna," and the "Wedding March" typify others still in use. It is probable that Stephen Foster composed more songs used today than any other composer of the 1800's.

Before electronics, a new song's popularity might carry over decades. "Mighty Lak a Rose," 1891; "Give My Regards to Broadway," 1904; "Ah, Sweet Mystery of Life" and "A Perfect Day," 1910; and "The Sweetheart of Sigma Chi," 1912, remained as high in favor as ten-year-olds. After fifty years at least three of them still remain high in use.

Publishers' records show how many copies of sheet music or discs have been sold. Beyond that, ASCAP, which looks after the interests of composers, authors, and publishers to whom a song is property like a home or a car, can account pretty well for the times a copyrighted song is used in public performance. Muzak's lists of compositions played unobtrusively in public places indicate use. So do the reports of radio and TV stations and others that use great numbers of recordings. All are needles on the gauge of use measurement, but they do not pinpoint usage. No slide rule or computer can calculate the number of times a song was played or sung yesterday in the home or repeated by recordings because someone liked it particularly. No computation can hint at how often it was sung, whistled, or hummed, at work or play or in cars scurrying about the nation. Tunes pop out anywhere, almost everywhere.

Even if an accurate gauge of song usage could jot down the number of times a tune has been uttered everywhere in every way, its findings this week would be different from a week in 1950 or earlier or since. Certain songs could be at their high tide of public performance (think of "Whistle While You Work"), others at the ebb that usually follows flood. Flood applies to more than song usage. The reports of the Register of Copyrights at the Library of Congress indicates an inundation. The musical compositions registered for copyright in 1961 numbered 65,000. They increased annually until in 1965 the total registration was 80,881. Few of that enormous number have engendered enough enthusiasm among professional musicians nor among those who musicalize for the fun of it to make them "standards," like "Whispering."

These and other contingencies put hazards on the course of anyone bold, or foolish, enough to compile the songs that have been among the most used over a half century or so. There are enough pitfalls to make one approach a selection only after fasting and incantations to Lady Luck. Hundreds of thousands of songs have been published.

The compilation that follows is not a list of personal favorites. I wouldn't give kennel space to a few of the musical dogs that have been among our most used. Conversely, I'd like to add several that are real gems, though they never attained the popularity that they deserved. "Says who?" Says i, humbly.

Nearly all hymns must be eliminated because of comparatively infrequent use. That applies particularly to Christmas hymns heard rarely at other seasons. The mention of Christmas hymns brings to mind a trend, noticeable to many in the late 1960's, toward injecting modern to futuristic harmonies and even changed notes into the traditional melodies of "Silent Night," "The First Noel" and others.

With such updating of centuries-old Christ-mas music, it is no surprise to also hear newly composed songs in the Holidays theme that blend hard rock with Dixieland. How long before moderns begin re-writing the Declaration of Independence, Lincoln's Gettysburg Address and "Star Spangled Banner" in Hippiese?

If we want to know about the popularity of a song of the late 1800's or early 1900's, ask those who've lived with them. The methods of their selection here are unorthodox, comparable to the seat-of-the-pants flying techniques of World War I, because of the lack of instruments for gauging song use over more than half a century.

The compiler's face will glow red because of songs that, obviously, should have been included. At times, Sigmund Spaeth felt that way about his epochal *History of Popular Music in America*. To quote "the wonder grew that one small head could carry all he knew" gave him slight comfort. In the preface to Julius Mattfeld's colossal *Variety Music Cavalcade* he wrote: "Omissions? There are plenty, as the compiler knows. They are the lacunae that disturb every biographer's sense of detail—the inevitable disappointments attending his most careful efforts." The wonder grows that those two musicographers made so few omissions that nit-pickers find slim pickings in either book.

So, this compiler of those songs that have been among the most used is out on a limb. Hand me that saw:

1,000

TOPS IN THEIR TIMES

Age and Memory Testers—1800's into 1950's

A Bundle of Nostalgia for Some—A Glimpse into the Unexplored for Others

Abadaba Honeymoon	*1914*
Abdulla Bulbul Ameer	*1800's*
Absent	*1899*
Absinthe Frappé	*1904*
Ach du Lieber Augustin	*old German*
Adeste Fidelis	*1851*
After the Ball	*1892*
After You've Gone	*1918*
Ah, Sweet Mystery of Life	*1910*
Ain't Dat a Shame?	*1901*
Ain't She Sweet?	*1927*
Ain't We Got Fun?	*1921*
Alexander's Rag Time Band	*1911*
Alice Blue Gown	*1919*
All Aboard for Blanket Bay	*1910*
All Aboard for Dixieland	*1913*
Allah's Holiday	*1916*
All Alone (H. Von Tilzer)	*1911*
All Alone (Berlin)	*1924*
All Coons Look Alike to Me	*1896*
All of Me	*1931*
All the World Will Be Jealous of Me	*1917*
Aloha Oe	*1878*
Along Came Ruth	*1914*
Always	*1925*
Always in the Way	*1903*
America	*1832*
America the Beautiful	*1895*
Am I Blue	*1929*
Among My Souvenirs	*1927*
Anchors Aweigh	*1906*
Angry	*1925*
Annie Laurie	*1838*
Annie Rooney (Little)	*1890*
Anona	*1903*
Any Little Girl That's a Nice Little Girl Is the Right Little Girl for Me	*1910*
Any Rags?	*1902*
Apple Blossom Time (I'll be with you in)	*1920*
April Showers	*1921*
Arkansas Traveller	*1851*
Army Air Corps Song	*1939*
Are You from Dixie?	*1915*
Are You Lonesome Tonight?	*1926*
Are You Sincere?	*1906*
Around the World (in Eighty Days)	*1956*
Arrah Wanna	*1906*
As Time Goes By	*1943*
At a Georgia Camp Meeting	*1897*
At Dawning	*1906*
A-tisket A-tasket	*1938*
At Sundown	*1927*
Auf Wiedersehn	*1915*
Auld Lang Syne	*1799*

Aura Lee	*1861*
Avalon	*1920*
Babes in the Wood	*1800's*
Babes in the Wood (Kern)	*1915*
Baby Face	*1926*
Baby Shoes	*1916*
Back Home in Indiana	*1917*
Back Home In Tennessee	*1915*
Ballin' the Jack	*1913*
Band Played On (The)	*1895*
Barcarole	*1864*
Barney Google	*1923*
Battle Hymn of the Republic	*1862*
Beautiful Dreamer	*1864*
Beautiful Garden of Roses	*1910*
Beautiful Isle of Somewhere	*1897*
Beautiful Lady in Blue	*1935*
Beautiful Ohio	*1918*
Because	*1902*
Because You're You	*1906*
Bedelia	*1903*
Beer Barrel Polka	*1939*
Begin the Beguine	*1935*
Believe Me If All Those Endearing Young Charms	*1808*
Bells of St. Mary's	*1917*
Be My Little Baby Bumblebee	*1912*
Ben Bolt	*1848*
Best Things in Life Are Free	*1927*
Be Sweet to Me, Kid	*1908*
Betsy from Pike (Sweet)	*1854*
Betty Co-ed	*1930*
Bill	*1927*
Bill Bailey, Won't You Please Come Home?	*1902*
Billy	*1911*
Billy Boy	*old English*
Bird in a Gilded Cage	*1900*
Blow the Smoke Away (Melody identical with "What's the Use of Dreaming")	*1906*
Blue Bell	*1904*
Blue Moon	*1934*
Blue Room	*1926*
Blue Skies	*1927*
Body and Soul	*1930*
Bowery (The)	*1892*
Boy of Mine (Dear Little)	*1918*
Break the News to Mother (Just)	*1897*
Bring Back My Bonnie to Me	*early 1800's*
Bring the Wagon Home, John	*1800's*
Brother, Can You Spare a Dime?	*1932*
Buffalo Girls	*1844*
Buttons and Bows	*1948*
Button Up Your Overcoat	*1928*
By a Waterfall (Just a Cottage Small)	*1925*
Bye Bye, Blackbird	*1926*
Bye Bye Blues	*1930*
By the Beautiful Sea	*1914*
By the Light of the Silvery Moon	*1909*
By the River Saint Marie	*1931*
By the Watermelon Vine (Lindy)	*1904*
Caisson Song (Field Artillery)	*1908*
California and You	*1913*
California, Here I Come	*1924*
Call Me Up Some Rainy Afternoon	*1910*
Camptown Races (De)	*1850*
Can't Help Loving' Dat Man	*1927*
Can't Yo Heah Me Callin', Caroline?	*1914*
Can't You See I'm Lonely?	*1905*
Carolina in the Morning	*1922*
Carolina Moon	*1928*
Carry Me Back to Old Virginny	*1878*
Casey Jones	*1909*
Cecelia	*1925*
Charmaine	*1926*
Chattanooga Choo-Choo	*1941*
Chattanooga Shoe Shine Boy	*1950*
Cheerful Little Earful	*1930*
Cheer Up, Mary	*1906*
Cheyenne (Shy Ann)	*1906*
Children's Marching Song	*1959*
Chinatown, My Chinatown	*1910*
Chloe	*1927*
Ciribiribin	*1909*
Cocktails for Two	*1934*
Come, Josephine, in My Flying Machine	*1910*
Come Over and Love Me Some More	*1913*
Come Take a Trip in My Airship	*1904*
Comin' Round the Mountain (She'll Be)	*American folk*
Comrades	*1894*
Constantinople	*1928*
Cool Water	*1936*
Coon! Coon! Coon!	*1901*
Creole Belle	*1900*
Cruising Down the River	*1945*
Cubanola Glide	*1909*

Cucaracha (La)	1934
Cuddle Up a Little Closer	1908
Cup of Coffee, A Sandwich and You	1925
Curse of An Aching Heart	1913
Daisies Won't Tell	1908
Daisy Bell (Bicycle Built for Two)	1892
Dancing Around	1913
Dancing with Tears in My Eyes	1930
Danny Boy	1913
Dardanella	1919
Dark Eyes (Otchi Tcharniya)	1926
Darktown Strutters' Ball	1917
Darling Nellie Gray	1856
Davy Crockett (Ballad of)	1955
Day Dreams, Visions of Bliss	1909
Dearie (Kummer)	1905
Dearie (Hilliard and Mann)	1950
Dear Little Boy of Mine	1918
Dear Old Girl	1903
Dear Old Pal of Mine	1918
Deep in My Heart, Dear	1924
Deep in the Heart of Texas	1941
Deep Purple	1934
Deep River	1917
Didn't He Ramble (Oh)	1902
Dinah	1925
Dipsy Doodle	1937
Dixie (Dixie's Land)	1860
Doan You Cry, Mah Honey	1899
Doggie in the Window (That)	1953
Doin' What Comes Natur'lly	1946
Don't Fence Me In	1944
Don't Take Me Home	1908
Down Among the Sheltering Palms	1915
Down Among the Sugar Cane	1908
Down by the Old Mill Stream	1910
Down in Jungle Town	1908
Down in the Old Cherry Orchard	1907
Down in the Valley	1943
Down on the Farm (H. Von Tilzer)	1902
Down on the Farm (I Want to Go Back to Michigan—Berlin)	1914
Down South	1912
Down Went McGinty	1889
Down Where the Cotton Blossoms Grow	1901
Down Where the Wurburger Flows	1902
Do You Ever Think of Me?	1920
Dream (A)	1895
Dream A Little Dream of Me	1931
Dreaming	1906
Dream Melody	1922
Drifting and Dreaming	1925
Drink to Me Only with Thine Eyes	1780
Dunderbeck (Johnny Rebeck)—tune Solomon Levi—	early American
Easter Parade	1933
Ebenezer Frye (Wal I Swan)	1907
Elsie from Chelsea	1896
Empty Saddles	1926
Evaline (Oh, Eva, Iva, Ova)	1800's
Everybody's Doing It Now	1911
Everybody Two-Step	1912
Everybody Works But Father	1905
Every Little Movement	1910
Far Above Cayuga's Waters (Annie Lisle—adapted to Cornell and other colleges)	1860
Fatal Wedding	1893
Feather Your Nest	1920
Ferdinand the Bull	1938
Five Foot Two, Eyes of Blue	1925
Five Minutes More	1946
Florodora Sextette (Tell Me, Pretty Maiden)	1900
Flow Gently, Sweet Afton (tune adapted to many songs)	1838
Flying Trapeze (Man on the)	1868
Forgotten	1894
For He's a Jolly Good Fellow (Tune of Malbrouck)	early 1700's
For Me and My Gal	1917
Forty-five Minutes from B'way	1905
Frankie and Johnny (date unknown; probably mid to late 1800's)	
Freckles	1919
Funiculi Funicula	1880
Gallagher and Shean (Oh, Mr. Gallagher)	1922
Garden of Your Heart (In the)	1914
Garland of Old Fashioned Roses	1911
Gee! But There's Class to a Girl Like You	1908
Georgia Camp Meeting	1897
Georgia on My Mind	1930
Get Out and Get Under the Moon	1928
Girl Friend (The)	1926

Girl of My Dreams	1927
Girl That I Marry (The)	1946
Give Me a Night in June	1927
Give Me the Moonlight, Give Me the Girl	1917
Give My Regards to Broadway	1904
Glow Worm (The)	1907
God Bless America	1939
Gold Mine in the Sky (There's a)	1937
Gondolier (The)	1904
Goodbye, Boys	1913
Goodbye, Broadway, Hello, France	1917
Goodbye, Dolly Gray	1900
Goodbye, Eliza Jane	1903
Goodbye, Girls, I'm Through	1914
Goodbye, Little Girl, Goodbye	1904
Goodbye, My Lady Love	1904
Goodbye, My Lover, Goodbye	1880's
Goodbye, Rose	1910
Good Morning, Mr. Zip Zip Zip	1918
Good Morning to All (Happy Birthday to You)	1893
Good Night, Dear	1908
Good Night, Irene	1950
Good Night, Ladies	1867
Good Night, Little Girl, Good Night	1898
Good Night, Nurse	1912
Good Night, Sweetheart	1931
Go 'Way Back and Sit Down	1901
Grizzly Bear	1910
Gypsy Love Song	1898
Hail, Hail, the Gang's All Here	1908
Hallelujah	1927
Happy Birthday to You (Good Morning to All)	1893
Happy Days Are Here Again	1929
Harbor of Love	1911
Harrigan	1907
Has Anybody Here Seen Kelly?	1909
Have You Ever Been Lonely	1933
Hawaiian Butterfly	1917
Heart of My Heart (Story of the Rose)	1899
Hearts and Flowers (instrumental)	1899
He'd Have to Get Under . . . to Fix Up His Automobile	1913
Heigh-Ho (Dwarfs in Snow White)	1938
Hello, Central, Give Me Heaven	1901
Hello, Frisco	1915
Hello, My Baby	1899
Here Comes the Showboat	1927
He's a Cousin of Mine	1906
He's a Rag Picker	1914
Hey, Look Me Over	1960
Hiawatha	1901
Hindustan	1918
Hi, Neighbor	1941
Hinky Dinky Parlay Voo	1918
Hold Me	1920
Holy City	1892
Holy Night (Silent Night)	1818
Home on the Range Copyrighted	1905
Home Sweet Home	1823
Honey Boy	1907
Honeymoon (The Waning)	1908
Honeysuckle Rose	1929
Honey That I Love So Well	1898
Hot Time in the Old Town Tonight (There'll Be a)	1896
How Are Things in Glocca Morra?	1946
How Can I Leave Thee (old German)	1851
How Come You Do Me Like You Do?	1924
How Deep Is the Ocean?	1932
How Dry I Am (Tune of "Oh Happy Day," a hymn)	1891
How'd You Like to Spoon with Me?	1915
How Ya Gonna Keep 'Em Down on the Farm?	1919
Huckleberry Finn	1917
Humoresque (instrumental)	1894
I Ain't Got Anybody	1916
I Believe	1953
I Can't Do This Sum	1903
I Can't Give You Anything But Love	1928
I Can't Tell Why I Love You But I Do-oo-oo	1900
I Could Have Danced All Night	1956
Ida! Sweet as Apple Cider	1903

Note: In a collection of popular songs the "I" file is the largest, showing who's most important. "M" for "My" bulks large. "What," "where" and "when" make "W" a big one. "Y" is loaded with "You" and its derivatives.

I Didn't Raise My Boy to Be a Soldier	1915
I'd Leave My Happy Home for You	1899
I'd Love to Live in Loveland with a Girl Like You	1910
I Don't Know Where I'm Going But I'm On My Way	1917
I Don't Know Why	1931
I Don't Know Why I Love You (But I Do)	1903
I Don't Want to Get Well	1917
I Don't Want to Play in Your Yard	1894
I Dreamt I Dwelt in Marble Halls	1843
I Fah Down Go Boom	1928
If All Moons Were Honeymoons	1909
If All My Dreams Were Made of Gold	1911
If I Had a Talking Picture of You	1929
If I Had My Way	1913
If the Man in the Moon Were a Coon	1905
If We Can't Be the Same Old Sweethearts, We Can Still Be the Same Old Friends	1917
If You Knew Susie	1925
If You Talk in Your Sleep, Don't Mention My Name	1911
If You Were the Only Girl in the World	1925
I Get the Blues When It Rains	1929
I Got Mine	1901
I Got Rhythm	1930
I Had a Dream Dear	1908
I Like Mountain Music	1933
I'll Be with You in Apple Blossom Time	1920
I'll Make a Ring Around Rosie	1910
I'll See You in My Dreams	1924
I'll String Along with You	1934
I'll Take You Home Again, Kathleen	1876
I Long to See the Girl I Left Behind	1893
I Love a Lassie	1906
I Love Life	1923
I Love Love	1911
I Love My Wife, But Oh You Kid	1909
I Love the Ladies	1914
I Love the Name of Mary	1910
I Love the Silver in Your Hair	1915
I Love You (Little Jesse James)	1923
I Love You in the Same Old Way	1896
I Love You Truly	1906
I'm Afraid to Come Home in the Dark	1907
I'm Always Chasing Rainbows	1918
I'm An Old Cowhand	1936
I'm Awfully Strong for You	1908
I'm Drifting Back to Dreamland	1913
I'm Falling in Love with Someone	1910
I'm Forever Blowing Bubbles	1919
I'm Going Back to Carolina	1913
I Miss You Most of All	1913
I'm Just Wild About Harry	1921
I'm Looking over a Four-Leaf Clover	1927
I'm On My Way to Dublin Bay	1915
I'm On My Way to Mandalay	1914
I'm Sitting on Top of the World	1925
I'm Sorry I Made You Cry	1918
In a Cozy Corner	1901
In a Little Spanish Town	1926
In a Shanty in Old Shanty Town	1932
Indiana (Back Home in)	1917
Indian Love Call	1924
In Honky Tonky Town	1917
In My Harem	1913
In My Merry Oldsmobile	1905
In My Sweet Little Alice Blue Gown	1919
In Old New York	1906
International Rag (That)	1913
In the Baggage Coach Ahead	1896
In the Evening by the Moonlight	1880
In the Garden of My Heart	1908
In the Good Old Summer Time	1902
In the Hills of Old Kentucky	1914
In the Shade of the Old Apple Tree	1905
In the Sweet By and By	1868
In the Valley of the Moon	1933
Ireland Must Be Heaven, for my Mother Came from There	1916
I Remember You	1908
Irene (Goodnight)	1950
Isle d'Amour	1913
Isle of Capri	1934
Isle of Our Dreams (Red Mill)	1906
Is There Still Room for Me 'Neath the Old Apple Tree?	1915
It Ain't Gonna Rain No Mo'	1923
Italian Street Song	1910
It Had to Be You	1924
It Looks Like a Big Night Tonight	1908

It's a Long Way to Tipperary	1912
It's a Sin to Tell a Lie	1936
It's Been a Long Long Time	1945
It's Lonesome Tonight	1906
It's Tulip Time in Holland	1915
I Used to Love You But It's All Over Now	1920
I've Been Workin' on the Railroad (Levee Song)	1894
I've Got a Feelin for You (Way Down in My Heart)	1904
I've Got My Love to Keep Me Warm	1937
I've Got Rings on My Fingers	1909
I've Got You Under My Skin	1936
I Want a Girl	1911
I Want to Be Happy	1924
I Want to Be in Dixie	1912
I Wish I Had a Girl	1909
I Wish You Were Jealous of Me	1926
I Wonder How the Old Folks Are at Home	1909
I Wonder What's Become of Sally	1924
I Wonder Who's Kissing Her Now	1909
Jada	1918
Japanese Sand Man	1920
Jealous	1924
Jeannie with the Light Brown Hair	1854
Jeannine I Dream in Lilac Time	1928
Jingle Bells	1857
Jingle Jangle Jingle	1942
Joan of Arc, They Are Calling You	1917
John Brown Had a Little Indian (old round)	early American
John Brown's Body—and other variants of the Battle Hymn	1862
Johnny Rebeck (Dunderbeck)	early American
Joshua Ebenezer Frye	1907
Juanita	1850
June Night	1924
Just a Baby's Prayer at Twilight	1918
Just a Cottage Small by a Waterfall	1925
Just a Dream of You, Dear	1910
Just a Gigolo	1930
Just a Little Love a Little Kiss	1912
Just a Memory	1927
Just As the Sun Went Down	1898
Just a Wearyin' for You	1901
Just Because She Made Dem Goo-Goo Eyes	1900
Just Like a Butterfly That's Caught in the Rain	1927
Just Like a Gypsy	1919
Just One Girl	1898
Just Tell Them That You Saw Me	1895
Just Try to Picture Me—Back Home in Tennessee	1915
Kashmiri Song	1903
Katinka	1916
Keep the Home Fires Burning	1915
Keep Your Sunny Side Up	1929
Kentucky Babe	1896
Kiss in the Dark (Just a)	1922
Kiss Me Again	1905
Kiss Me, My Honey, Kiss Me	1910
K-k-k-Katy	1918
Lady, Be Good	1924
Last Night on the Back Porch	1923
Last Night Was the End of the World	1912
Last Roundup	1933
Lazybones	1933
Lazy River (Up a)	1931
Learn to Smile	1921
Leave Me with a Smile	1921
Lemon in the Garden of Love (I Picked a)	1906
Let Me Call You Sweetheart	1910
Let's All Sing Like the Birdies Sing	1932
Let's Have Another Cup of Coffee	1932
Let the Rest of the World Go By	1919
Life Is Just a Bowl of Cherries	1931
Li'l Liza Jane	1916
Lily of the Valley	1917
Linger a While	1923
Listen to the Mocking Bird	1855
Little Annie Rooney	1890
Little Bit of Heaven (A)	1914
Little Brown Church	1865
Little Brown Jug	1869
Little Bungalow (A)	1925
Little Grey Home in the West	1911
Little Lady Make Believe	1935
Little Lost Child (A Passing Policeman)	1894
Little Love a Little Kiss (Just a)	1912
Little Man, You've Had a Busy Day	1934
Little Old Ford It Rambled Right Along	1914
Little Old Lady	1937

Little Street Where Old Friends Meet (It's Just a)	1932
Little White Lies (Those)	1930
London Bridge Is Falling Down—Londonderry Air old English	1855
Lonesome and Sorry	1926
Lonesome Road (Look Down That)	1938
Long Long Ago	1843
Long Long Trail	1913
Look for the Silver Lining	1920
Love in Bloom	1934
Love Is the Sweetest Thing	1933
Loveliest Night of the Year	1951
Love Me, and the World Is Mine	1906
Love Me Tender (Aura Lee)	1861
Love Me While the Lovin' Is Good	1912
Love Nest (Just a)	1920
Lover, Come Back to Me	1928
Love's Old Sweet Song	1884
Lullaby (Brahms)	1868
Lullaby of Broadway	1935
Lullaby of the Leaves	1932
MacNamara's Band	1917
Macushla	1910
Mademoiselle from Armentières (Hinky Dinky Parlay Voo)	1918
Maggie Murphy's Home	1890
Magic of Your Eyes (Oh the)	1917
Ma, He's Making Eyes at Me	1921
Maiden with the Dreamy Eyes	1901
Maine Stein Song	1910
Mairzy Doats	1943
Make Believe (Show Boat)	1927
Makin' Whoopee (spoken more than sung)	1928
Mammy (My)	1921
Mammy Jinny's Jubilee	1913
Mammy's Little Coal Black Rose	1916
Mandalay (I'm On My Way to)	1924
Mandy	1919
Mandy Lane	1908
Mandy Lee	1899
Man I Love	1924
Man on the Flying Trapeze	1868
Marcheta	1913
Marching Along Together	1933
March of the Toys (instrumental)	1905
Margie	1920
Mary	1920
Mary Lou	1926
Mary's a Grand Old Name	1905
Massa's in the Cold Cold Ground	1852
May the Good Lord Bless and Keep You	1950
Me and My Shadow	1927
Meet Me in St. Louis, Louis	1904
Meet Me Tonight in Dreamland	1909
Melancholy Baby	1912
Melody of Love (Lehar)	1911
Memories	1915
Memory Lane	1924
Merry Widow Waltz	1907
Message of the Violet	1902
Mexicali Rose	1923
Mickey	1918
Mighty Lak a Rose	1901
Minnie the Moocher	1931
Mississippi Mud	1927
Missouri Waltz	*Copyrighted* 1914 *(Played earlier)*
Mister Dooley	1902
Mister Gallagher-Shean	1922
Mocking Bird Hill	1949
Mood Indigo	1931
Moonbeams (Red Mill)	1906
Moonglow	1934
Moon Has His Eyes on You (The)	1905
Moonlight and Roses	1925
Moonlight Bay	1912
Moonlight on the Ganges	1926
Moon Love	1939
Moon over Miami	1935
Moth and the Flame (The)	1898
M-o-t-h-e-r	1915
Mother Machree	1910
Music Goes 'Round and 'Round	1935
Music! Music! Music!	1950
My Baby's Arms	1919
My Belgian Rose	1918
My Blue Heaven	1927
My Bonnie (Bring Back)	*early* 1800's
My Buddy	1922
My Castle on the Nile	1901
My Croony Melody	1914
My Gal Is a High Born Lady	1896
My Gal Sal	1905
My Heart Stood Still	1927
My Hero	1909
My Home in Tennessee	1915
My Isle of Golden Dreams	1919
My Little Dream Girl	1915
My Little Girl	1915

My Little Persian Rose	*1912*
My Man	*1921*
My Melancholy Baby	*1912*
My Mother's Rosary (Ten baby fingers)	*1915*
My Mother Was a Lady (If Jack Were Only Here)	*1896*
My Old Kentucky Home	*1853*
My Old New Hampshire Home	*1898*
My Pony Boy	*1909*
My Sweetheart's the Man in the Moon	*1892*
My Wife's Gone to the Country	*1913*
My Wild Irish Rose	*1899*
Naughty Lady of Shady Lane (The)	*1954*
Navajo	*1903*
Nelly Was a Lady	*1849*
Never in a Million Years	*1937*
Night and Day	*1932*
Night Is Young (The)	*1936*
Nights of Gladness	*1913*
Nobody	*1905*
Nobody Knows	*1919*
Nobody's Sweetheart Now	*1924*
Nola (instrumental)	*1916*
No! No! A Thousand Times No	*1934*
No, No, Nora	*1923*
Not Because Your Hair Is Curly	*1906*
Now Is the Hour	*1946*
Now the Day Is Over	*1869*
Oceana Roll	*1911*
Of Thee I Sing	*1931*
Oh, by Jingo	*1919*
Oh, Didn't He Ramble	*1902*
Oh! Gee Be Sweet to Me, Kid	*1907*
Oh, How I Hate to Get Up in the Morning	*1918*
Oh, How I Miss You Tonight	*1923*
Oh, Johnny, Oh, Johnny, Oh!	*1917*
Oh, Promise Me	*1889*
Oh, Susanna	*1848*
Oh! What a Beautiful Morning	*1943*
Oh! What a Pal Was Mary	*1919*
Oh! You Beautiful Doll	*1911*
O Katharina	*1924*
Old Black Joe	*1860*
Old Fashioned Garden (An)	*1919*
Old Folks at Home (Swanee River)	*1851*
Old Grey Mare	*1915*
Old Lamp-lighter (The)	*1946*
Old MacDonald Had a Farm	*American folk*
Old Man River	*1927*
Old Oaken Bucket	*1826*
Old Refrain	*1915*
Old Rugged Cross	*1913*
Old Spinning Wheel	*1933*
On a Bicycle Built for Two (Daisy Bell)	*1892*
On a Slow Boat to China	*1948*
On a Sunday Afternoon	*1902*
One Horse Open Sleigh (Jingle Bells)	*1857*
One, Two, Three, Four	*1917*
One Wonderful Night	*1914*
On Miami Shore	*1919*
On Mobile Bay	*1910*
On the Atchison, Topeka and the Santa Fe	*1945*
On the Banks of the Wabash	*1897*
On the Beach at Waikiki	*1915*
On the Mississippi	*1912*
On the Old Fall River Line	*1913*
On the Road to Mandalay	*1907*
On the Shores of Italy	*1912*
On the Sunny Side of the Street	*1930*
On the Trail of the Lonesome Pine	*1910*
On Top of Old Smoky	*American folk*
On Wisconsin	*1909*
One Alone	*1926*
Only a Rose	*1925*
O, Tannenbaum (old German)	*1820's*
Oui Oui, Marie (Wee Wee)	*1918*
Over the Rainbow	*1939*
Over There	*1917*
Over the River and Through the Woods	*early American*
Pack Up Your Troubles (Smile Smile Smile)	*1915*
Pagan Love Song	*1929*
Painting the Clouds with Sunshine	*1929*
Paper Doll	*1915*
Parade of the Wooden Soldiers	*1911*
Paradise	*1932*
Pardon My Southern Accent (spoken more than sung)	*1934*
Peanut Vendor	*1931*
Peggy O'Neil	*1921*
Peg o' My Heart	*1913*

Pennies from Heaven	*1936*
Perfect Day (When You Come to)	*1910*
Picnic for Two (A)	*1905*
Pistol Packin' Mamma	*1943*
Play That Barber Shop Chord (Mr. Jefferson Lord)	*1910*
Please Don't Talk About Me When I'm Gone	*1930*
Please Go 'Way and Let Me Sleep	*1902*
Polly-Wolly-Doodle	*American folk*
Poor Butterfly	*1916*
Poor Pauline	*1914*
Pop Goes the Weasel	*American folk*
Powder Your Face with Sunshine	*1948*
Preacher and the Bear (The)	*1904*
Prelude in C-sharp Minor (Rachmaninoff instrumental)	*1898*
Pretty Baby	*1916*
Pretty Girl Is Like a Melody (A)	*1919*
Prisoner's Song	*1924*
Put Me Off at Buffalo	*1895*
Put On Your Old Gray Bonnet	*1909*
Put Your Arms Around Me, Honey	*1910*
Quaker Down in Quaker Town (There's a)	*1916*
Quilting Party (Aunt Dinah's)	*1830*
Ragtime Cowboy Joe	*1912*
Ragtime Violin	*1911*
Rainbow (Come be my)	*1909*
Ramona	*1927*
Rastus on Parade	*1895*
Rebecca of Sunny-Brook Farm	*1914*
Red River Valley	*American folk*
Red Rose Rag	*1911*
Red Roses for a Blue Lady	*1949*
Red Sails in the Sunset	*1935*
Red Wing	*1907*
Remember	*1925*
Rememb'ring	*1923*
Reuben and Rachel	*1871*
Rings on My Fingers (Bells on My Toes)	*1909*
Rio Rita	*1926*
Rip Van Winkle Was a Lucky Man	*1901*
River, Stay 'Way from My Door	*1931*
Roamin' in the Gloamin'	*1911*
Rock-a-bye, Baby	*1887*
Rock-a-bye Your Baby with a Dixie Melody	*1918*
Rocked in the Cradle of the Deep	*1840*
Rosary (Nevin)	*1893*
Rose Marie	*1924*
Rose of No Man's Land	*1918*
Roses of Picardy	*1916*
Row, Row, Row	*1912*
Row, Row, Row Your Boat	*old round*
Rudolph the Red-Nosed Reindeer	*1949*
Rufus Rastus Johnson Brown (what you goin' to do when)	*1905*
Running Wild	*1922*
Russian Lullaby	*1927*
Sailing Down the Chesapeake Bay	*1913*
St. Louis Blues	*1914*
Sally	*1921*
Salut d'Amour	*1889*
San Antonio	*1907*
Santa Claus Is Coming to Town	*1934*
Santa Lucia	*1849*
Save Your Sorrow for Tomorrow	*1925*
Say "Au Revoir" But Not "Good-bye"	*1893*
Say It Isn't So	*1932*
Say It with Music	*1921*
School Days	*1907*
Scotland's Burning	*old round*
Seeing Nellie Home (Quilting Party)	*1848*
Sentimental Journey	*1946*
Serenade (Romberg)	*1925*
Seventeen (When You and I Were)	*1924*
Seventy-six Trombones	*1957*
Shanty in Old Shanty Town	*1932*
She'll Be Comin' 'Round the Mountain	*date uncertain—1800's*
She May Have Seen Better Days	*1894*
She Was Bred in Old Kentucky	*1898*
Shiek of Araby	*1921*
Shine On, Harvest Moon	*1908*
Ship That Never Returned (tune became "Wreck of the Old '97")	*1860's*
Shortnin' Bread	*American folk*
Show Me the Way to Go Home	*1925*
Shuffle Off to Buffalo	*1932*
Side by Side	*1927*
Sidewalks of New York (East Side, West Side)	*1894*
Silent Night (Holy Night)	*1818*
Silver Moon	*1927*
Silver Threads Among the Gold	*1873*
Singin' in the Rain	*1929*

Sing Me to Sleep 1902
Sioux City Sue 1946
Sit Down, You're Rockin' the Boat 1913
Sleep 1923
Sleepy Head 1926
Sleepy Time Gal 1925
Smarty 1908
Smile, Darn Ya, Smile 1931
Smiles 1917
Smilin' Through 1915
Smoke Gets in Your Eyes 1933
Soldier's Farewell early 1800's
Solomon Levi date uncertain—early 1800's
So Long, Mary 1905
Somebody Loves Me—I Wonder Who 1924
Somebody's Coming to Our House 1913
Somebody Stole My Gal 1922
Someday I'll Find You 1931
Someday My Prince Will Come 1937
Some Enchanted Evening 1949
Some of These Days 1910
Something Seems Tingle-ingleing 1913
Sometimes I'm Happy 1927
Somewhere a Voice Is Calling 1911
Song I Love (The) 1928
Song Is Ended (The) 1927
Song of Love (The)—Romberg 1921
Sonny Boy 1928
South of the Border 1939
Spain 1924
Spaniard That Blighted My Life 1911
Star Dust 1929
Stars and Stripes Forever (Be Kind to your web) 1897
Stars Fell on Alabama 1934
Star-Spangled Banner 1814
Stay in Your Own Backyard 1899
Steamboat Bill 1910
Stein Song (Heidelberg) 1902
Stein Song (Maine) 1910
Stormy Weather 1933
Story of the Rose (Heart of My Heart) 1899
Streets of New York (In Old New York) 1906
Strike Up the Band 1927
Sugar Moon 1910
Summertime (H. Von Tilzer) 1908
Summertime (Gershwin) 1935
Sun Bonnet Sue 1906
Sunny Side of the Street (On the) 1930
Sunny Side Up (Keep Your) 1929
Sunshine of Paradise Alley 1895
Sunshine of Your Smile (The) 1915
Surrey with the Fringe on Top 1943
Susie (If You Knew) 1925
Swanee 1919
Swanee River Moon 1921
Sweet Adeline 1903
Sweet Afton (Flow Gently) 1838
Sweet and Lovely 1931
Sweet and Low early 1800's
Sweet Betsy from Pike 1854
Sweet Bunch of Daisies 1894
Sweet By and By (In the) 1868
Sweet Georgia Brown 1925
Sweetheart (Will You Remember?) 1917
Sweetheart of Sigma Chi 1912
Sweethearts 1913
Sweet Lady 1921
Sweet Little Buttercup 1917
Sweet Marie 1893
Sweet Rosie O'Grady 1896
Sweet Sixteen (When You Were) 1898
Sweet Sue 1928
Sylvia 1914
Sympathy (I Need) 1912

Take Back Your Gold 1897
Take Me out to the Ball Game 1908
Tale of the Bumblebee 1901
Tale of the Kangaroo 1900
Tammany 1905
Ta-ra-ra-boom-de-re 1891
Tea for Two 1924
Teasing 1904
Tell Me, Little Gypsy 1920
Tell Me, Pretty Maiden (Florodora) 1900
Tell Me Why (the stars do shine) date unknown
Ten Little Fingers and Ten Little Toes 1921
Tennessee Waltz 1948
Tenting on the Old Camp Ground 1864
Thanks for the Memory 1937
That Doggie in the Window 1953
That International Rag 1913
That Mysterious Rag 1911
That Old Black Magic 1942
That Old Gang of Mine 1923
That Old Girl of Mine 1912
That's Amore 1953

That's an Irish Lullaby (Too-ra-loo-ra)	*1914*
That's How I Need You	*1912*
That's My Weakness Now	*1928*
That's What the Daisy Said	*1903*
That's Why Darkies Were Born	*1931*
That's Why They Call Me "Shine"	*1910*
That Tumbledown Shack in Athlone	*1918*
The Little Old Ford It Rambles Right Along	*1914*
Then I'll Be Happy (I Want to Be Happy)	*1924*
Then You'll Remember Me	*1843*
There Goes My Heart	*1934*
There Is a Tavern in the Town	*probably earlier than 1883*
There'll Be a Hot Time in the Old Town Tonight	*1896*
There'll Be Blue Birds Over the White Cliffs of Dover	*1941*
There'll Be Some Changes Made	*1921*
There'll Come a Time Someday	*1895*
There Never Was a Girl Like You (verse modified by barbershop quartets to "Bright Was the Night")	*1907*
There's a Church in the Valley (Little Brown Church)	*1865*
There's a Girl in Havana	*1911*
There's a Girl in the Heart of Maryland	*1913*
There's a Gold Mine in the Sky	*1937*
There's a Little Spark of Love Still Burning	*1914*
There's a Long Long Trail	*1913*
There's a Quaker Down in Quaker Town	*1916*
There's a Rainbow 'Round My Shoulder	*1928*
There's No Business Like Show Business	*1946*
These Foolish Things Remind Me of You	*1935*
They Always Pick on Me	*1911*
They Called It Dixieland	*1916*
They Didn't Believe Me	*1914*
They Gotta Quit Kickin' My Dawg Aroun'	*1912*
They Go Wild Simply Wild Over Me	*1917*
This Is the Life	*1914*
This Ole House	*1954*
Those Wedding Bells Shall Not Ring Out	*1896*
Thou Swell	*1927*
Three Blind Mice	*old round*
Three Little Words	*1930*
Three O'clock in the Morning	*1922*
Tiger Rag	*1917*
Till the Clouds Roll By	*1917*
Till the Sands of the Desert Grow Cold	*1911*
Till We Meet Again	*1918*
Tip-toe Through the Tulips	*1926*
'Tis the Last Rose of Summer	*1813*
Tom Dooley	*1958*
Tomorrow	*1922*
Too Much Mustard (Très Moutarde)	*1911*
Too-ra-loo-ra (Irish Lullaby)	*1914*
Toot, Toot, Tootsie (Goodbye)	*1922*
Too Young	*1951*
Toyland	*1903*
Trail of the Lonesome Pine	*1913*
Tramp! Tramp! Tramp!, the Boys Are Marching	*1864*
Trees	*1922*
Tuck Me to Sleep in My Old "Tucky" Home	*1921*
Tulip Time in Holland (It's)	*1919*
Turkey in the Straw (Old Zip Coon)	*1834*
Twinkle, Twinkle, Little Star (several tunes to traditional words)	
Two Guitars	*1925*
Two Hearts in Three-Quarter Time	*1930*
Two Little Girls in Blue	*1893*
Two Little Love Bees	*1910*
Two Sleepy People	*1938*
Ukulele Lady	*1925*
Under the Anheuser Bush	*1903*
Under the Bamboo Tree	*1902*
Until the Real Thing Comes Along	*1936*
Up a Lazy River	*1931*
Valencia	*1926*
Vieni, Vieni	*1937*
Vilia	*1907*
Volga Boatman's Song	*Russian folk—popularized in States, 1920's*

Wabash Blues	*1921*
Wabash Moon	*1931*
Wagon Wheels	*1934*
Waiting at the Church	*1906*
Waiting for the Robert E. Lee	*1912*
Wait Till the Cows Come Home	*1917*
Wait Till the Sun Shines, Nellie	*1905*
Wal I Swan (Joshua Ebenezer Frye)	*1907*
Walkin' My Baby Back Home	*1930*
Waltz Me Around Again, Willie	*1906*
Waltz You Saved for Me (The)	*1930*
Wang, Wang Blues	*1921*
'Way down in My Heart I've Got a Feelin' for You	*1904*
'Way down Yonder in New Orleans	*1922*
Wearing of the Green date uncertain—probably in the	*1700's*
Wedding Bells Are Breaking Up That Old Gang of Mine	*1929*
Wedding of the Painted Doll	*1929*
Wee, Wee, Marie (Oui Oui)	*1918*
We'll Have a Jubilee in My Old Kentucky Home	*1915*
What Do We Do on a Dew-dew-dewy Day?	*1927*
What Do You Want to Make Those Eyes at Me For?	*1916*
What'll I Do?	*1924*
What's the Matter with Father?	*1910*
What's the Use of Dreaming? (same melody as "Blow the Smoke Away")	*1906*
What You Goin' to Do When the Rent Comes 'Round (Rufus Rastus Johnson Brown)	*1905*
When a Maid Comes Knocking at Your Heart	*1912*
When Day Is Done	*1926*
When I Dream of Old Erin I'm Dreaming of You	*1912*
When I Get You Alone Tonight	*1912*
When I Grow Too Old to Dream	*1935*
When I Leave the World Behind	*1915*
When I Lost You	*1912*
When Irish Eyes Are Smiling	*1912*
When I Take My Sugar to Tea	*1931*
When It's Apple Blossom Time in Normandy	*1912*
When It's Darkness on the Delta	*1932*
When It's Springtime in the Rockies	*1929*
When I Was a Dreamer	*1914*
When Johnny Comes Marching Home (usually parodied)	*1863*
When My Baby Smiles at Me	*1920*
When My Dream Boat Comes Home	*1936*
When Shall We Meet Again?	*1921*
When the Angelus Is Ringing	*1914*
When the Bees Are in the Hive	*1904*
When the Harvest Days Are Over, Jessie Dear	*1900*
When the Maple Leaves Were Falling	*1913*
When the Midnight Choo-Choo Leaves for Alabam	*1912*
When the Moon Comes over the Mountain	*1931*
When the Red, Red Robin Comes Bobbin' Along	*1926*
When Uncle Joe Plays a Rag on His Old Banjo	*1911*
When We Are M-A-double-R-I-E-D	*1907*
When You and I Were Seventeen	*1924*
When You and I Were Young, Maggie	*1866*
When You Know You're Not For-Gotten by the Girl You Can't Forget	*1906*
When You're a Long Long Way from Home	*1914*
When You're Away	*1914*
When You're Smiling	*1928*
When Your Hair Has Turned to Silver	*1930*
When You Were Sweet Sixteen	*1898*
When You Wish Upon a Star	*1940*
When You Wore a Tulip	*1914*
Where Did You Get That Girl?	*1913*
Where Do We Go from Here?	*1917*
Where Oh Where Has My Little Dog Gone?	*1864*
Where the Blue of the Night Meets the Gold of the Day	*1931*
Where the Morning Glories Grow	*1917*
Where the Morning Glories Twine	*1905*
Where the Red Red Roses Grow	*1913*
Where the River Shannon Flows	*1905*
Where the Southern Roses Grow	*1904*
Whiffenpoof Song Probably earlier than	*1918*
Whispering	*1920*
Whistle While You Work	*1937*

White Christmas	1942
White Cliffs of Dover	1941
White Wings (never grow weary)	1884
Who	1925
Who's Afraid of the Big Bad Wolf?	1933
Who's Sorry Now?	1923
Who Were You with Tonight?	1912
Why Do I Love You?	1927
Will You Love Me in December as You Do in May?	1905
Will You Remember? (Sweetheart, Sweetheart, Sweetheart)	1917
Winter Wonderland (Walking in a)	1934
Wishing (will make it so)	1939
Without a Song	1929
Wonderful One (My)	1922
Won't You Come over to My House?	1906
Workin' on the Railroad (I've Been)—Levee Song	1894
World Is Waiting for the Sunrise	1919
Would God I Were a Tender Apple Blossom (tune of "Danny Boy")	1894
or Londonderry Air	1855
Wreck of the Old '97 (tune of "Ship That Never Returned")	1860's
Yacka Hula Hickey Dula	1916
Yama Yama Man	1908
Yankee Doodle	1782
Yankee Doodle Dandy	1904
Yearning	1925
Yellow Bird	1961
Yellow Rose of Texas	1955
Yes, Sir, That's My Baby	1925
Yes! We Have No Bananas	1923
Yip-I-Addy-I-Ay	1909
Yoo-hoo	1921
You Are My Lucky Star	1935
You Are My Sunshine	1940
You Are the Ideal of My Dreams	1911
You Call Everybody "Darling"	1948
You'll Do the Same Thing Over	1911
You'll Never Walk Alone	1945
You Made Me Love You (I didn't want to do it)	1913
You're a Grand Old Flag (originally "Rag")	1906
You're a Great Big Blue Eyed Baby	1913
You're a Million Miles from Nowhere	1919
You're an old Smoothie	1932
You're As Welcome As the Flowers in May	1901
You're Driving Me Crazy	1930
You're in the Right Church But in the Wrong Pew	1908
You're the Cream in My Coffee	1928
You're the Flower of My Heart, Sweet Adeline	1903
Your Eyes Have Told Me So	1919
You Tell Me Your Dream	1908
You Were Only Foolin'	1948
Zing! Went the Strings of My Heart	1935
Zip-a-dee-doo-dah	1946
Zip Coon (Old)—Turkey in the Straw	1834

Obviously, the 1920's were the golden years of popular musical compositions that last and last and are used over and over again. But don't sell the Depression years of the 1930's short. Those years and the recovery from the roughing that the Depression gave many were amazingly productive of enduring music, hardly any of it in the theme of "Brother, Can You Spare a Dime?" That one symbolized the early 1930's when flipping it would decide whether to spend it for carfare after walking several miles toward home or at the grocery.

In countless homes the stock market crash of October 1929 landed with the devastating impact of a flash flood. Storm warnings had been raised, but most of the nation, riding the pleasant stream of prosperity, paid little heed. In consequence, wreckage of hopes, plans and expectations littered the country from its beaches to hilltops. As the torrents and gales continued into the 1930's, homes and businesses were shattered, often beyond recovery. But the Great Depression taught a lesson that those blessed with long memories can never forget: Dollars of themselves mean little because the worth of a dollar depends entirely upon its purchasing power, whether in the 1920's, 30's, 70's or sometime in the future. From the foregoing reprise of the depression blues we turn to other songs of those times. Some adult readers may contend that certain of the following depression-born numbers, selected from among many, should have been included among the 1,000 most used. So, the debate continues into the small hours.

A SMALL SAMPLING OF HIGH LIGHTS IN THE DARK DECADE

1929–1939

1929

I'll Always Be in Love with You
When the Organ Played at Twilight
Singin' in the Bathtub
Aren't We All
Great Day
I'm Just a Vagabond Lover
I'll See You Again
Moanin' Low

1930

Betty Co-ed
Embraceable You
Lady, Play Your Mandolin
St. James Infirmary
Sing Something Simple
Goofus
So Beats My Heart for You
Around the Corner

1931

Between the Devil and the Deep Blue Sea
Cuban Love Song
Got a Date with an Angel
I Don't Know Why
Barnacle Bill the Sailor
Dancing in the Dark
Home
I Found a Million Dollar Baby in a Five and Ten Cent Store
I Love a Parade
Night Was Made for Love
When the Blue of the Night Meets the Gold of the Day
When It's Sleepy Time Down South
Moonlight Saving Time

1932

All-American Girl
I'm Getting Sentimental Over You
It's Just a Little Street Where Old Friends Meet
Love Is the Sweetest Thing
Pink Elephants
When It's Darkness on the Delta
Let's Put Out the Lights
Soft Lights and Sweet Music

1933

Annie Doesn't Live Here Anymore
By a Waterfall
Did You Ever See a Dream Walking
In the Valley of the Moon
Jimmy Had a Nickel
Once in a Blue Moon
You've Got to Be a Football Hero

1934

Lost in a Fog
Fare Thee Well, Annabelle
I'll Follow My Secret Heart
Two Cigarettes in the Dark
Stay As Sweet As You Are
The Very Thought of You

1935

Beautiful Lady in Blue
In a Sentimental Mood
The Night Is Young
Cheek to Cheek
Lovely to Look At

1936

Is It True What They Say About Dixie?
It's D'lovely
Shoe Shine Boy

There's a Small Hotel
When My Dream Boat Comes Home
I've Got a Feelin' You're Foolin'

1937

Bei Mir Bist du Schoen
Harbor Lights
Merry-Go-Round Broke Down
Somebody Else Is Taking My Place
Sweet Leilani
That Old Feeling
Vieni, Vieni
It Looks Like Rain in Cherry Blossom Lane
Josephine
Nice Work If You Can Get It (Spoken more than sung)

1938

Flat Foot Floogie
My Heart Belongs to Daddy
September Song
You Must Have Been a Beautiful Baby
Jeepers Creepers

1939

Leanin' On the Old Top Rail
All the Things You Are
Do I Love You?
I'll Never Smile Again
South of the Border
Wishing Will Make It So

The Depression had its laughs, too, some of them fabricated from pretty thin material. About two o'clock one morning, Don Knowlton and I decided that nothing else was as important as writing a song to end all home-and-mother songs. So we wrote "Every Day Is Mother's Day in Home Sweet Home." It had the syrup of "The Waltz You Saved for Me" and "My Isle of Golden Dreams" agonized on a Wurlitzer theater organ. Depression days later, we wrote new lyrics:

Chorus

Ev'ry day is mother's day in home sweet home
Send today a big bouquet where e'er you roam
She is still your dear old mother
You will never have another
And ev'ry day is mother's day in home swee-eet home,

and sent the opus to a florists' association. It was played at the annual meeting of the national directors. They were "impressed favorably," it was reported, over the possibilities of the song as a theme for their national radio program. An advertising agency, newly selected at that meeting, promptly put the association's ad dollars into magazine pages. Ah, music!

Regardless of possible embarrassing omissions in the Top in Their Times or disagreements about their merits, they represent a melodic panorama of America, including history, language, incidents, manners and modes, names in the news, thoughts, attitudes, and sentiments. In the originals and in the parodies written around many of them, they present every aspect of America set to music.

Parodies Prove Popularity

A literary composition that imitates the style or theme of an original one is called a parody. A song parody presents new words for an established tune, exemplified by many singing commercials of radio and television. Home talent shows in musical theme often include parodies that point toward a person or local incident with which the audience is familiar. To the tune of "The Old Grey Mare," "The old gay mayor's just as good as he used to be" delights his electorate and the grinning mayor. "Good publicity." Other parodies of that song would need explanation to a motorized generation unfamiliar with whiffletrees.

Usually, a parody injects humor into what may have been a serious subject in the composition that's parodied. As little as a transposed word can twist the original into quite different meaning, as in centuries-old "Au Claire de la Lune." Americans who've been exposed to grade-school French recognize "Ouvri moi ta porte pour l'amour de Dieu" (open your door for the love of God). Generations of Frenchmen have parodied it gleefully "pour le Dieu d'amour" (for the God of love).

Until about the time of World War I, well-known songs were often heard on stage in parody form, most often on burlesque's boards when burlesque lived up to its name. If the melody was well enough known to be recognized as from the classics, so much the better. Incongruity heightened the impact. Not from the stage but widely known, a parody on Dvořák's "Humoresque" originated from the traditional sign in the rest rooms of Pullman cars concerning sanitation.

Passengers will please refrain
From flushing toilets while the train
Is standing in the station—(I love you-ou-ou).

For years I heard it attributed to the late Ted Robinson, Jr., of *Time,* though Ted regretted sincerely that he couldn't claim paternity. Wagner's "Wedding

March" is best known as "Here Comes the Bride" whose versions beyond that opening take off in many directions. Composer Lincke's near-classic "The Glow Worm" couldn't dodge "Nix on the 'Glow Worm,' Lena, Lena/Play something else on your concertina," which indicates the general level of humor found in most parodies.

No one knows how many parodies have been superimposed upon the old English tune "William and His Dinah," usually cockneyized to "Villikens." As is true with most ancient songs, several versions of the "original" exist:

> *'Tis of a merchant I'm going to tell*
> [*or—who in London did dwell*]
> *He had but one daughter, an uncommon gal*
> [*or—unkimmon gal*].

Our "Little Mohee" and "Sweet Betsy from Pike," associated with the pioneers' westward trek, are to the tune of "Villikens." The late Leonard Payne of Sarnia, Ontario, brought with him from England more than fifty years ago what was then a very old parody:

> *I'm a poor lonely sailor, as you plainly see*
> *Come list to my tale, or have pity on me*
> *I'm just from the workhouse, I've been in one year*
> *For chewing a chunk from young Fitzgerald's ear.*

Succeeding verses describe life in that institution, including "an army of bedbugs and a navy of lice."

Another version, as sung by the late Frank Ward of Albany, New York, dealt with another "unkimmon" daughter whose "age it was red and her hair was sixteen." When her father became infuriated at a young man who'd been infesting his living room, "he drew a horse pistol he'd raised from a Colt." "Villikens" may be the most parodied song among the English-speaking peoples, though a simpler tune of French origin, "Malbrouck," might outrank it.

References to "Malbrouck" crop up in the early 1700's. By the mid-1800's it had become in one parody form "We Won't Go Home Till Morning." Today it's better known as "For he's a jolly good fellow, which nobody can deny." Other versions include "The bear went over the mountain to see what he could see"; "My father and mother were Irish and I was Irish too"; and "We'll all go down to Rauser's to drink some lager beer." To the tune of "The Old Oaken Bucket" most adults are familiar with "the old family toothbrush that hung in the sink."

The tune of "Hail, Hail, the Gang's All Here" is lifted from a chorus in Gilbert and Sullivan's *Pirates of Penzance,* which in turn had been borrowed from Verdi's "Anvil Chorus." All that have been cited conform to the humorous treatment. An exception that was sung last night in countless sessions throughout the country, whether oldsters or juniors, is "The Wreck of the Old '97." It's a parody on Henry C. Work's original of the 1860's which told an equally doleful tale of "The Ship That Never Returned." Paul Dresser's sad ballad "Just Tell Them That You Saw Me—and they will know the rest" was reshaped in burlesque into "Just tell them you saw me but you didn't see me

Parodies Prove Popularity

saw" as sung by a tramp who was offered food *if* he'd saw some stove wood.

Even our hymns have not escaped the humorous treatment, as witness "Nero my dog has fleas" to the tune of "Nearer, My God to Thee." All sorts of words have been grafted upon "The Battle Hymn of the Republic," whose words parody another older hymn, "Brothers, Will You Meet Us?" One version recalls the famous Kansas abolitionist of Civil War times, "John Brown's body lies a mouldering in the grave." Also in the North it was sung as "Hang Jeff Davis to a sour apple tree." Its parodies included juveniles, such as Mary Ann—who went to gather clams—"but she couldn't find a slam-bam clam." (Slam-bam is a euphemism.) During several generations, the "Battle Hymn" has also been sung, "The big grasshopper jumped right over the little grasshopper's back" in endless procession. "They were only playing leapfrog" instead of the original "Glory, glory, hallelujah."

A daring parody on "At the Cross" recounted "At the bar at the bar where I smoked my first cigar . . . It was there by chance that I tore my Sunday pants/ And now I wear them every day." The hymn "Oh Happy Day" became "Nobody knows how dry I am. Nobody seems to give a damn." Another, "Revive Us Again," provided the tune for "Hallelujah, give us a handout to revive us again." That one is recalled by some as "Hallelujah, I'm a Bum." In that vein, a song of the Wobblies, a defunct we-won't-work organization, was based upon "The Sweet By and By": "There'll be pie in the sky, by and by." Of course "Rocked in the Cradle of the Deep" could hardly escape "locked in the stable with the sheep." "There Is a Happy Land Far Far Away" became "There Is a Boarding House Far Far Away—where they serve ham and eggs three times a day."

The Civil War's "Tramp, Tramp, Tramp, the Boys Are Marching" carried into this century and the Philippine insurrection that followed the Spanish-American War. As always, those in the army of occupation suffered from nostalgia exemplified in the last line of the chorus: "And beneath the starry flag/ Civilize 'em with a Krag [service rifle]/Then we'll go to our own beloved homes." A musical incident related to that occupation of 1898, though not to parodies, should be in a record of musical Americana. The U.S. troops marched into Manila behind a regimental band singing "There'll Be a Hot Time in the Old Town Tonight." Thinking that the tune must be the liberators' national anthem, a Philippine band reciprocated with its own version of the song, played by ear after one hearing. That war also brought Cuba's liberation. The most popular parody in the states was "There'll Be a Hot Time in Cuba Tonight."

Years later, the highly popular "My Home in Tennessee" went to Europe with the American Expeditionary Forces of World War I. It returned from England with the doughboys in far more humorous vein than it had gone. As is the case with all unwritten folk songs, the versions vary a bit:

I paid a bob to see a tatooed Scotch lady-ee
Tatooed from head to knee
She was a sight to see
For over her jaw[r]
Was the Royal Flying Corps [cawr]

And on her back was the Union Jack
How could one ask for more?
But up and down her spine
Was the Queen's Own Guard in line
While all around her hips
Was a fleet of battle ships
And over each kidney
Was a birdseye view of Sydney
But what I like best
Right across her chest
My home in Tennessee.

A parody that was borrowed from the repetitive echoes of "Say 'Au Revoir' But Not 'Goodbye'" and "We Never Speak As We Pass By," and probably from an echo of "Sweet Adeline," too, is still heard in junior camporee circles concerning Bill Grogan's goat who was feeling fine, and "ate three red shirts from a clothes line." His angry owner took him "to a railroad track and tied him there upon his back." But the clever goat "coughed up the shirts and flagged the train." A sentimental version to that same melody was sung nationally by barbershop harmonists under the gaslights. Maurice Gross of Cleveland learned it in Baltimore, the late George O'Brien in Saginaw, Michigan, while I learned it in Missouri and have heard it in South Dakota and in California:

Goodnight, my love (goodnight, my love)
The hour 'tis late (the hour 'tis late)
The moon shines bright (the moon shines bright)
On silv'ry lake (on silv'ry lake)
'Tis then our hearts ('tis then our hearts)
In joy repeat (in joy re–pe-e-ea–eat)
"Goodnight, my love" ("goodnight, my love")
"Goo-ood-night, my-y-y-y swee-eet" (goodnight, my sweet").

To that same tune, a different parody went like this—with repeats of each line, as above:

Oh, When I die
Don't bury me at all
Just pickle my bones
In alcohol
Put a bottle of booze
At my head and feet
So these old bones
Will surely keep.

The last line may differ in different sections of the country, none of the variations end rhyming with "feet" to my knowledge—not that it matters. The same sentiments are in "Old Rosin, the Beau" which was parodied in several political campaign songs of long ago.

Parodies Prove Popularity

The double meaning and pun reached its peak in our songs during the first decade of the 1900's when it was the fashion to parody established songs. Regardless of the different interpretations of "corn" and "corny," it is probable that "The Irish Jubilee" came direct from the granary. An Irishman named Doherty had been elected to the Senate by a very large majority. He decided to give the finest supper ever given on this continent. This hints at the menu:

When everyone was seated, they started out to lay the feast
Cassidy said: "Rise up and give us each a cake of yeast. . . ."
There was pig's head and goldfish, mocking birds and ostriches
Ice cream, cold cream, Vaseline and sandwiches
Blue fish, green fish, fish hooks and partridges
Fish balls, snow balls, cannon balls and cartridges . . .
Reindeer and snowdeer, dear me and antelope
And the women ate so mushmellon the men said they cantelope.

Granivorous! Quite a corn meal!

Here is one treatment given in burlesque to the ancient "Wearing of the Green."

I was born in Cincinnati up in Iceland 'way down south
Sure that is just the reason why the voice is in my mouth
'Twas a hot and frosty morning and quite windy, I believe
The great big trees were making boughs for they were going to leave. . . .

My brother owned a great big store, he owned it in his mind
He put a shutter on the roof, he did it for a blind
A girl laid down beside a sewer and by that sewer she died
And at the coroner's inquest they called it sewerside. . . .

Oh the camphor ice was frozen and the bells were ringing wet
The chamber maids were making beds to do them up, you bet
The crows were making crowbars and the grass was making hay
The bumblebees were making bums—ta-ra-ra-boom-de-yay.

But there is precedent for such literary mayhem. Here is an excerpt from revered Stephen Foster, almost identical in treatment:

It rained all night the day I left, the weather was so dry
The sun so hot I froze myself, Susanna, don't you cry.

Why are the first two corny while Foster's is lightly humorous? Draw your own conclusions. May you draw aces!

Parodies were at their peak from about 1905 to the teens before the movies and radio changed America's amusement-seeking habits. A much abused song was "She Was Bred in Old Kentucky." One version claimed:

She was bread in old Kentucky
She was pie in New Orleans
She was cake in Cincinnati
But in Boston she was beans,

and still another, written obviously by an ignorant eastern outlander who didn't know that Kentucky has even a Bourbon County: "I was bred in old Kentucky Where the rock and rye is pure."

"In the Shade of the Old Apple Tree" is one of the best ballads ever written. As proof of its deserved popularity, it was parodied in versions from the humorous to the ribald. One of them was about a man beside a rural brook who went swimming in the altogether. A lady came and sat down beside his clothing: "She came at nine and didn't leave till three."

In the shade of the old apple tree
The water was up to my knee
I had to bend down while the lady was 'round
Till only my face she could see
While the bees they were stinging my nose
The fishes were biting my toes
I stayed there all day till that lady went 'way
From the shade of the old apple tree.

Songwriters for the burlesque circuits seized upon any song of any type for material. One of the truly great songs of mourning is Berlin's "When I Lost You," the poignant sentiment in words matched with the lovely melody. On the burlesque stage even that one was subverted into "I lost the house that I lived in/And all my furniture too."

Paul Dresser's nostalgic "On the Banks of the Wabash," Indiana's state song, is an example of sentiments subverted into laughs when parodied. Here is a bit of it exhumed from the memory file:

There's a mortgage on my Indiana homestead
And to lift that debt has never been my craze
But one day a cyclone struck down on the Wabash
And the mortgage got the lift I couldn't raise
Oh the fever and the ague's often found there
And the chills are situated there to stay
They use a lightning bug to light their lamps with
(Alternate: The people there still vote for Andrew Jackson)
On the banks of the Wabash far away.

Parodies usually came out on the burlesque stage, then went into national circulation in pamphlets that included the words only. (Everybody was supposed to know the tune of a song popular enough to be parodied.) The two principal publishers of these gems of Americana were Will Rossiter in Chicago and William W. Delaney in New York. Their song pamphlets are important contributions to American musical lore.

Rossiter holds a unique place in the field of early 1900 music. Under the pesudonym of W. R. Williams, he was a successful songwriter whose successes include "When the Moon Plays Peek-a-boo," the melodious "Don't You Remember the Time?" "Gee! But There's Class to a Girl Like You," all of them hits. Today one of his best-known songs is "I'd Love to Live in Loveland with a Girl Like You." Many of the Williams-Rossiter songs received accolades in the barber's shop before clippers were wired for sound, and when the "tonsorial

Parodies Prove Popularity

parlor" was often the headquarters for those with an urge to harmonize. The Williams songs had melodies suited to natural harmonization.

He not only wrote but published his own songs. Other songwriters have yearned to take all by publishing, but few of them have had the business acumen needed for success in this dog-eat-dog field of competitive enterprise. Paul Dresser, composer of "My Gal Sal," "On the Banks of the Wabash," "The Blue and the Grey," "Just Tell Them That You Saw Me," and other ballads sung nationally, exemplifies other composers whose abilities were geared to composition but not to business. But Rossiter was adept in composing and successful in publishing. He succeeded also in the role of an editor scouting for new song-writing talent. He helped young songwriters to develop; then he published their output. In the roles of composer, lyric writer, talent scout, developer, and astute publisher, Will Rossiter was truly unique. As a businessman, he produced pamphlets of words, music, or both, including great numbers of parodies.

In New York, William W. Delaney was less successful as a composer. To some degree he compensated for his musical frustrations by becoming as widely known in the song-pamphlet publishing field as his rival. Though the Delaney pamphlets were largely compendiums of words written by others, nearly every edition included the music of a song or two credited to "Ned Yale" or "Willie Wildwave," otherwise known as Delaney. His creative spark glowed perennially, though it couldn't quite burst into flame. Among the many that he composed under those pseudonyms are "Scorn Not the Convict," "My Little Roof Garden Girl," "Before the Ball" (composer-publisher Charles K. Harris had made a national success of "After the Ball"), and "Down in the Lehigh Valley"—all of them forgotten today.

In addition to songs and parodies, both the Rossiter and Delaney sheets included pages of recitations, jokes, poetry, and great numbers of advertisements for their other stocks-in-trade. These included dream books, German at sight, and "standard choice novels" that were shockers for that era: *The Stranglers of Paris, Wife in Name Only, She;* and in Delaney's case, *Dr. Jekyll and Mr. Hyde* and Verne's *The Tour of the World in Eighty Days* on which the Mike Todd movie of the 1950's was based.

One means of getting the pamphlets into circulation was through the theatrical road companies whose one- or two-night stands were common to small towns along the railroads. Between acts, an actor who had just played a serious part might come before the curtain as a zany comedian singing parodies on current hits, while fellow actors sold song pamphlets through the aisles. Audiences along the Quincy, Omaha & Kansas City railroad (Q.O. and Come Slow to embittered citizens along the line) and in comparable hinterlands expected to hear parodies. In the parody of "Come Take a Trip in My Airship," the verse told of a boyfriend's arrival while his date was still in the bathtub upstairs. Her mother called to her to "slip on a dress or a gown. She slipped on some soap on the top step/And I think she came all the way down/O-o-o-h! Come take a trip in my airship."

The hot sports, archaic term for cool cats, stamped on the floor since their hands were busy shelling out twenty-five-cent pieces for the "Official Album of Vocal Gems" from Rossiter or Delaney. Usually, it carried a page or two of Hot

Stuff Jokelets. A quick sampling, *circa* 1906: "How long did Cain hate his brother?—As long as he was Abel." "What makes a lamp chimney smoke?—Because it can't chew." The "albums" were on cheap paper such as the sheets of pirated songs prized by bobby-soxers in the 1920's. Rossiter and Delaney gave credit to the publishers of the songs they used in the original or in parody.

Current news made good material to parody, particularly when well-known names were involved. Often, parodies expressed thought and popular attitudes toward incidents or conditions. When they became outmoded, crowded out by new incidents or changed conditions, the parody lost its point. Without an explanation, the parody on "Just As the Sun Went Down" would leave a modern audience coldly puzzled. It was popular when the 1900's arrived.

Foreword: In the ancient days an organization of fanatics directed its activities against Catholicism in ways comparable with Ku Klux Klan tactics. It was referred to as the A.P.A. An associate who had an enormous assortment of cuss words reached his climax when he referred to someone as a "dirty A.P.A. such and such." This was not necessarily because that person *was* one. It was dredged up from the very lowest epithet in his vocabulary. Now, with the scenery in place, we raise the curtain on a character in a burlesque or road show as he sings the climactic line of the parody on "Just As the Sun Went Down":

The son called his father an A. P. A.
Just then the son went down.

Glug!

Though such a one has lost its point, a parody that depends upon dateless humor can go on and on as in the case of "Be kind to your web-footed friends/ A duck may be somebody's mother" to the tune of bandmaster John Philip Sousa's "Stars and Stripes Forever."

The late Sigmund Spaeth believed that there is no higher compliment to an original musical composition than a parody which lasts. Parodies that range from excellent satire through sharp criticism into far-fetched nonsense and down into the subcellar of versifying could fill a hefty tome, though the extent of its contribution to our culture might be debatable.

That also applies to parodies for private performance, such as "Shame on You, Evelyn Thaw" to the tune of "Colleen Bawn." Evelyn (Nesbit) Thaw was the third corner of a love triangle that involved her with a murder and national notoriety in 1905. Among others, that are usually sung sub rosa, the parody on ancient "John Peel," "Sweet Violets," "The Little Old Red Shawl That Maggie Wore" switched to another garment, "The Sailor's Hornpipe" in the British Navy version, "Christopher Colombo," and the many parodies on "Ta-ra-ra-boom-de-re," always sung "boom-de-yay."

Many of the singing commercials of radio and television are parodies, new words set to an old established melody. Before radio, there were songs that of themselves were singing commercials.

"Oh, You Spearmint Kiddo"

Soon after radio went into national broadcasting of its programs, certain songs that introduced a program became the "theme" songs associated with bands or entertainers: "When the Moon Comes over the Mountain"—Kate Smith; "Sleep"—Fred Waring; and "The Waltz You Saved for Me"—Wayne King. Then an advertising man with sadistic tendencies linked words in praise of his product with a well-known tune, and the first singing commercial new-style was launched.

In general, advertisers have been as sheep-minded as the songwriters who watched their competition hawklike in order to design a song that resembled any current hit. (Automobile designers have had that same monkey-see-monkey-do ingenuity, if you recall rumble seats, teardrop designs, trick transmissions, fins, and the rest.) When manufacturers heard radio's early singing commercials, they commanded their ad departments to turn out songs "like our competition. We oughta had it first." The commercials were set to well-known tunes as simple as "Jingle Bells," "The Blue Tail Fly," or "Camptown Races." Much later, products attained the dignity of special music to carry an ad. A few of them are so well conceived and executed that they might well be nuclei of national song hits. Others are as pleasing as a door squeak.

In more ancient days, before radio, certain of our songs were singing commercials in effect, though not written with that intent. "In My Merry Oldsmobile," which nearly every adult recognizes, exemplifies that class. Today's singing commercials are written with the knowledge that they'll be used for a month or other limited time, only to be replaced by new ones. The singing commercial old-style had no such intention back of it. It was written as popular music. Rarely, a composer might have a nudge from a manufacturer's advertising department, but in the main songs such as "Take Me Out to the Ball Game" were published with an eye toward the rewards from sheet-music sales and later, 78 recordings. The two songs mentioned ran into vast numbers of copies as did others that were recorded on the heavy discs and for tinkly music boxes and paper rolls for pianolas—as songs not advertisements. They were popular among bands, calliope thumpers when the circus came to town ("Oh, You Circus Day" was one of their favorites), strolling organ grinders, and hurdy-gurdy players on the streets.

The songwriters' and publishers' targets were commercial, but they aimed at music counters rather than at the sale of filtered hams or Tweezled Twinx in the giant economy size—it's kloranated. (Incidentally, TV is here to stay. It survived that ghastly green chlorophyll year in the 1950's. Remember the singing ads that promoted chlorophyll to sweeten wet dogs, human breath, and overworked toilet bowls?)

In a few instances, the attempts to mold public preference by writing songs about products are older than radio's oldest crystal set. Some were written in ad departments, for reasons as obvious as today's singing commercials. "My Kola Girl" of 1895 was published as sheet music for giveaway in stores selling sweets:

She chews good Kola gum, the best that's made, they say
She chews sweet Kola gum, she chews both night and day
She chews fine Kola gum, she'd rather chew than play
She chews sweet Kola gum both night and day.

Radio and television might not have survived that one, had they been in existence.

A bit later, still in the sheet-music era, "Oh, You Spearmint Kiddo with the Wrigley Eyes" was also about a girl who just loved gum. Her sweetheart was a "gumster," and to her he did say in the chorus that every kiss was loaded with bliss "peptonized." It is unlikely that Wrigley, Sr., subsidized the song. Jerome and Schwartz, the writers, were successful writers of popular songs. They were unusually adept at picking up bits, incidents, news, names, almost anything from the current scene, and converting them into a subject for a song. Wrigley's ads were everywhere, hence were newsy subjects.

That applies also to "The Yellow Kid," a song of 1904 based upon a comic strip that had taken hold nationally. "Mr. Dooley," a syndicated column of current comment, was another. It will be amplified later under names in the news that were picked up in song. By comparison, the Kola number came directly from an ad department where mere mention of a brand name was sweet music. Most such songs had anemic melodies, limping harmonies, and lyrics that needed chlorophyll.

To my knowledge, no one knows the authorship of a widely sung old-style "commercial" that seems to have just growed without parents, the ballad of "Lydia Pinkham." Back of it was heavy advertising that had run for years to promote the sale of Lydia's "vegetable compound" for female ills. An ancient chromolith trade card in my collection shows the new Brooklyn Bridge (1883) with a Vegetable Compound sign suspended, by the artist, full length beneath it. These colorful trade cards were given away in hundreds of thousands. Visitors from inland must have been surprised to find that the new and famous bridge carried no Pinkham ad beneath it. One verse among the several versions, went like this:

Makers of another patent medicine, whose blue bottles are still seen on drugstore shelves and in bathroom cabinets, capitalized early upon America's ornate parlor organs by printing sheet music with Bromo Seltzer ads on the covers and distributing them almost gratis. In case anyone wants to peep into the remote 1870's and 1880's to see what the country was singing then, here are a few titles from my Bromo collection:

Annie Laurie
Ben Bolt
Columbia My Country
Dream Faces
Flee As a Bird
Grandma's Shamrocks
Home Sweet Home
In the Gloaming
Juanita
Kathleen Mavourneen
Listen to the Mocking Bird
Nearer, My God, to Thee
Over the Moonlit Sea
Rocked in the Cradle of the Deep
Take Back the Heart
When the Swallows Homeward Fly

Another heavy advertiser of that era was Dr. Munyan. A song about him carries his picture on the cover, with forefinger pointing upward. His well-advertised slogan "There Is Hope" was not included. Still in the patent-medicine field, Hamlin's Wizard Oil song pamphlets carried the oil's trademark, an elephant in a top hat, on the cover, which featured "Let Dr. Wizard Cure Your Ills." Songs, such as in the Bromos, alternated with ad pages. "America" and "The Lord's Prayer" led the collection, with "Heaven Is My Home" and "Good Night, Ladies" ending it. Opposite "Sweet and Low," the advertisement commanded the reader "Whip Your Liver . . . an occasional whipping. That is what Wizard Liver Whips are for."

The Pure Food and Drug Act of 1906 was good news to some of the patent-medicine makers because it required the listing of ingredients that were in the package. In this case "Contains 65% Alcohol" prominently displayed on the oil package could hardly have hurt sales in dry territories, since it was to be taken internally when not rubbed on. Among the seventy humans ills listed for which the oil was "prescribed . . . you are following the directions of a practicing physician" were Ankles (sprained), Asthma, Biliousness, Bites (dog or reptiles), Cancer, Chilblaines, Catarrh, Corns, Deafness, Hemorrhage, Hydrophobia, Nipples (Sore), Pneumonia, Sour Stomach, Sunburn, Warts, and Whooping Cough. Can TV top that?

Other free song pamphlets presented well-known tunes with words by the advertisers, as in early radio. I don't know whether Lion coffee still exists as a brand, but in the early 1900's the manufacturer distributed a song leaflet whose words, to the tune of "Rally 'Round the Flag," a Civil War song, went beautifully with a mandolin or Jew's-harp background:

We're all for the Lion
Hurrah, boys, hurrah
Shouting its praises
Wherever you are
And we'll rally 'round the brand, boys
Rally once again
Showing the praise of Lion coffee.

An eastern Massachusetts lyricist must have rhymed "hurrah" with "are." More later about sectional background as it shows through the words.

"The Jolly Thresherman," 1880, was composed by a Distinguished American

Song Writer, it says on the cover. Inside, Arthur Sullivan receives credit for the tune, which is his "Little Buttercup" from the veddy British *Pinafore*. Manufacturers of farm machinery published it for giveaway. Obviously, the thresherman's life was replete with joys of that unsophisticated era. But why that frowsy bird in the medallion at the top? Ah, my city friend, you see the sad plight of a starveling. A chicken was turned out to seek calories around a straw stack whose straw had been through an Aultman & Taylor threshing machine. Separation of grain from straw was so efficient that all the wheat or oats went into the farmer's granary. Slim pickin' made a slim chicken. Purty cute, we, who see it all at a glance, chuckle. No comment about corn, please. That goes through a sheller not a thresher.

On the back of "Beautiful Ohio," (not the one you know) was "the latest and greatest success" in motordom, the 1914 Royal at $1,275. The general sales manager was also the composer and publisher of this and eleven other songs listed inside the cover.

Current singing commercials are frank bids for business—advertising in every sense. Many of the old songs that referred in one way or another to products or services might have emanated from the public-relations (publicity) department, molding public opinions or preference as they did (the soft sell). In the field of communications, use was often the theme as in "Hello, My Baby," "I Guess I'll Have to Telegraph My Baby," "Call Me Up Some Rainy Afternoon," "All Alone" (both Von Tilzer's and Berlin's), and "Hello, Frisco," which recognized the completion of transcontinental telephone service in 1915. The "image" on the song covers was that of the instrument in use (good indirect public relations). In the field of transportation "On the Old Fall River Line" outlived the Boston–New York boat trains and ships that inspired it, while a diesel "On the 5:15" hauls commuters, as it does "When That Midnight Choo-Choo Leaves for Alabam." In some cases the references to use were in the lyrics, not the title, as in "I'm Going Back to Carolina."

Among the early songwriters, some were bibulous, so alcohol may be praised or blamed for the songs with dithyrambs in praise of *Wines, Liquors & Cigars* (as many signs read) that dotted the years before Prohibition (1920). (The present-day roadside version: *Eat JOE'S Liquor* or the reverse.) The only straightforward singing commercial that comes to mind concerning wine is that coy "Hello, Virginia [Dare]." Herbert's "Absinthe Frappe" is still good music. So is the rousing "In Bohemia Hall." It might be possible to identify songs in every letter of the alphabet that touted drinking, or pointed to penalties.

A few examples are:

Absinthe Frappe
Behind Those Swinging Doors
Beer Barrel Polka
Brown October Ale
Champagne Charlie
Cocktails for Two
Drinking Song—Student Prince
Drinking, Drinking, Drinking
Drunkards' Doom

Father, Dear Father, Come Home with Me Now
Germanyland (Where the Sauerkraut Grows)
Hitting the Bottle—Earl Carroll Vanities 1930
Heidelberg—Prince of Pilsen
Landlord Fill the Flowing Bowl
Maine Stein Song
Saloon—E. R. Llab (Ernest R. Ball)
Show Me the Way to Go Home
To Anacreon in Heaven (melody of "Star Spangled Banner")
We Won't Go Home Till Morning

Though it was never set to music, Disraeli's comment about Gladstone (1878) being "inebriated by the abundance of his own pomposity" had a swing to it that should have invited a musical setting.

"Down Where the Wurzburger Flows" and "The Maine Stein Song," associated with Rudy Vallee's early radio days, were good promotion for the brewers. As popular as those two, the echoes of "Under the Anheuser Bush" bounced around every summer park in the country as the band competed, usually in a different key, with the merry-go-round's mechanical version. Its "drink some Budweis with me" was a restrained suggestion, but four years later "Budweiser's a Friend of Mine" was an outright singing commercial.

Smaller breweries took note of a host of potential consumers who were paying money at the music counters for songs advertising the big competitor's product (we oughta had it first), and soon a flood of songs in praise of local Grossvaters, Pilseners, and Heinie Gabooblers flowed out, free to the public. But the locals' giveaway songs had no more inspiration than a long-drawn seidel. Few recipients played them more than once.

Distillations had their musical fling, too, but more in the theme of prohibition than promotion. Before those years, comedy actress Florence Moore floated down "the Old Green River," a brand of bottled goods, and the nation was treated to "Mr. Wilson—that's all," the name and slogan of another whiskey. Came Prohibition and "Everybody Wants a Key to My Cellar," also "Show Me the Way to Go Home." The Volstead Act was so slightly prohibitory that "Prohibition, You Have Lost Your Sting" was among the several dozen songs inspired by the act.

A song that was the essence of singing commercialism concerned a silent movie serial, "The Perils of Pauline." The late Pearl White played Pauline who displayed athletic abilities and daring comparable with the actual later accomplishments of "Babe" Didricksen Zaharias. Week after week, Pauline's skill, strength, daring, and ingenuity kept her just ahead of a gang that wanted to rub her out by any foul means. Let a verse and chorus speak for themselves:

I'm as worried as can be, all the movie shows I see
Have that awful mystery "Pauline and Her Perils"
On a rope they dangle her, then they choke and strangle her
With an axe they mangle her, always something new
To make you shake they give her Paris green
Of course her horse will neigh "Nay, Nay Pauline."

"Oh, You Spearmint Kiddo"

CHORUS:

Poor Pauline, I pity Poor Pauline
One night she's drifting out to sea
Then they tie her to a tree
I wonder what the end will be
This suspense is awful
Bing! Bang! Biff! they throw her off a cliff
They dynamite her in a submarine
In the lion's den she shakes with fright
Lion starts to take a bite
Zip goes the film—"Goodnight"
*Poor Pauline.**

It should be explained to an increasingly urbanized readership that Paris green was an arsenical poison to kill potato bugs and such pests. "Goodnight" refers to the slide shown on the screen at the end of 1914 "fillums." When a film snapped, as it did frequently, the operator flashed his "Just a Minute Please" slide comparable with today's "Due to mechanical difficulty, we return you to the station until..." The movie's makers and the box office men in theaters showing the serial listened to America singing "Poor Pauline"—and smiled.

Song for political campaigns are also singing commercials. Most of our Presidents have had songs about them during the campaigns. Probably "Honest Abe" Lincoln had the most. "Our Landon" was a dud in 1936. Ohioans were responsible for 1938's "Elect Bricker Governor." That was a year after "Mr. Roosevelt, Won't You Run Again?" The Democrats' tuneful plea "Don't Let Them Take It Away" referred to his administration.

Songwriters hailed all phases of motoring as natural subjects for songs, to be commented upon later. But, lest it be missed, one point should be clarified here. "In My Merry Oldsmobile" was not written as a singing commercial, though it's heard on the air today. It was a national waltz whose popularity continued for years. Like others, it became a record of things with which America has lived, things that in many cases have vanished from the language. In the Oldsmobile song "They love to spark in the dark old park as they go flying along/She says she knows why the motor goes/The sparker's awfully strong," the double entendre slang word "spark" also referred smoochily to spooning, necking, and such and to their quaint habit of flying along rather than parking. But was that awfully strong "sparker" merely a "spark plug"?

* Copyright 1914 by Broadway Music Corporation, 135 West Fiftieth St., New York, N. Y.

Language and Slanguage

Dialects, Allusions, and Pleasantries

To greater extent than in other published literature, the words of popular songs reflect the language of the people over succeeding eras. Time marches on, memories are short, and, between generations, meanings can shift so far that allusions which were clear originally, as in the A.P.A. case cited or in the changed meaning of "square," have become obscure or lost entirely. In consequence, songs preserve the obsolete meanings of words, slang, catch phrases, and pleasantries common to a particular generation, as an example, "spoon," once so recurrent in the moon-June-tune cycle.

Lyrics constitute an anthology of word use long after a combination such as "twenty-three skiddoo" has become meaningless to most. Tad Dorgan, one of the best-known early cartoonists, is credited with it. It signified go away, get out, scram, or git lost. The song of that name stemmed from Dorgan's slang. In reverse order, some songwriters have created words, phrases, or meanings that entered and spiced the language.

Like a few others who write for a living, some of the successful songwriters had little formal education. Sometimes our slips show. Other lyricists have held degrees in English but were weak in the techniques of versifying when, conventionally, poetry included end rhymes such as spark with park. (With the new freedoms, much of the output is as bare of rhyme or rhythm as a stockyard report of receipts.) In the main, regardless of who wrote them, our songs' lyrics project more meaning than the language of most social scientists and of the financial seers who ravel doubtful thoughts into tangled skeins of obfuscation.

It is quite possible that a lyricist may be an authority on verse, blank or other, but he faces the task of fitting words into a pattern of music already provided by a collaborator. Gilbert and Sullivan, Jerome and Schwartz, Hough, Adams and Howard, the Gershwin brothers, Rodgers and Hart or Hammerstein, and Loewe and Lerner are representative of song-writing teams, each with its own method of cooperation. When words must fit music already composed, the lyricist may have the exact word or phrase to continue a sequence of thought but he's short or long by a syllable or more that's needed to fill the musical framework provided by the composer. Regretfully, the word wielder may be forced to abandon "The moon above knows I'm in love" and substitute "The moon above, maybe, knows I'm in love, baby."

Slang may be used by a lyricist who takes his English poets seriously but who is more serious about the immediate objective of turning out a song hit, he hopes. Hits are not necessarily grammatical. Usage may bring acceptance of what was frowned upon. "Like" for "as" is an example in "If You Knew Susie." To my ear, the lyrics would lose if you knew her *as* I know her. That ancient "That's How I Need You" (like a baby needs its mother), 1912, has six "likes" compressed into the chorus. In 1966 the subject cropped up again in *Saturday Review*. Subsequent letters to the editor were like/as before, expressions that ranged from loathing to approval. As yet, no one has quoted the final authorities, the stars of screen, radio, and TV who say "like I do" when speaking without script. Who would dare criticize? "There are a few, kind sir." (That's a line from the Floradora Sextette, "Tell Me, Pretty Maiden," 1900.)

We'd lose much if our songs were tailored to fit the patterns long established by grammarians. Look into this song mirror of 1908, "Be Sweet to Me, Kid":

Aw Gee! Be sweet to me, kid
I'm awfully fond of you
Aw Gee! When you're cross with me
Nothing looks good I'm so blue
On the square, kid
I'm crazy about you for fair
Love me the way you did
Fill me with joy, My Honey Boy
Go on, be sweet to me, kid.

Much of the language, slanguage, and allusion of sixty years ago is still current, though "square," "for fair" and "Honey Boy" are dated. The last one makes double reference to minstrel man Honey Boy Evans and the 1907 song "Honey Boy" dedicated to him with his picture on the cover. The lyrics were by a most literate university graduate, Franklin R. Adams, not to be confused with Franklin P. Adams, the deceased conductor of the deceased New York *World*'s "Conning Tower" column and a connoisseur of our old sad ballads.

Lyricist Franklin R. collaborated with Will M. Hough as librettist of a series of musical comedies for which Joseph E. Howard wrote the music. They include *A Stubborn Cinderella; The Time, the Place and the Girl; The Umpire* ("for the umpire is a most unhappy man"); *The Girl Question; The Prince of Tonight; Honeymoon Trail,* whose theme song of the same name set a high mark in lyrical verse writing, though the show flopped; and *The Isle of Bong Bong,* which included the best "Illinois" song ever written, says this commentator. "My Illinois" lay dormant for more than a half century. Happily, with the cooperation of Charles Wilcox of Freeport, Illinois, it is revived and in the repertoire of several SPEBSQSA choruses in the state where, I can hope, it will continue.

As in the two-way flow of folk music into popular and the reverse, the language has contributed to song titles; and conversely, titles or catch lines from songs have become part of the language, sometimes temporarily as in "I Fah Down Go Boom," "That's My Weakness Now," "Go 'Way Back and Sit Down," "Ain't We Got Fun?" "Makin' Whoopee," "Aren't We All?" "Sit Down, You're Rockin' the Boat," and "I'm Putting All My Eggs in One Basket." "Paddle Your Own Canoe," meaning be independent, and others like it fitted earlier outdoor and rural conditions. Mechanization and trends cityward blunted their points and popularity.

The eggs in one basket song had a corollary or at least a relationship to a song, probably of the 1870's (which came first, the chicken or the egg?), that an aunt used to sing as a lesson in consequences when one brags about expectations:

Young Fred'rick Augustus in love with a girl
He twists his mustaches up into a curl
He tells all the boys he'll be married next June
And sings silly songs by the light of the moon
But, while he is talking of what is to be,
Another young man comes along, don't you see?
From under his nose the fair girl has been snatched
He counted his chickens before they were hatched.

While contributing to or borrowing from the language, the songwriter may also reveal something of his early sectional background. Most frequently it shows in his use of *r, ar, er,* or *ir*. They may be smothered, according to mid-American speech which must be considered the criterion since it is the standard from the Berkshire Hills of Massachusetts to the West Coast, in the section north of the Mason-Dixon line. A lyric writer's use of a smothered *r* is a clue to his early exposure to phonetics. In "Betsy's the Bell of the Beach," Richard Carle rhymed *charms* with *qualms* because he heard them that way. In "Gee But I Like Music with My Meals," a restaurant owner had the right *idea*(*r*), he pleased the appetite and delighted the *ear*. Nearly everyone recognizes *Ida*(*r*) and her sweetness comparable with apple *cider*. In "The Bowery," on the night when I struck New *York* I went out for a quiet *walk*. In "Just Behind the Times," a sob song, a church's board notified a veteran preacher, by letter, that he'd soon be dropped: "Your voice is *gone* and none will *mourn,* for you're just behind the times." (He died in the pulpit in the second verse.)

At Christmas time "Heavenly hosts sing *halleluja*(*r*)," in New England a section that still preserves original English pronunciation to greater extent than elsewhere, though sound tracks, radio, and TV are bleeding its individuality drop by drop. It will be a sad day when precedent no longer allows dropping of the final *g* in *ing* endings (town meetin') while accenting others as in the late President Kennedy's *in-te-rest.* Mid-America says *intrst.* The perfect example of the split syllable is the northeast coastal *ay-yuh,* meaning aye or yes as in old English. Diacritical marks have not yet been devised to fully reproduce the phonetics of "goin' to park the car," according to Mid-America speech standards.

The song "Down at Toity-toid and Toid" exemplifies Mid-Atlantic as heard in a small area(r) centered upon Manhattan. It is commonly called the Brooklyn accent, but it thrives as far away as "Over on the Jersey Side." I was fortunate to preserve it by limerick in a *Cleveland Press* poetry column:

A Brooklyn refiner of spoim irl
And other irls, such as wheat goim irl
Once said to his girl
"You can tell when they birl
By the odor and bubbles and toimurl."

Commonly limericks are spoken. But "when good fellows get together" ("Heidelberg" from *The Prince of Pilsen,* 1902), a rousing session is assured when an individual sings a limerick, and then the group enters into the chorus lustily, as in Lindroth's earlier comment about hymns. Thus:

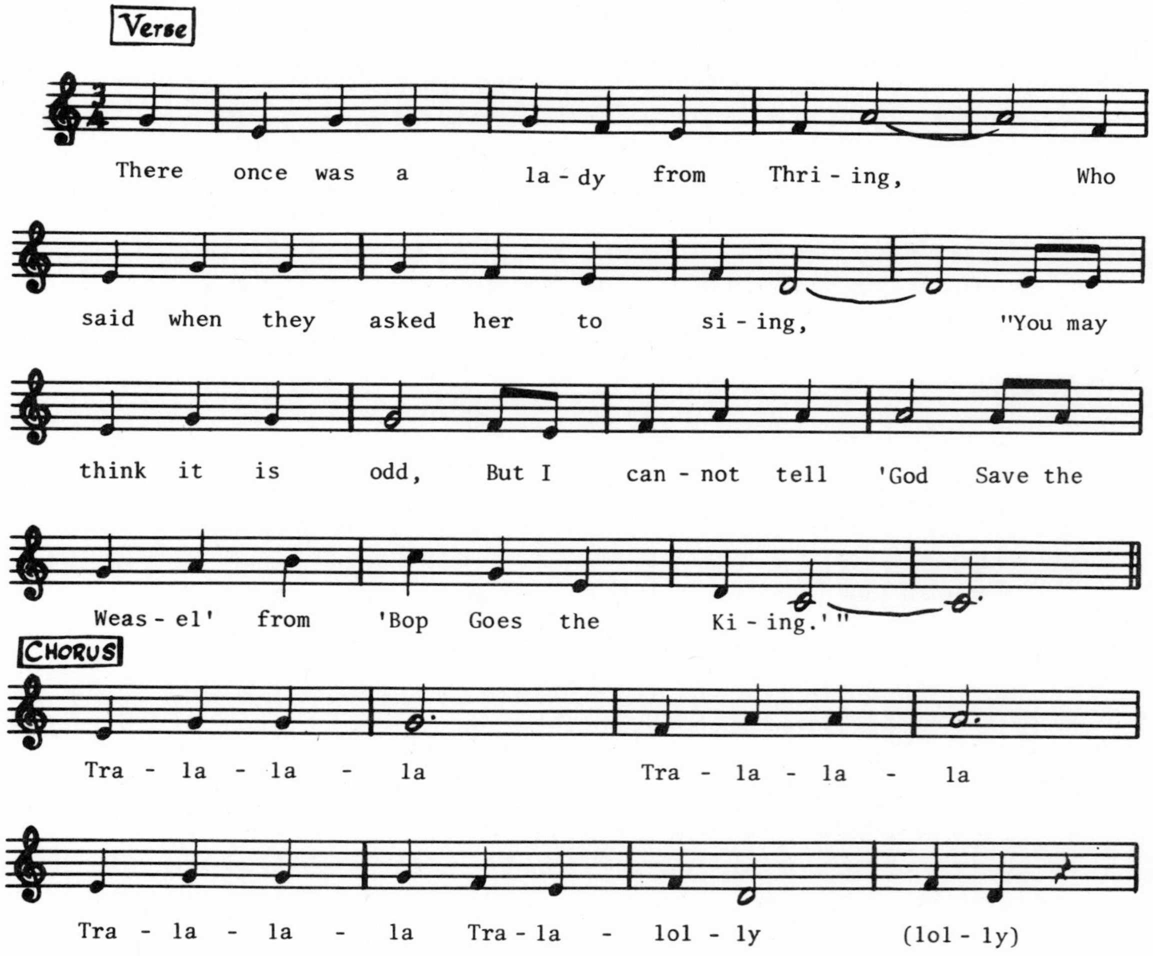

Tra - la - la - la Tra - la - la - la
Tra - la - la - la Tra - la la - Tra - la lol - ly.

Two more are in Appendix L for those interested in singing limericks. The tune fits them, whether ta-tum or ta-ta-tum, iamb or anapest. "An' a pest on both," you may say, paraphrasing FDR's famous squelch.

To those who find euphony in free verse, it doesn't matter that the forced rhymes in many songs, particularly hymns, would have no terminal if laid end to end. "There's a land that is fairer than day/And by faith we can see it *afar*/For the Father waits over the way/To prepare us a dwelling place *there*." Thar she blows in the opening of "In the Sweet By and By." Secularly, in the verse of "Oceana Roll," "on the cruiser *Alabama* he was there at that *piano*." Such citations are not criticism. They point out the oddities that help to fill us with pleasant expectation of what may be just around the corner. We can smile affectionately with our old songs without laughing at them.

Listeners determine whether music is worth repeating. What is taken seriously by one audience may be corny to another, even in the same era. And corn or corny can have quite different meanings to two or more persons. It may be called corny because it is overly sentimental or because it is outmoded or because of a double meaning or pun as in "Hearts Win, You Lose," 1913. It depends upon the interpretation placed by an individual on corn—as inexact in usage as "dig" in the early 1960's. Dig (see) that blonde; I don't dig (understand) that; they didn't dig (recognize) me, etc.

Current trends to the contrary, a speaking acquaintance with grammar does no harm in writing song lyrics, though it is no assurance of success. Wes Lawrence, formerly book review editor of Cleveland's *Plain Dealer,* once commented upon a columnist's painful task when throwing away his accumulation of substandard poetic contributions: "There lies the verse that rhymes deem with preen, the limerick whose last line is tangled in its five feet (instead of the standard three) . . . all destined to become a little pile of ashes," like the hopes of many who have written a sure-fire song hit but can only get it published at their own expense. Less sympathetically, John Ciardi referred in *Saturday Review* (November 5, 1966) to specimens such as Lawrence's as "drivel."

"Pardon My Southern Accent," 1934, should have been included in the group of songs that have spiced the language. It is still heard among oldsters as an allusion meaning "pardon me" and other nuances. Phonetically, the native Missourian refers to the "Mizzourah Waltz." "The Hutsut Song" of the 1920's gives the effect of an ancient Norse ode.

Many of the oldies were used less as songs than as pleasantries covering a broad range of meanings. In common usage "I Picked a Lemon—in the garden of love" meant that I made a wrong choice. Dresser's "Just Tell Them That You Saw Me" could mean anything from good-bye, to, say hello to the family for me. Other pleasantries carried meanings beyond the words themselves: "Why Don't You Try?" "Who's Sorry Now?" "Would You Care?" "I Love Me," "Everybody Works But Father," "Good Night, Nurse," and "Daisies Won't Tell" as examples. "Not for Joe" goes back to the mid-1860's as a song; when spoken, it provided a snappy comeback or retort meaning no thank you or other refusal.

One characteristic connects the majority of songs that are hummed or whistled because they stick in memory. Their lyrics are in the theme of boy-meets-girl. What occurs after that provides themes for the entire range of somber thoughts—doleful ballads of parting ("Till We Meet Again") or regret ("You Always Hurt the One You Love")—as well as every nuance of the gayer ones. Some were baked in the oven of love (not a bad title, that) as in "The Cook-book of Love," 1909, whose cover shows Cupid in a chef's cap reading a recipe that starts with "2 young hearts."

Honey and sugar have always been useful ingredients in our songs. "Stop Stop Stop" includes the suggestion to fry kisses in honey. "Sugar Moon" and "When I Take My Sugar to Tea" represent the confectionery group. In "The Honeysuckle and the Bee," "I'd like to sip the honey sweet from those red lips, you see." That line of thought became quite syrupy in the 1909 song "If You Were a Big Red Rose":

I would dine on the nectar sweet
As forth from your lips it flows
I'd choose the life of a honey bee
If you were a big red rose.

But our songwriters have also gone as contrariwise as Tweedle-Dee in their declarations of independence: "No Wedding Bells for Me," "Gee! But I'm Glad That I'm Single," "Don't Take Me Home," or "My Wife's Gone to the Country—Hurrah! Hurrah!" The collaborator on that one, George Whiting, became a highly successful composer of popular hits that include "Japanese Sand Man," "Till We Meet Again," and "Mammy's Little Coal Black Rose," after his apprenticeship as a piano player on an Illinois River showboat.

So, to the multitudes of reasons why our popular songs have such potentials for pleasure beyond the music, add their portrayal of the American language in all its meanings and allusions over generations of usage.

77
P.T. BARNUM'S
GREAT
CLOWN
EUROPE
ASIA
AFRICA
ASIA
AFRICA
SONGSTER
N.Y. POPULAR PUB. CO.—32 BEEKMAN ST NEW YORK.

The Gal with the Balmoral

POETRY BY

FRED. WILSON,

J. H. BUFFORD'S LITH. BOSTON.

3

MUSIC BY

R. J. HERRERO.

BOSTON.

Published by RUSSELL & PATEE, 61 Court Street.

RUSSELL & TOLMAN, Boston. | W. PAINE, Portland.

RESPECTFULLY INSCRIBED TO MISS MARY E. SOUTH, TERRE HAUTE IND.
ON THE BANKS OF THE WABASH, FAR AWAY.
SONG & CHORUS BY
PAUL DRESSER.
5
Song . . . 50c.
Waltz . . . 50c.
Mandolin and Piano . . . 40c.
Two Mandolins and Piano . . . 50c.
Mandolin, Guitar and Piano . . . 50c.
Two Mandolins, Guitar and Piano . 60c.
Mandolin Solo . . . 30c.
Mandolin and Guitar . . . 40c.
Two Mandolins and Guitar . . 50c.
Orchestra Accompaniment to Song . 25c.
Waltz, Orchestra, 10 Pts. and Piano . 55c.
Waltz, Orchestra, 14 Pts. and Piano . 75c.
Transcription . . . 50c.
Band . . . 50c.
PUBLISHED BY
HOWLEY, HAVILAND & CO.,
4 EAST 20th STREET, NEW YORK.
LONDON, CHAS. SHEARD & CO.
SYD. DAVIES.

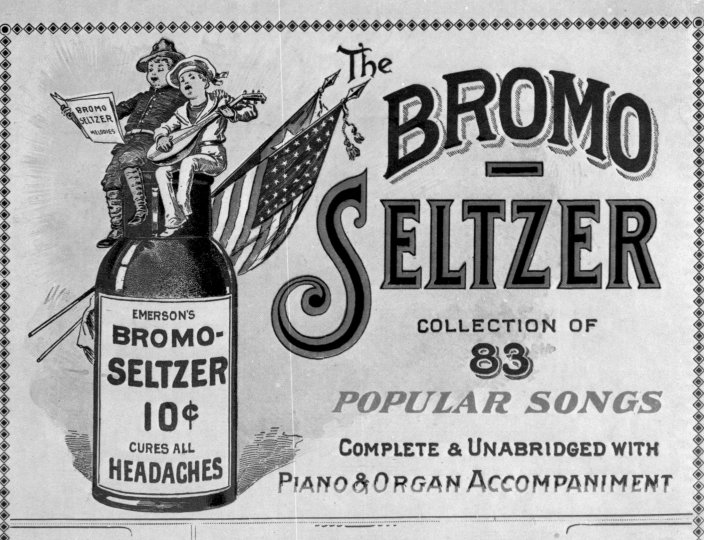

The BROMO-SELTZER

COLLECTION OF

83

POPULAR SONGS

COMPLETE & UNABRIDGED WITH
PIANO & ORGAN ACCOMPANIMENT

"Afterwards."

MARY MARK LEMON. JOHN W. MULLEN.

SELECTIONS.

VOCAL.

Afterwards.
Alice, Where Art Thou.
Annie Laurie.
At the Gate.
Auld Lang Syne.
Beautiful Moonlight, (Duet.)
Ben Bolt.
By Normandie's Blue Hills.
By the Sad Sea Waves.
Comin' Thro' the Rye.
Do They Think of Me at Home.
Dream Faces.
Ehren on the Rhine.
Ferryman John.
Gathered Flowers, (Duet.)
Green Palms, Les Rameaux.
Home, Sweet Home.
How Can I Leave Thee.
I Dreamt I Dwelt in Marble Halls.
I Love My Love.
Juanita, (Duet.)
Kathleen Mavourneen.
Keep for me a Trusting Heart.
Larboard Watch.
Last Night (Sehnsucht.)
Last Rose of Summer.
Let Me Dream Again.
Listen to the Mocking Bird.
Love's Old Sweet Song.
Love's But a Dream.
Love, I Will Love You Ever.
"Lullaby" from the Opera of "Erminie."
My Old Kentucky Home.
My Sweetheart at the Door.
Old Folks at Home.
Rocked in the Cradle of the Deep.
Sailing.
Sweethearts and Wives.
Take Back the Heart.
The Bridge.
The Heart Bowed Down.
The Miller and the Maid.
The Old Oaken Bucket.
The Old Ship.
The Sweetest Girl of All.
Then You'll Remember Me.
Thine Eyes So Blue and Tender.
Warrior Bold.
When the Swallows Homeward Fly.

INSTRUMENTAL.

Adelaide Polka Mazurka.
Bacio, (The Kiss) Waltz.
Belle of Cuba Quickstep.
Black Key Polka Mazurka.
Carnival of Venice.
Hornpipe Polka.
Intermezzo (Cavaliera Rusticana.)
Jolly Brother's Gallop.
Just a Little Sunshine, Waltz.
Marie Waltz.
Old Barn Polka.
School-Bell March.
Schubert's Serenade.
Silver Brook Schottische.
Starlight Polka.
Sweethearts' Waltz.
The Arrow Dance.
University Polka.

NEW SELECTIONS ADDED, JANUARY 1st, 1899.

America.
De Gal I Dream About.
Hail, Columbia.
Home Again.
Katie Callahan.
Loves Golden Dream.
Mary of Argyle.
Never to Part.
Since Mollie Moved Away.
Strangers Yet.
The Old Cottage Clock.
The Red, White and Blue.
The Star Spangled Banner.
The Song for Me.
Were We Lovers Then.
What are the Wild Waves Saying.

Any TWO pieces of the above music will be sent to any address upon receipt of a two-cent stamp and a Wrapper from a ten cent bottle of Bromo-Seltzer. Should you desire four pieces, send two stamps and two wrappers, and so on. Address MUSIC DEPARTMENT.

EMERSON DRUG CO., BALTIMORE, MD.

COMPLIMENTS OF
Frank H. Broad, Phar. in Mass. & R. I. 108 Union St. Cor. Green, Lynn, Mass

Margaret C. Kissick

See Description Inside.

THE BURNING OF ROME

MARCH-TWOSTEP.

BY E.T. PAULL.

PUBLISHED BY E.T. PAULL MUSIC CO. 46 WEST 28th ST.
NEW YORK

PHILADELPHIA, PA. M. D. SWISHER.
SPRINGFIELD, MASS. A. H. GOETTING.
PHILADELPHIA, PA. JOS. MORRIS.
NEW YORK NEW YORK MUSIC SUPPLY CO.
NEW YORK CROWN MUSIC CO.
NEW YORK ENTERPRISE MUSIC CO.
LONDON, ENG. W. PAXTON & CO.
CHICAGO, ILL. F. J. A. FORSTER CO.
TORONTO, CAN. W.R. DRAPER
BOSTON, MASS. COUPON MUSIC CO.
J. A. ALBERT & SON, SYDNEY, AUSTRALIA.

5 PIANO SOLO
10 FOUR HAND
5 SIMPLIFIED

LITH BY A HOEN & CO. RICHMOND VA.

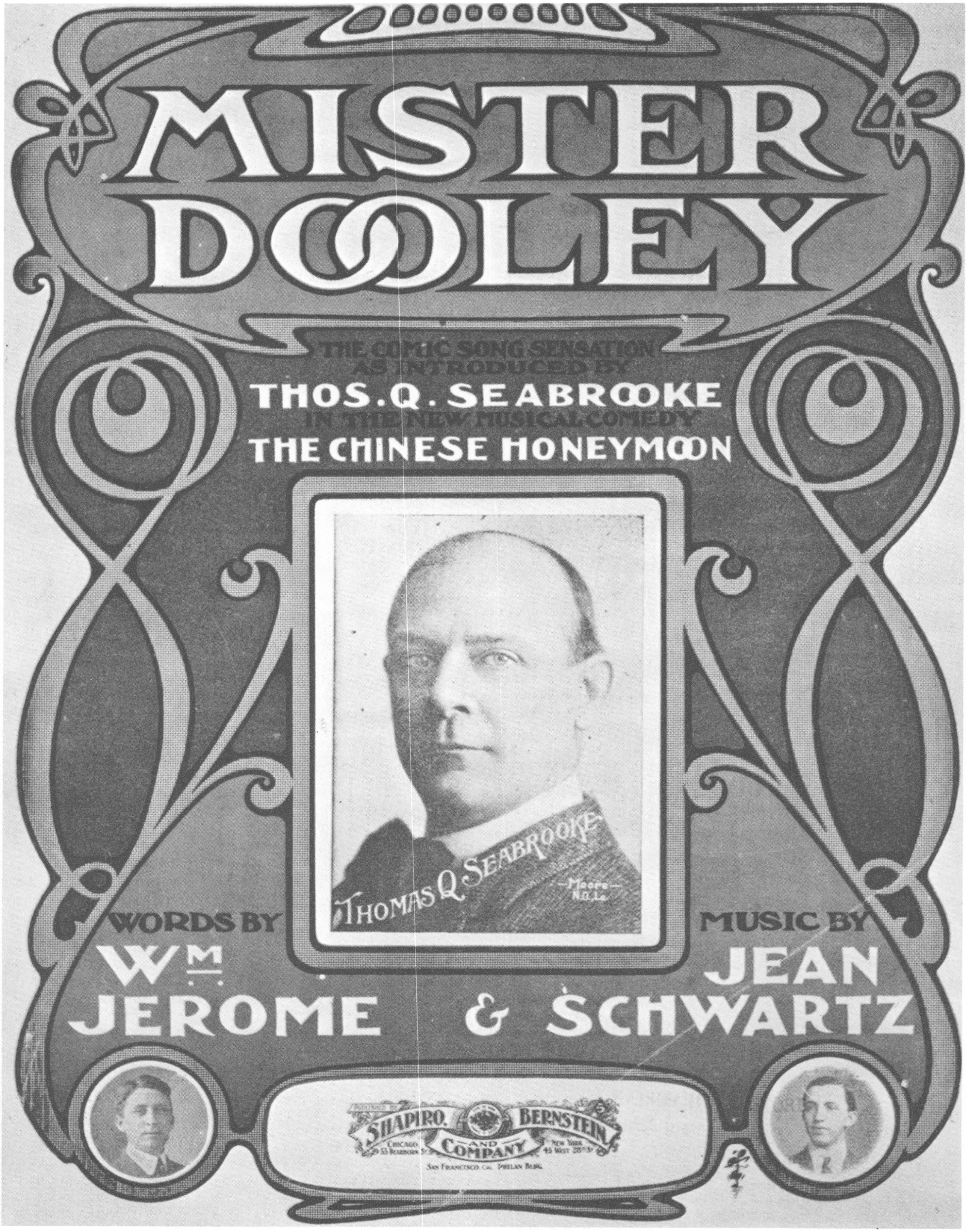
MISTER DOOLEY
THE COMIC SONG SENSATION
AS INTRODUCED BY
THOS. Q. SEABROOKE
IN THE NEW MUSICAL COMEDY
THE CHINESE HONEYMOON
THOMAS Q SEABROOKE
WORDS BY
Wm. JEROME
MUSIC BY
JEAN SCHWARTZ
SHAPIRO, BERNSTEIN AND COMPANY
CHICAGO 53 DEARBORN ST.
NEW YORK 45 WEST 28TH ST.
SAN FRANCISCO, CAL. PHELAN BLDG.

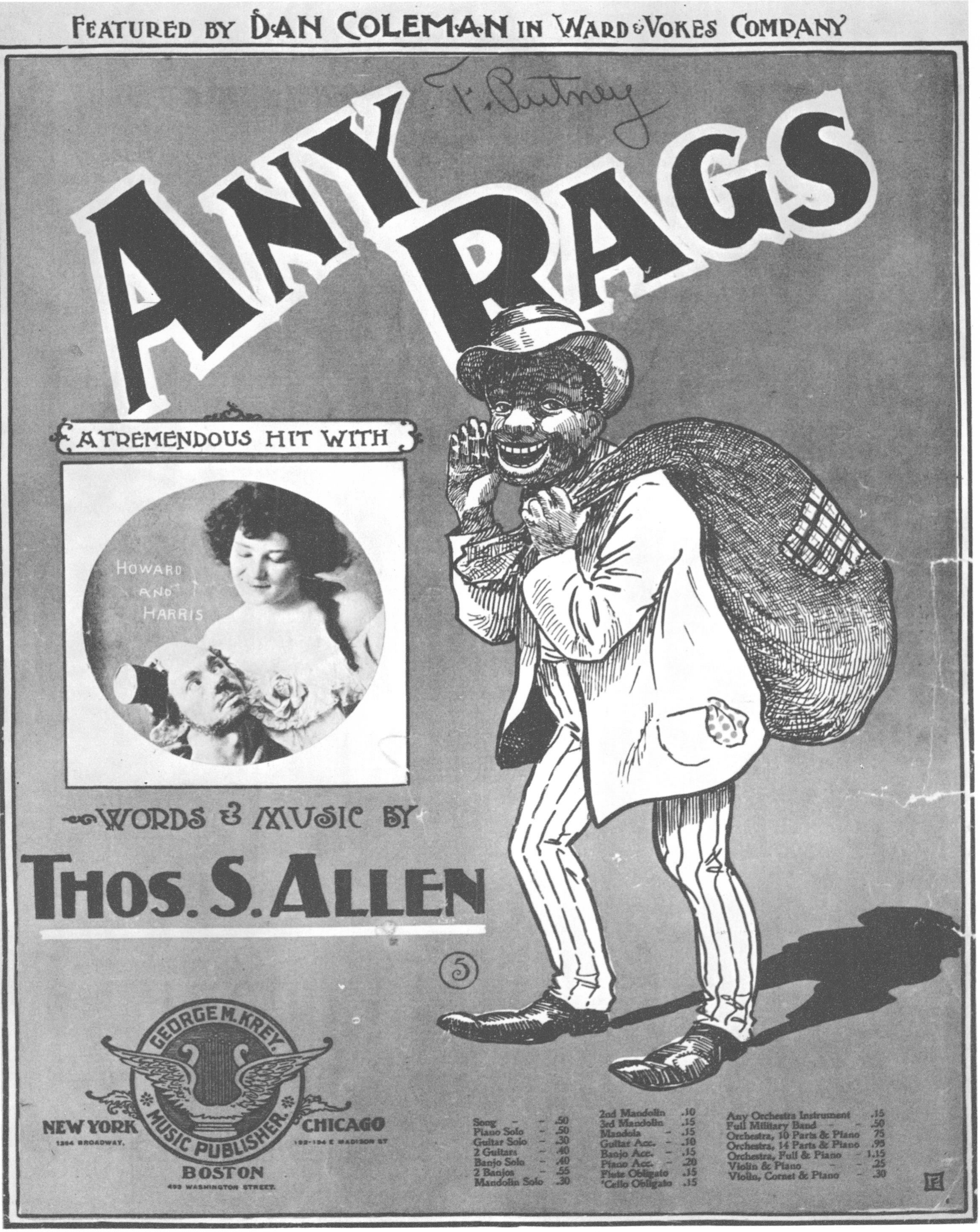
FEATURED BY DAN COLEMAN IN WARD & VOKES COMPANY
ANY RAGS
A TREMENDOUS HIT WITH
HOWARD AND HARRIS
WORDS & MUSIC BY
THOS. S. ALLEN
5
GEORGE M. KREY MUSIC PUBLISHER
NEW YORK
CHICAGO
BOSTON
Song - - .50
Piano Solo - .50
Guitar Solo - .30
2 Guitars - .40
Banjo Solo - .40
2 Banjos - .55
Mandolin Solo .30
2nd Mandolin .10
3rd Mandolin .15
Mandola - .15
Guitar Acc. - .10
Banjo Acc. - .15
Piano Acc. - .20
Flute Obligato .15
'Cello Obligato .15
Any Orchestra Instrument .15
Full Military Band - - .50
Orchestra, 10 Parts & Piano 75
Orchestra, 14 Parts & Piano .95
Orchestra, Full & Piano - 1.15
Violin & Piano - - .25
Violin, Cornet & Piano - .30

Paul Revere's Ride
MARCH-TWOSTEP
BY
E.T. PAULL
RESPECTFULLY INSCRIBED TO THE DAUGHTERS OF THE AMERICAN REVOLUTION
PUBLISHED BY E.T. PAULL MUSIC Co. 46 WEST 28th ST.
NEW YORK
PHILADELPHIA, PA. M.D. SWISHER.
SPRINGFIELD, MASS. A.H. GOETTING.
PHILADELPHIA, PA. JOS. MORRIS.
NEW YORK. NEW YORK MUSIC SUPPLY CO.
NEW YORK. CROWN MUSIC CO.
NEW YORK. ENTERPRISE MUSIC CO.
LONDON, ENG. W. PAXTON & Co
CHICAGO, ILL. F.J.A. FORSTER Co
TORONTO, CAN. CANADIAN-AMERICAN MUSIC CO. LTD.
BOSTON, MASS. COUPON MUSIC CO.
COPYRIGHT FOR ALL COUNTRIES.
5 PIANO SOLO
10 FOUR HAND
4 SIMPLIFIED
Copyright MCMV. By E.T. PAULL.
LITH. BY A. HOEN & CO. RICHMOND, VA.

PUBLISHED BY E.T. PAULL MUSIC Co 46 WEST 28th ST.
NEW YORK

5 PIANO SOLO
10 FOUR HAND

PHILADELPHIA, PA.
M. D. SWISHER.

SPRINGFIELD, MASS.
A. H. GOETTING.

PHILADELPHIA, PA.
JOS. MORRIS.

NEW YORK
NEW YORK MUSIC SUPPLY CO.

NEW YORK
CROWN MUSIC CO.

NEW YORK
ENTERPRISE MUSIC CO.

LONDON, ENG.
W. PAXTON & CO.

CHICAGO, ILL.
F. J. A. FORSTER CO.

TORONTO, CAN.
CANADIAN-AMERICAN MUSIC CO., LTD.

BOSTON, MASS.
COUPON MUSIC CO.

J. A. ALBERT & SON, SYDNEY, AUSTRALIA.

LITH BY A HOEN & CO RICHMOND, VA

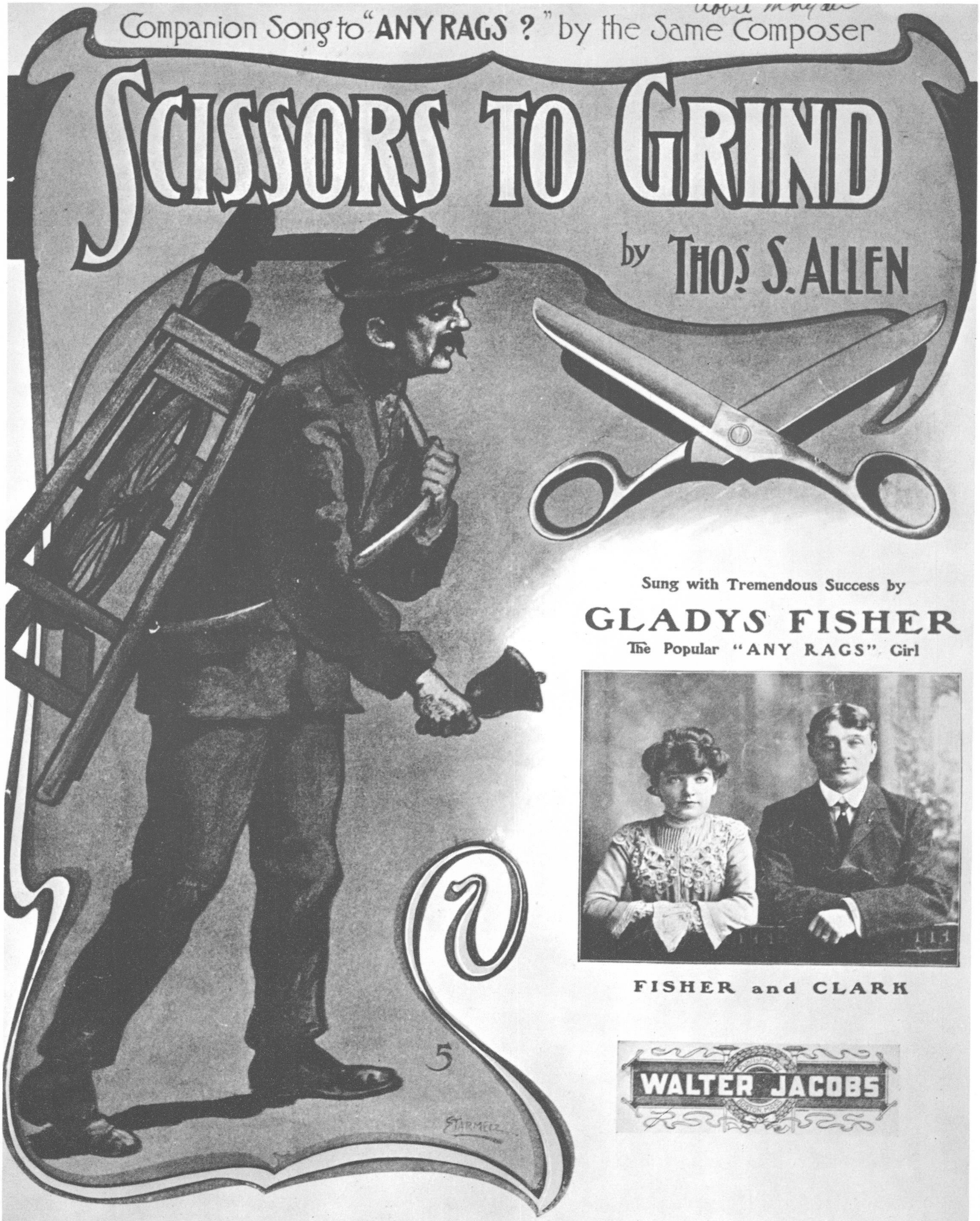
Companion Song to "ANY RAGS ?" by the Same Composer
SCISSORS TO GRIND
by THOS. S. ALLEN
Sung with Tremendous Success by
GLADYS FISHER
The Popular "ANY RAGS" Girl
FISHER and CLARK
5
WALTER JACOBS

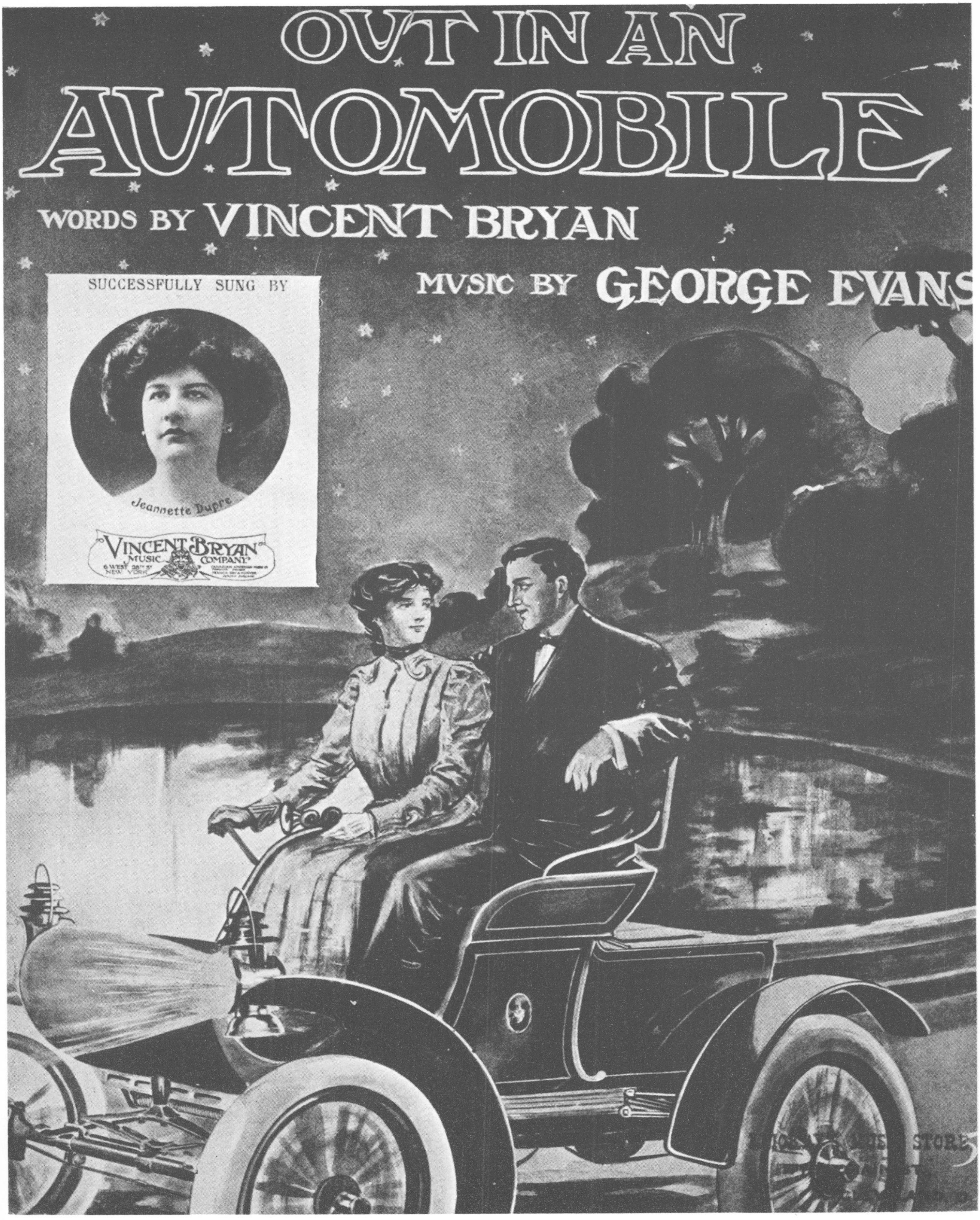
OUT IN AN
AUTOMOBILE
WORDS BY VINCENT BRYAN
MUSIC BY GEORGE EVANS
SUCCESSFULLY SUNG BY
Jeannette Dupre
VINCENT BRYAN MUSIC COMPANY
6 WEST 28TH ST
NEW YORK

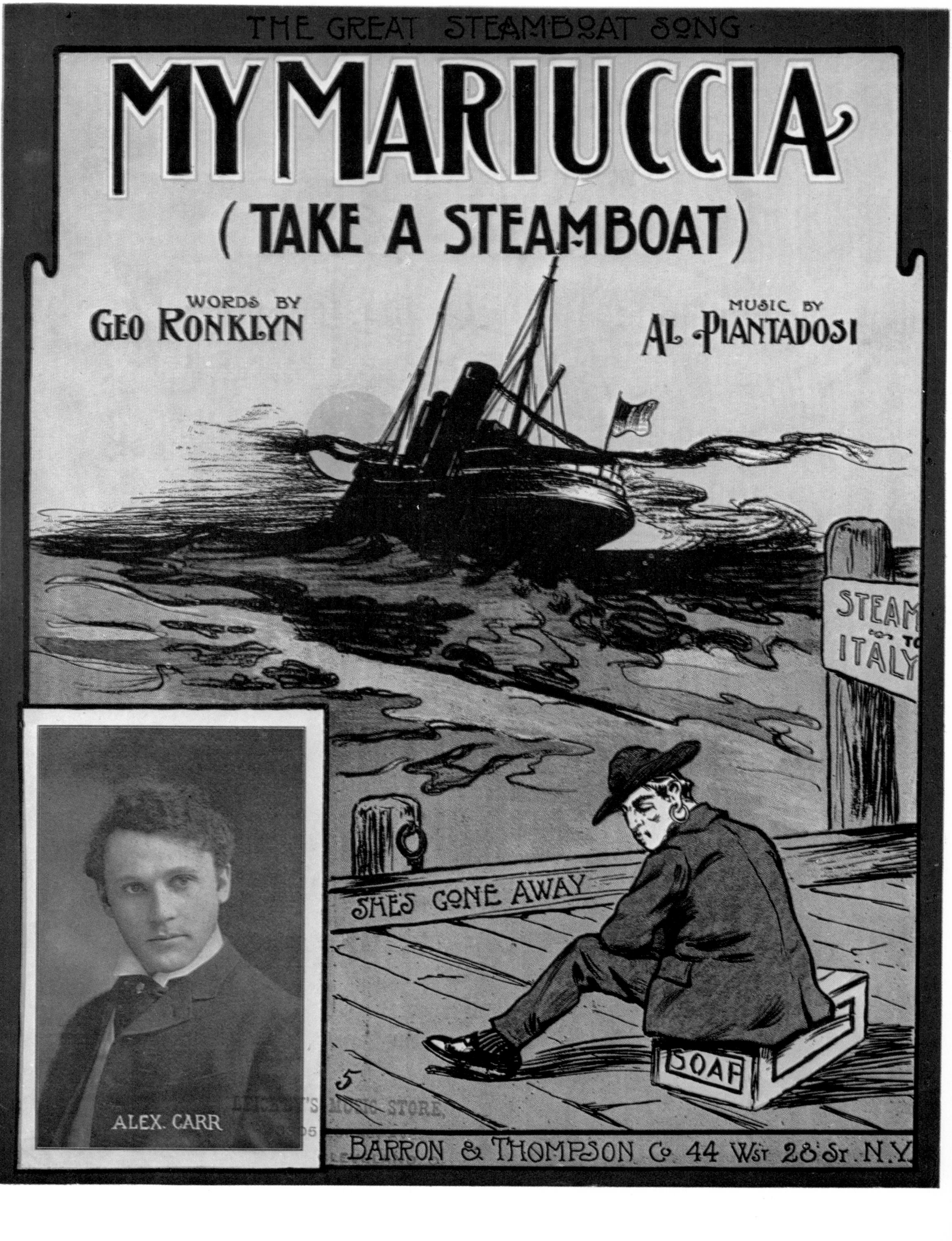
THE GREAT STEAMBOAT SONG
MY MARIUCCIA
(TAKE A STEAMBOAT)
WORDS BY
GEO RONKLYN
MUSIC BY
AL PIANTADOSI
STEAM
TO
ITALY
SHE'S GONE AWAY
SOAP
ALEX. CARR
BARRON & THOMPSON Co 44 W^ST 28TH ST. N.Y.

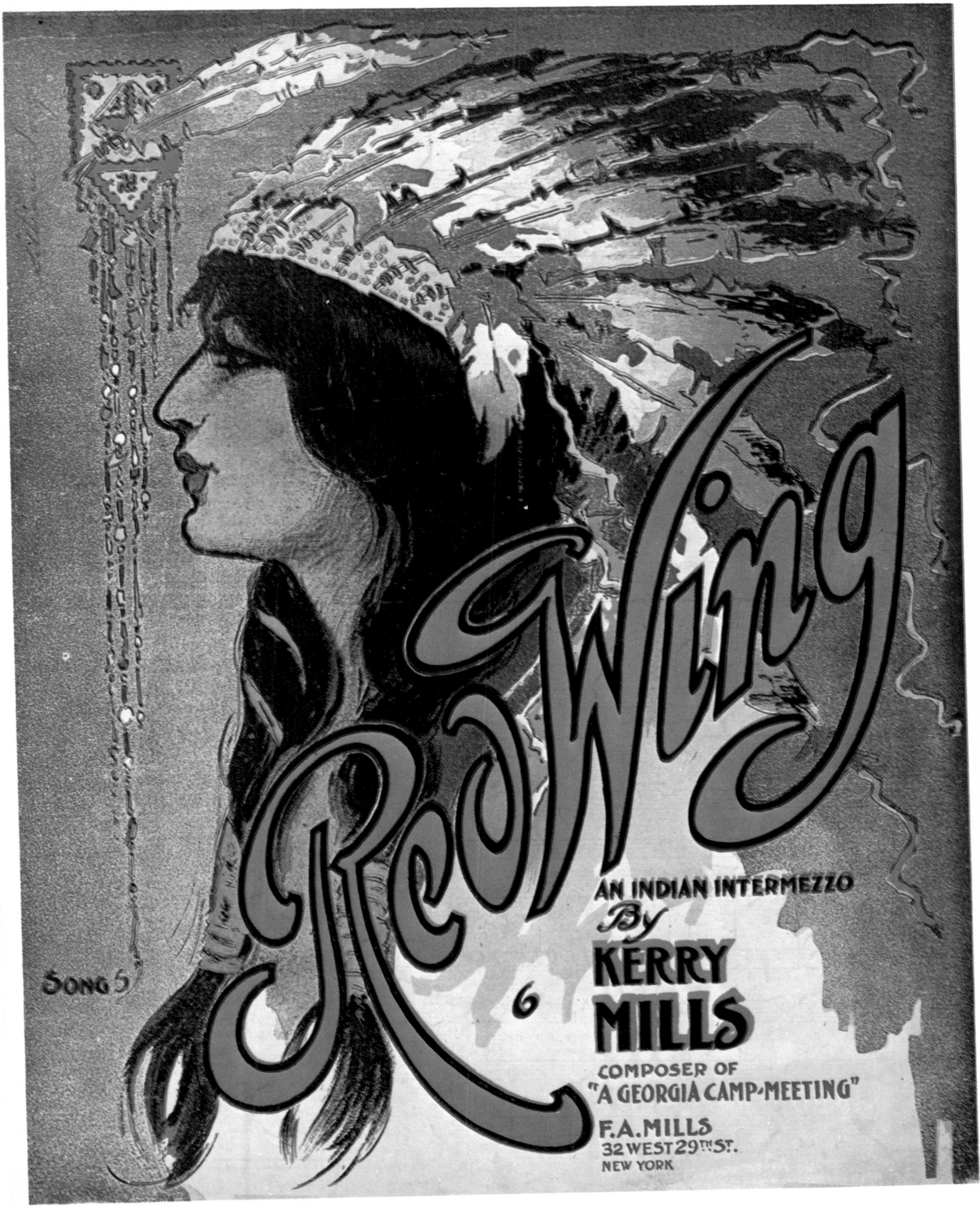
Red Wing
AN INDIAN INTERMEZZO
By
KERRY
MILLS
COMPOSER OF
"A GEORGIA CAMP-MEETING"
F. A. MILLS
32 WEST 29TH ST.
NEW YORK
SONG 5
6

I've Got Your Number
23
WORDS BY
Alfred Bryan
MURRAY WHITEMAN
MUSIC BY
Geo. W. Meyer
5
F. B. HAVILAND PUB. CO.
NEW ZEALAND BUILDING NEW YORK BROADWAY & 37TH ST.

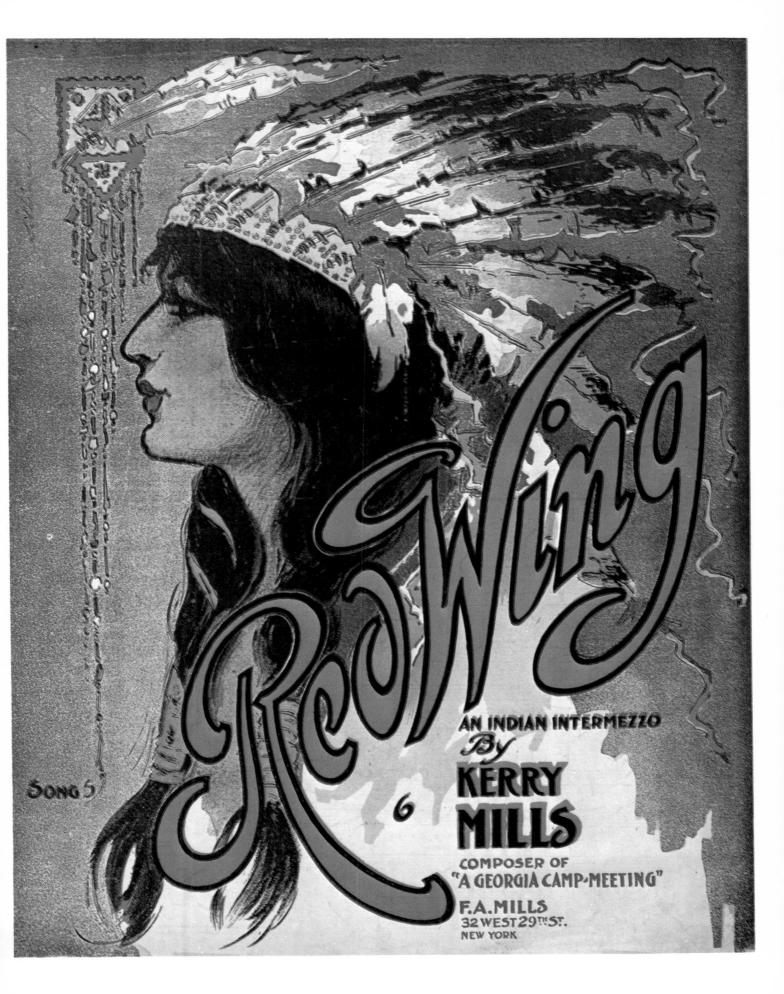

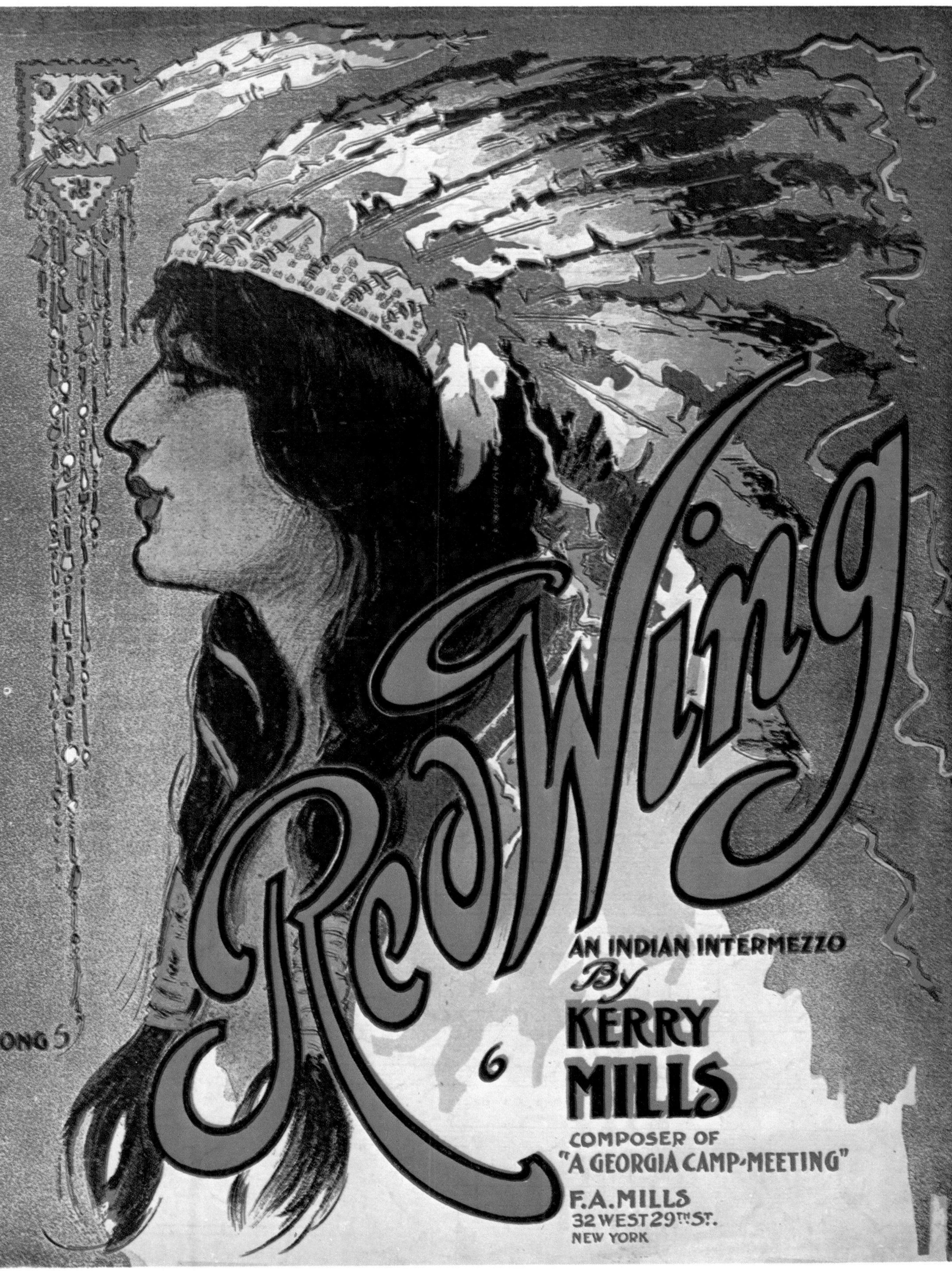
Red Wing
AN INDIAN INTERMEZZO
By
KERRY
MILLS
COMPOSER OF
"A GEORGIA CAMP-MEETING"
F.A. MILLS
32 WEST 29TH ST.
NEW YORK
SONG 5
6

In My Merry Oldsmobile
TIMELY WALTZ SONG
THOS. J. QUIGLEY
Sung with Great Success by
THOS. J. QUIGLEY.
WORDS BY VINCENT BRYAN
MUSIC BY GUS EDWARDS
M. Witmark & Sons.
New York. London. Chicago

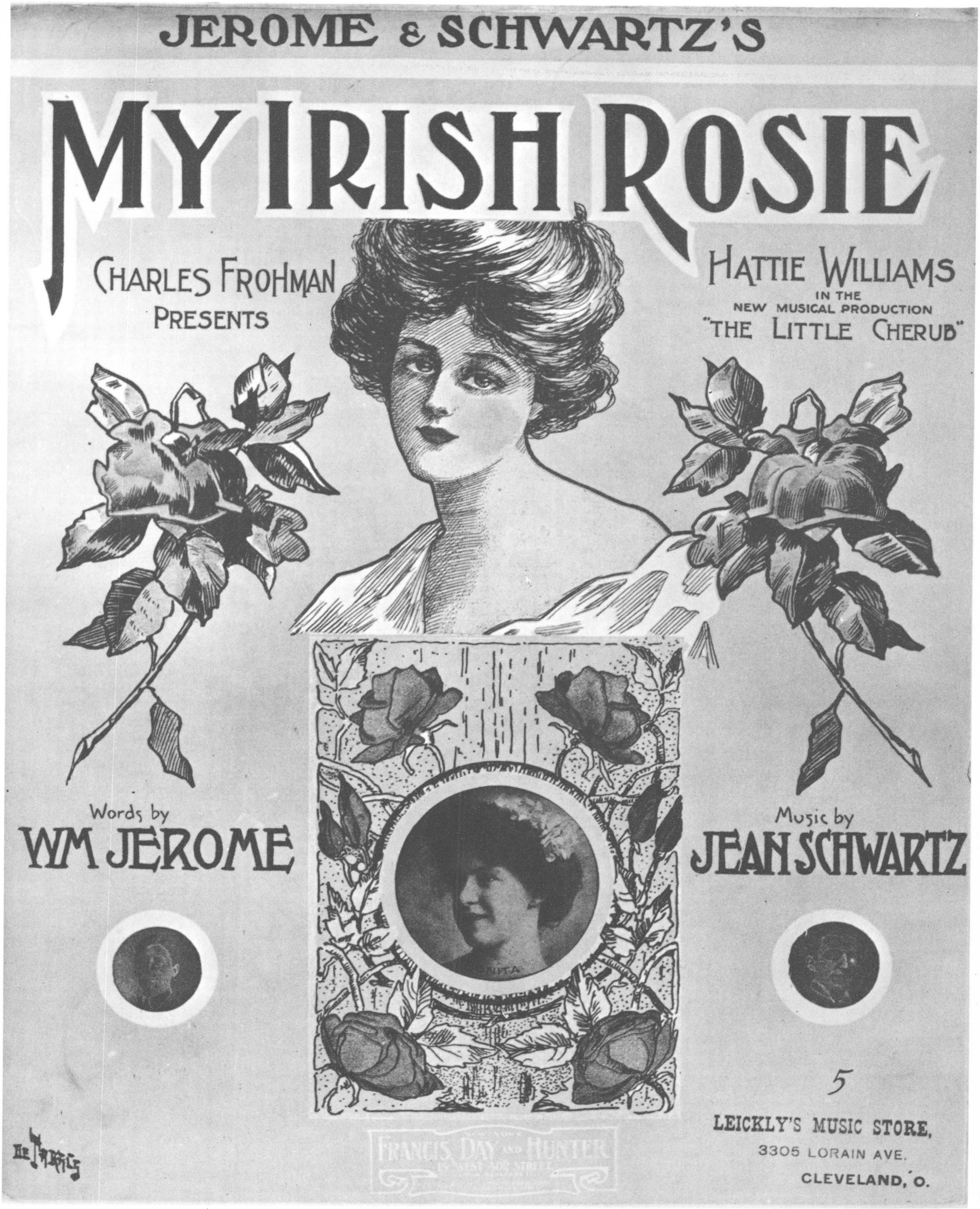
JEROME & SCHWARTZ'S
MY IRISH ROSIE
CHARLES FROHMAN
PRESENTS
HATTIE WILLIAMS
IN THE
NEW MUSICAL PRODUCTION
"THE LITTLE CHERUB"
Words by
WM JEROME
Music by
JEAN SCHWARTZ
5
FRANCIS, DAY AND HUNTER
LEICKLY'S MUSIC STORE,
3305 LORAIN AVE.
CLEVELAND, O.

PLAY THAT BARBER SHOP CHORD

PROMINENTLY FEATURED BY

BERT WILLIAMS

Words by **WM. TRACEY**

Music by **LEWIS F. MUIR**

J. FRED HELF COMPANY
136 WEST 37th ST. N.Y. CITY
Successor to HELF & HAGER COMPANY

Lillian Forg

"LEWIS & BROWN'S HOME RUN HIT."

BASE BALL

WORDS BY

ROGER LEWIS,

MUSIC BY

AL. W. BROWN.

5

PUBLISHED BY
THE THOMPSON MUSIC CO.
CHICAGO, ILLS.

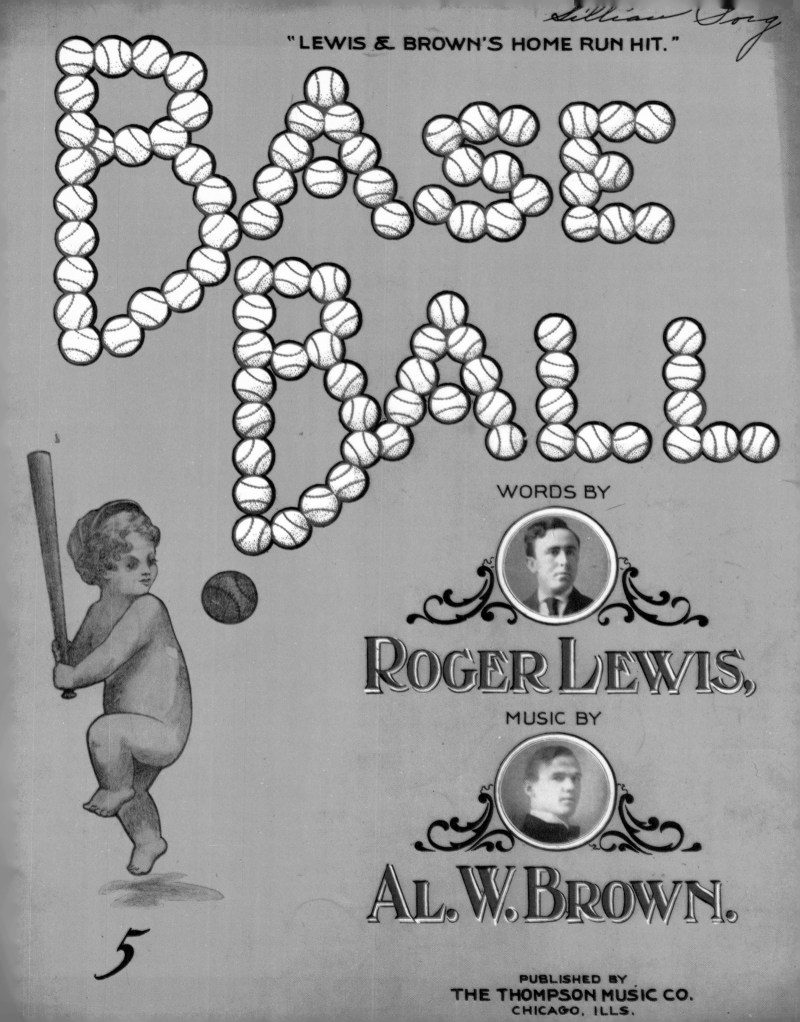

YOU'RE A GRAND OLD RAG
A SONG-HIT FROM THE LATEST MUSICAL PLAY
GEORGE WASHINGTON JR.
WRITTEN AND COMPOSED BY
GEO. M. COHAN
F. A. MILLS
48 WEST 29TH ST
NEW YORK
5

COME JOSEPHINE
IN MY FLYING MACHINE
(UP SHE GOES!)
BLANCHE RING
STARMER
Words by ALFRED BRYAN
Music by FRED FISCHER
Published by "Shapiro" Music Publisher
Cor. Broadway & Thirty Ninth Street, New York.

5

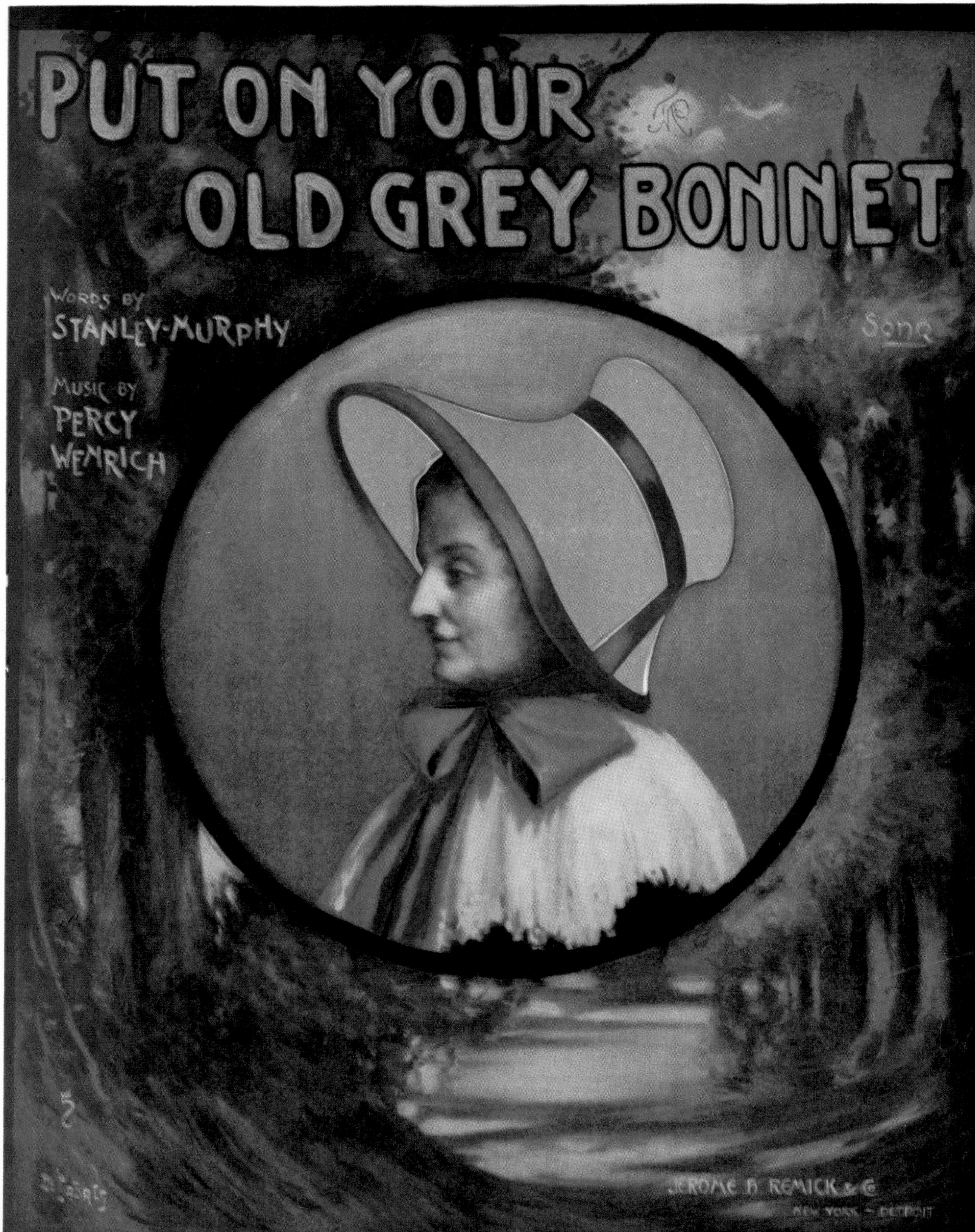
PUT ON YOUR
OLD GREY BONNET
WORDS BY
STANLEY-MURPHY
Song
MUSIC BY
PERCY
WENRICH
JEROME H. REMICK & Co
NEW YORK - DETROIT

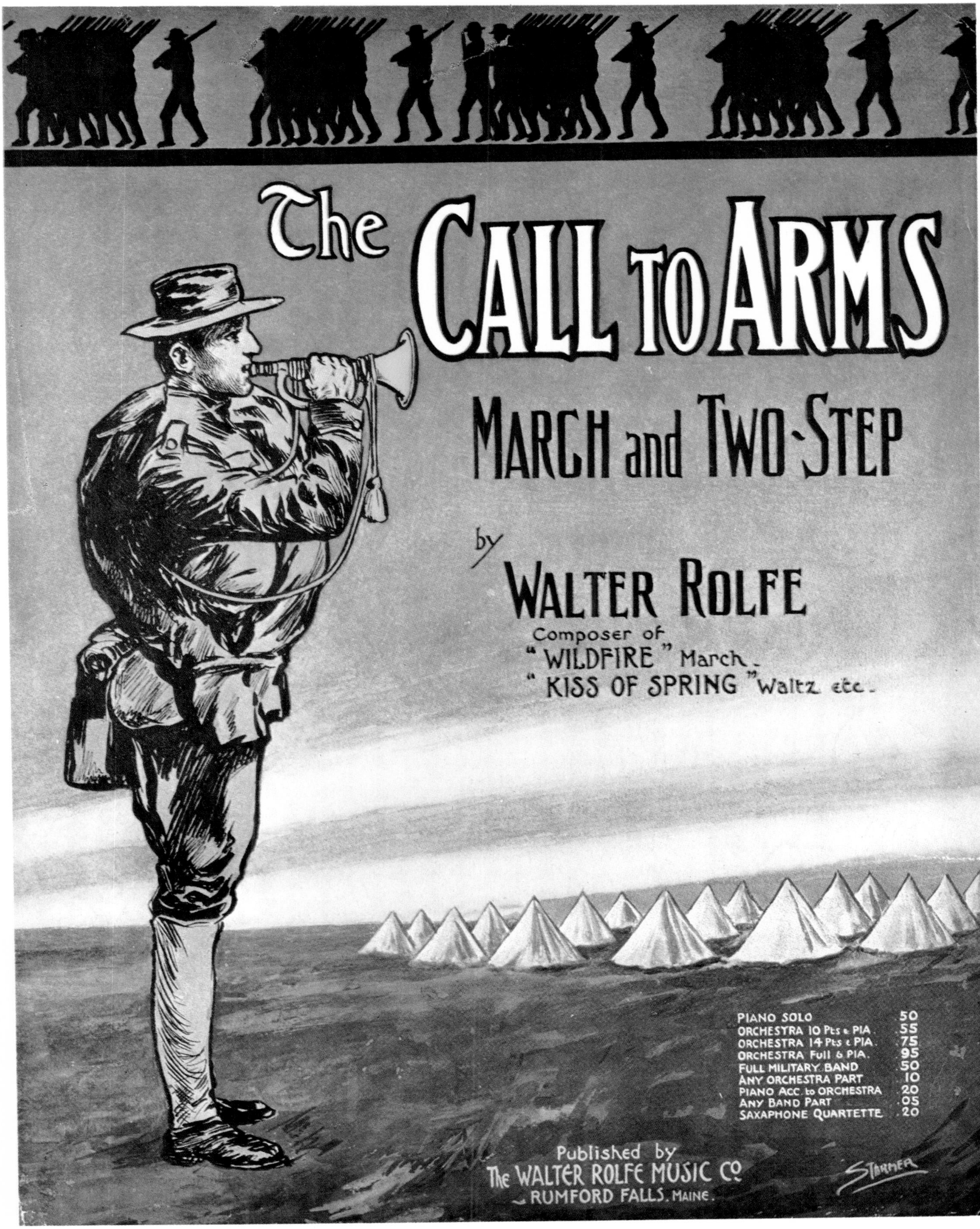
The CALL TO ARMS
MARCH and TWO-STEP
by
WALTER ROLFE
Composer of
"WILDFIRE" March
"KISS OF SPRING" Waltz etc.
PIANO SOLO .50
ORCHESTRA 10 Pts & PIA. .55
ORCHESTRA 14 Pts & PIA. .75
ORCHESTRA Full & PIA. .95
FULL MILITARY BAND .50
ANY ORCHESTRA PART .10
PIANO ACC. to ORCHESTRA .20
ANY BAND PART .05
SAXAPHONE QUARTETTE .20
Published by
The WALTER ROLFE MUSIC Co.
RUMFORD FALLS, MAINE.
STARMER

I've Got
Your
Number
23
WORDS BY
Alfred Bryan
MURRAY WHITEMAN.
MUSIC BY
Geo. W. Meyer
5
E.P.C
F. B. HAVILAND PUB. CO.
NEW ZEALAND BUILDING
NEW YORK
BROADWAY & 37th ST.

I'M A LITTLE BIT AFRAID OF YOU, BROADWAY
L. H. Hooper
Mar 28th '14
NEW YORK
TIMES
INTRODUCED BY
Miss SADIE BURT
OF WHITING AND BURT
IN
"The PASSING SHOW of 1913"
AT THE NEW YORK WINTERGARDEN
WORDS BY
GEORGE WHITING
MUSIC BY
HARRY VON TILZER
HARRY VON TILZER
MUSIC PUBLISHING Co.
5

Beautiful Ohio
Song
by
Mary Earl
Lyric by
Ballard Macdonald
INSTRUMENTAL
PIANO SOLO (Waltz)
FULL ORCHESTRA
MILITARY BAND
VOCAL
SONG (Key E flat)
SONG ORCHESTRATION
MALE QUARTETTE
PRICE SIXTY CENTS
PUBLISHED BY
SHAPIRO, BERNSTEIN & CO. INC
Music Publishers
224 West 47th Street
NEW YORK
THIS NUMBER ON
PHONOGRAPH REC
AND MUSIC ROL

I'M SIMPLY CRAZY OVER YOU
LYRICS BY
WILLIAM
JEROME
and RAY
GOETZ
MUSIC BY
JEAN
SCHWARTZ
AL BARBELLE
PUBLISHED BY
IRVING BERLIN
INC.
No 1571 B'WAY
N.Y.

JUST TRY TO PICTURE ME
BACK HOME IN TENNESSEE
WORDS BY
WM. JEROME
MUSIC BY
WALTER DONALDSON
WATERSON BERLIN & SNYDER CO.
Music Publishers
Strand Theatre Bldg
NEW YORK

OH, JOHNNY! OH, JOHNNY! OH!
Featured By
"NORA BAYES"
in Her Production
"Songs as is
and
Songs as was"
Words By
Ed. Rose
Music By
Abe. Olman
FORSTER MUSIC PUBLISHER INC CHICAGO.

ALICE, WHERE ART THOU GOING
March Song
M. JOHNSON
WORDS BY:
WILL A. HEELAN
MUSIC BY:
ALBERT GUMBLE
Composer of "Jessamine"
5
JEROME H. REMICK & CO.
Successors to
WHITNEY WARNER PUB. CO.
New York – Detroit

GIVE ME THE MOONLIGHT
GIVE ME THE GIRL
AND LEAVE THE REST TO ME
5
LYRIC BY
LEW BROWN
MELODY BY
ALBERT VON TILZER
BROADWAY MUSIC CORPORATION
WILL VON TILZER PRESIDENT
145 WEST 45TH ST NEW YORK

POPULAR EDITION
HOME COMING
WEEK IN FRANCE
Song
Words and Music by
Seneca G. Lewis
5
DETROIT
JEROME H. REMICK & Co.
NEW YORK

FOR IF KISSES ARE INTOXICATING AS THEY SAY
PROHIBITION
YOU HAVE LOST YOUR STING
SUCCESSFULLY SUNG AND INTRODUCED BY
SOPHIE TUCKER AND HER
5
KINGS
OF
SYNCOPATION
Apeda N.Y. 16
Words and Musi
J. RUSSEL ROBINSON
AL SIEGEL
BILLY CURTIS
MEYER COHEN MUSIC PUB. CO. INC
1531 BROADWAY, NEW YORK
DUNK. N.Y.

Are You Sincere?
Song
WORDS BY
ALFRED BRYAN
MUSIC BY
ALBERT GUMBLE
5
JEROME H. REMICK & Co
NEW YORK
DETROIT

Names Make News—and Songs

"The Billiken Man," 1909, is cited primarily as evidence that our popular songs present almost every phase of Americana that, a songwriter thinks, is a popular song subject. Billiken was a grotesque grinning little figure somewhere between man and monkey that leaped into public favor and became such a fad that Billiken statues replaced many of the Speak No Evil, See No Evil, Hear No Evil monkey trios as bric-a-brac in countless homes. Reproduced in three dimensions and for varied uses in publication, the figure became big business, like Davy Crockett and Hula-Hoops in the 1950's. The song was published "by special arrangement with the Billiken Co." E. Ray Goetz, Irving Berlin's brother-in-law, wrote the lyrics of eleven verses, most of them topical, right out of the news of the times. Typically:

Have you seen the smile that Taft's got?
Like the Billiken man
He will be the country's mascot
On the Roosevelt plan
He beat Bryan by a mile
'Cause he wears a sunny smile
(Yes?) Like a Billiken, (Oh!) a Billiken man.

Roosevelt was former President "Teddy" who supported Taft as his successor. Teddy was the subject of another song that same year, "Moving Day in Jungle Town." It referred to his African hunting trip. On the cover the animals are pictured running in all directions because "Here comes Teddy with his gun, gun, gun." A year later, 1910, "When Teddy Comes Marching Home" heralded his return.

Nestling alongside Billiken in the file is "Billy Boy," another 1909 song, subtitled "The Kidnapped Child." His picture is on the cover. "This is an exact photo of Billy Whitla just as he was when taken from school" in Sharon, Pennsylvania. Until that time, the Whitla kidnapping was the most highly publicized case in American history. The song's cover includes a reward offer of $1,000 from the Scripps-McCrea newspapers. In the chorus, the line "I want my dear daddy to hear me when I kneel down to pray" sets the tone of the words and music throughout. National suspense, the few sales of "Billy Boy," and the enormous newspaper coverage ended when he was released, unharmed, in Cleveland. News can make song subjects.

Now to William Jennings Bryan, three-time candidate for President. At Dayton, Tennessee, on July 24, 1925, John T. Scopes was found guilty of teaching Darwin's theory of evolution in a Tennessee school, contrary to state law. Bryan came out of semi-retirement to aid the prosecution. Clarence Darrow, famous criminal lawyer of that era, was chief counsel for Scopes. Two days after the widely publicized "monkey trial," Bryan died in Dayton. Not long after, a country music old-style (hillbilly) ballad recorded Bryan's part in the trial. This is as I remember it:

Listen now, all you good people
And a story I will tell
About a man named Mr. Bryan
A man that we all loved so well
He believed the Bible's teaching
And he fought for what was right
He was firm in his convictions
And for them he'd always fight.
Now he's gone 'way up to heaven
Where he'll find an open door
But the lessons that he taught us
They will live for evermore.
When the good folks had their troubles
Down in Dayton far away
Mr. Bryan went to help them
And he worked both night and day
There he fought for what was righteous
Till the vict'ry it was won
Then the Lord called him to heaven
For his work on earth was done.
If you want to go to heaven
When your work on earth is through
You must believe with Mr. Bryan
You will fail unless you do.

For a fundamentalist, there doesn't seem to be a halfway ground. Since then, it is rumored that there have been several failures.

Earlier, Jerome and Schwartz were mentioned as songwriters unusually alert to names, incidents, and references in the news ("Oh, You Spearmint Kiddo with the Wrigley Eyes"). They're about to be cited again for a 1911 song that utilized even more names than "Dearie," years later. Its title is the clue—"They're All Good American Names." These lines from the second of three verses lead into the name-calling chorus:

There's not a game like baseball, it's the best of all our games
The players are Americans, with good old Yankee names

CHORUS:

Jennings and McGann, Doyle and Callahan
Hanlon, Scanlon, Kirk and Donlin, Devlin, Keeler, Walsh
and Conlin
Joe McGinnity, Shea and Finnerty
Farrel, Carroll, Darrell and McAmes
Connie Mack and John McGraw, all together shout Hurrah!
They're all good American names.

Perhaps that should have been in the section of songs about the Irish.

In 1902 the J. & S. writing team had turned out a national song hit based upon the syndicated newspaper column "Mr. Dooley" written by Finley P. Dunne, whose delight was to deflate the pretentious, particularly the politicians. Dunne used the character Mr. Dooley as the commentator to his bartender friend, Hennessey, about the national scene, much as Gleason and others have done on television. Quite naturally a song about Mr. Dooley was in character in terms of names. For example:

New Wireless Telegraphy is cutting quite a dash
And messages across the sea are sent now like a flash
With all the great inventors it has made an awful hit
And but few of them acknowledge that the man invented it
Was Mr. Dooley, Mr. Dooley
To Edison he taught a thing or two
And young Marconi eats macaroni
Along with Mr. Dooley-ooley-ooley-oo.

Young Marconi's wireless telegraphy had sent the first message overseas in 1901. Other references in the dozen verses, each with a topical chorus, were to saloon-smashing Carrie Nation, George Washington and the cherry tree, "Bill the Kaiser" (Germany), Ward McAllister, the socialite "who led the merry pace" of New York's 400, and, among others, to Chauncey Depew, the most famous public speaker of his times, known particularly for his wit:

It's Mr. Dooley, Mr. Dooley
Who writes the jokes for Chauncey M. Depew
It seems that Chauncey took quite a fauncy [*sic*]
To jokes of Mr. Dooley-ooley-ooley-oo.

Ever alert to the news, Jerome and Schwartz wrote "Mr. Lawson the Man from Boston" in 1905 as financier Thomas W. Lawson's exposé of the methods employed by Big Business shocked the readers of *McClure's Magazine*. Reference in the song to the man who'd "made a lot with gas/But hasn't indigestion or a private Bible class" brought John D. Rockefeller into it. His crackers-and-milk diet had been widely publicized along with his Bible class and the dimes he doled out.

We hark back to the era of the "Mikado's" battle hymn that was mentioned in connection with Japan's and Russia's "quarrel." Moderns who heard "What's the Use of Dreaming" in the movie *I Wonder Who's Kissing Her Now,* based upon the life of Joseph E. Howard, could have been mystified by the lines as sung originally in the Opium Den Scene of the District Leader.

Then I heard the Czar of all Russia say
"You can have every ship and boat
That the Japs destroyed in the last affray
Only you must make them float."

That referred to the sinking of the Russian fleet in the Russo-Japanese War when overpowered by the superiority of the Japanese under Admiral Togo. President Theodore Roosevelt induced the combatants to sign a peace treaty in 1905 at Portsmouth, New Hampshire. Another verse recalls other pages in world history:

And then I can hear complacently
*The Sultan of Turkey * say to me*
"My boy, I'm getting old, that's true
So I'll give my wives to you"
But what's the use of dreaming.

Coming closer to home, the singer under a ghastly green spotlight in the opium den was "dreaming that Andrew Carnegie, Morgan and Rogers and John D. got tired of being rich, you see, so they gave their wealth to me." The music is identical with "Blow the Smoke Away" in *The Time, the Place and the Girl,* 1906. Howard said that they needed another number for the District Leader, so the lyricist wrote new words to fit the scene that was a forerunner of LSD pads.

In 1925, "The Wreck of the Shenandoah" recorded the early morning crash near Cambridge, Ohio, and the subsequent world news of the loss of another lighter-than-air dirigible balloon. That same year, Floyd Collins' entrapment in Sand Cave (Kentucky) drew news media of all sorts to that rural area. His death after strenuous efforts to free him is on the song record as "The Death of Floyd Collins." The composer forgot to give credit to the ancient "Little Old Sod Shanty on the Plains" for much of the melody.

Of course, our musical Americana includes the names of all sorts of famous places that have been in the news perennially or temporarily because of some incident. In the early 1900's few outlanders made a trip to New York without a visit to Coney Island's amusements ("Goodbye, My Coney Island Baby") and the famous Bowery, symbol of adventure in a strange polyglot world where "anything goes" seemed to be the slogan and practice. Here's a quick glimpse of what could happen to an innocent, as sung in Charles H. Hoyt's "Trip to Chinatown," 1892. "On the night when I struck New York I went out for a quiet walk." He'd been advised to stay on Broadway, but he chose the Bowery.

I went into an auction store
I never saw any thieves before
First he sold me a pair of sox
Then he said "how much for a box?"

* Abdul-Hamid II (1842–1918) credited with having several hundred wives in his harem. Commonly called the Sick Man of Europe.

Someone said "two dollars" I said "three"
He emptied the box and gave it to me
I sold you the box, not the socks, said he
I'll never go there any more . . .
[Oh] the Bowery, the Bowery
They say such things and they do strange things
On the Bowery, the Bowery
I'll never go there any more.

The tough characteristics of the Bowery were in Richard Outcault's cartooning the "The Yellow Kid," among the earliest if not the first cartoon color strip syndicated to the nation's newspapers. He was an illiterate little guy in contrast with modern delinquents who burn down the home because Dad made them drive to the prom in the Plymouth instead of the Cadillac. His dialect lives in an 1897 song: "Just watch dis kid from Hogan's alley/Dis tune's de stuff for me, you bet . . . I'm de Yellow Kid, don't you forget."

In another field of published art, magazine illustrations, the names of Flagg, Christy, Leyendecker, Rockwell, Neysa McMein, John Held, Jr., Petty, and Charles Dana Gibson are among others that are associated with individualistic styles. Gibson's subjects were the antithesis of the "Kid." They gave the impression that his contacts were exclusively with society's patrician 400, symbol of the haute monde attainable only through great wealth, however gathered. His black-and-white illustrations were usually of haughty young socialites recognized nationally as "Gibson Girls." The "song hit of Ziegfeld's Follies of 1907," it says on the cover, was "The Gibson Bathing Girl." These lines from it record the beginnings of a trend that brings toplessness into the news.

We have shown you the charms of our shoulders and arm
And we really don't think you can blame us
But we hated to hide other beauties beside
And we fumed at the artists' omission
So one day we arose in revolt at long clothes.

The name of dainty demure "Mary Pickford—The Darling of Them All," 1914, might well have been included with "Poor Pauline" among the old-time singing commercials. That and "Little Mary Pickford" stressed her winsomeness in juvenile parts. "Mickey," "Respectfully Dedicated to Miss Mabel Normand," grew like a flower of the mountains, according to the chorus, into the impish character recalled by those who remember Mack Sennett comedies. Neil Moret (Charles N. Daniels) wrote the music. More frequently, his name recalls "Hiawatha," "Silver Heels" (another sprightly song about an Indian maiden in the long succession of them), "You Tell Me Your Dream" ("I Had a Dream, Dear"), "On Mobile Bay," and "Moonlight and Roses." Many other names of stage and screen appear in song titles or in the lyrics, as "When Chauncey Olcott Sings."

Noticeably during World War I, many songs were name-droppers—"We're Going to Hang the Kaiser Under the Linden Tree" (Unter den Linden was the most famous avenue in Berlin) and "Just Like Washington Crossed the Delaware, General Pershing Will Cross the Rhine." Like other name songs and the songs about incidents or attitudes, fads, styles, and more, the war songs about a specific person lost their appeal when the war was no longer page-one news. The war with Spain of 1898 was won by a knockout in the second round. In the first one, Commodore George Dewey attacked the Spanish fleet in Manila harbor and sank it "before breakfast," as reported. Naturally, Dewey stepped into the national spotlight. The chorus of "What Did Dewey Do to Them?" is enough. It is among the better ones about the commodore who soon was an admiral.

What did Dewey do to them
What did Dewey do?
He did them up so thoroughly
He only left a few
It wasn't to the Queen's taste
That's a pun and very true
He didn't do a thing to them
What didn't Dewey do?

The adage, as dead as yesterday's newspaper, applies to practically all songs that hung on a news peg.

Let's Go

When I was a very small child, "The horse knows the way to carry the sleigh through the white and drifted snow-ow" flashed into my young mind a weird vision of a horse walking on its hind legs through snowdrifts while it cradled a sleigh with me in it, as tenderly as Eliza carrying her baby through the white and drifting ice illustrated in a dog-eared copy of *Uncle Tom's Cabin*. Much later, I learned first-hand that "carry" could also mean "pull" in a section where a rural school bus was a "barge." That horse exemplifies a primitive means of transportation recorded in our songs of succeeding eras.

Mankind has always wanted to go places. In consequence, songwriters have written into the record of Americana all sorts of transport methods from canoes to helicopters. In 1945 Buffalo's Grosvenor Library, now the Buffalo and Erie County (New York) Public Library, compiled under the direction of Margaret (McNamara) Mott a bibliography of its songs about transportation. The foreword expanded the thoughts that have been expressed here in several ways, that our popular songs record incidents and our mass interests and attitudes. "All who are familiar with our popular songs," Mrs. Mott wrote, "know that the moment an event of local or national significance occurs, some person is on hand to describe it in a song. Often the connection between the event and the lyrics is tenuous. Sometimes it is found in the title alone."

By now, it must be apparent here also that a flavorful bit of Americana may appear in a song where least expected if it is appraised only by the title. As yet, no songs about space capsules or moon rockets have become popular, but, with so many sights pointed skyward, it's possible that "My Sweetheart's the Man in the Moon" may be updated to a man *on* the moon. A criterion, "Come Take a Trip in My Airship," was published in 1904:

Come, take a trip in my airship
Come, take a sail 'mong the stars
Come, have a ride around Venus
Come, have a spin around Mars

No one to watch while we're kissing
No one to see while we spoon
Come, take a trip in my airship
And we'll visit the man in the moon.

However, such speculations deal with airborne futures. Let's return to the actualities of canoes. In 1870 "Paddle Your Own Canoe" expressed the philosophy of personal responsibility and became a catch phrase for independence. It was comparable with the pioneers' axiom "Let every tub stand on its own bottom." Both reveal the archaic thinking of an era which hadn't learned that a bureau's directive, in triplicate, properly channeled, must finalize procedures identified with areas of ideology, activating and tending to condition the mass mind.

"In My Tippy Canoe" must have been used in the 1840 presidential campaign of Harrison when his nickname, based upon his record in the Indian wars, headed the slogan "Tippecanoe and Tyler Too." Much later, "Paddlin' Madeline Home" had zip as well as alliteration. Irving Caesar wrote "In a Little Canoe." A safe rule for handling canoes and other small craft, "Sit Down, You're Rocking the Boat" is firmly embedded in our language.

In this category of small boats, exemplified by "Row, Row, Row," "The Gondolier" was on most parlor organs about 1905. It remained popular until the piano makers induced trade-ins comparable with later-day sales of television sets when some conservatives bought only because they were tired of explaining the absence of video in the home. The Grosvenor booklet lists "the only song about a rowing machine" as "Floating Down a Moonlight Stream," whose 1918 music was by none other than young Sigmund Romberg.

"Low Bridge! Everybody Down or Fifteen Years on the Erie Canal" is the best-known song about canal travel. Its command to duck or bend down brought "low bridge" into common use. Frank M. Warner of Old Brookville, New York, a pioneer searcher for authentic American folk songs and a delightfully robust singer of them, includes in his repertoire a song that preserves techniques of the early 1800's when hay-burner power on the towpath pulled barges on the canal:

Haul in your tow lines and take in your slack
Take a reef in your britches and straighten your back
Mind what I tell you and don't you forget
To tap the mules gently when the cook's on the deck.

Later in the 1800's, steam-propelled ferryboats attracted the attention of songwriters as a "Twickenham Ferry—It's only a penny to Twickenham Town." Songs about ferries continued into the 1930's and 1940's with songs such as "The Man on the Ferry," which plied between Hoboken and Manhattan.

Of course, songs about sailing vessels are as old as song literature. Tennyson's "Crossing the Bar" lives in several musical settings, as well as in spoken verse used often at memorial services. Today's dyed-in-the-rag sailors know that the ancient "Wet Sheet and a Flowing Sea" has no reference to washday. "White Wings—they never grow weary" of 1884 sings as smoothly as the sailing yacht glides on its cover. Songs about sail include the rollicking 1919 opus in broken

Italian-American about "Christo Colombo" who, traditionally, sailed the first ships to our shores:

He go to Frisco
Drinks forty quarts of whisko
Eat too much Uneeda Bisco
Get-a-sick-a in the bell'
Make a bigga funeral
[*always sung funer-el, of course*].

A list of songs about sailing ships would be comparable in size with the roster of "The Queen's Navee," heard perennially in repetitions of Gilbert and Sullivan's *Pinafore*.

As surely as steam succeeded sail, the songs followed that development. "My Mariuccia Take a Steamboat" was in the spirit of "Christo." "Sailing on a Steamer to Kahula" and "On a Slow Boat to China" exemplify scores of them that steamed into popularity. Some chronicled specific ships and events. "Lost on the *Lady Elgin*" records the sinking of a Great Lakes passenger steamer. We've already mentioned the song that told about the *Lusitania*'s tragic end. The world's largest steamship until the 1920's was the subject of "The Big Ship *Leviathan*." "Bobbin' Up and Down" is reminiscent of the earlier "Oceana Roll" in which stools and chairs waltzed in the cabin as they sang "I Don't Care," a reference to an older song made famous by Eva Tanguay.

Coastal travel left its mark in "Sailing Down the Chesapeake Bay," "On Mobile Bay," and "On the Old Excursion Boat" as examples. "On the Old Fall River Line" sings of transportation no longer available between Boston and New York. The series of riverboat songs is enormous. The most famous race on the Mississippi is memorialized in "The *Natchez* and the *Robert E. Lee*." The floating counterpart of 1909's "Casey Jones" and his famous railroad wreck is "Steamboat Bill" (1910). It is only one of the many examples of copycatting by songwriters when a song in certain theme makes a national hit, though in this case "Bill" is as good a song as "Casey." "Tugboat Joe" of 1913 couldn't get away from the wharf.

When we step ashore to inspect the songs about land transportation, the procession in merely horse-drawn or horseback themes stretch beyond the horizon. As to dates, "Wait for the Wagon—and we'll all take a ride" of 1851 is well up front. "Put on Your Old Gray Bonnet—while I hitch old Dobbin to the shay" of 1909 is still heard when young or old sing just for fun. Later, "Thanks for the Buggy Ride" and "The Surrey with the Fringe on Top" became allusions beyond the songs. "Wagon Wheels" features a mule for variety. "Shabby Old Cabby" was on every radio only a few years ago. Many of the songs of the "rube" persuasion included equine items natural to rural living. Of these, I believe I like best the verse in "Ebenezer Frye" (1907) where:

I drove the old mare over to the County Fair
Took first prize on a load of summer squash
Stopped at the cider mill coming over by the hill
Come home tighter than a drum, by gosh!
I was so durn full I give away the old bull

Dropped both reins right out on the thill
Got hum so darn late couldn't find the barn gate
Ma says "Joshua, 'taint possibil"
Wal, I swan! I mus' be gittin' on
Giddap, Napoleon! It looks like rain
Wal, I'll be switched! The hay ain't pitched
Come in when you're over to the farm again."

[A variant on the next-to-last line: "Wal, I'll be durned! The butter ain't churned."]

In different vein, many of the songs in western themes took the riding horse for granted as the only means of going places, "Cheyenne [Shy Ann] . . . on my pony from old Cheyenne" as example. In "San Antonio" she hopped on a pony and rode away with Tony. "Rag Time Cowboy Joe," "Pride of the Prairie," "Riding down the Canyon," "Home on the Range," and others of that school seem to have been written from cow saddles. By inference, the horse is present in great numbers of western folk songs, such as "Git Along, Little Dogeys." There is no question about the theme in "Horses, Horses, Horses" of 1926.

Two pithy maxims that were common before the auto ousted the horse exemplify others that fell into disuse when the nation was unhorsed. To a generation reared with horseless carriages the equine origins need explanation.

"A short horse is soon curried" is not a culinary reference as in curried shrimp, but a curry comb is involved. It was a flat comb with several rows of stubby metal teeth. The shorter the horse, the less currying to do. So the maxim applied to any small task.

"Don't look a gift horse in the mouth" refers to a horse's teeth, which, like humans', wear shorter with age. A horse trader didn't refer to a serial number on the chassis. He looked a horse in the mouth to estimate its age and worth. Applied to any gift, the maxim warned against too critical appraisal.

Songwriters alert to new material could hardly overlook the bicycle. In the 1890's adult Americans pedaled in millions while athletic youths pumped away on transcontinental relays, over rutted dirt roads, with official messages from the mayor of one city to another, to prove the speed and reliability of the new "safety" bikes. They had replaced the solid-tire high-wheeler which spilled its rider headfirst at every, or no, opportunity. Practically all adults recognize "Daisy Bell—on a bicycle built for two." But before "Daisy" and the tandem, the high-wheel boys had a song "The Bicycle Glide—respectfully dedicated to the Philadelphia Bicycle Club." Even before that, *three* wheels had invaded the horse's domain. A ride on "The Flying Velocipede" must have been hair-raising as it peeled rubber at four miles an hour, on the level.

The Rambler was one of the early "safety" bikes, chain-driven. It and other speedsters were cause for legislation to control "scorching" (hot-rodding) after bicycles had wheeled into popular songs about them. Then came gasoline power which pushed horses, the two-wheelers, and their songs onto detours. Most of them were lost there permanently. Showing again how songs follow fads and trends, of twenty-seven songs about bicycles listed in the Grosvenor bibliography, twenty-two were published in the 1890's, the early period of bicycle ascendancy when "Mulrooney on a Bike" reflected current news and interest. "Courting on a Wheel" referred to techniques unknown to rumble seaters and today's drivers of convertibles. "Bang Bang Went the Rubber Tire" in 1897, when a blowout to the mile was not unusual. "My Bicycle Girl" by Oscar Hammerstein II arrived belatedly in 1940, and the two-wheelers rolled a bit farther that year with "Rolleo Rolling Along."

True to song-writing traditions, the advent of steam engines on tracks produced a national eruption of songs about trains. Locomotives need stop only long enough to be watered and fed. An engine didn't stop to catch its breath after pulling up a hill, and it didn't require rest at night. One speeding railroad car could carry as much as a caravan of wagons bumping over dirt roads at three miles an hour. In consequence, bards everywhere dipped their pens.

A George F. Root song of 1874 is evidence that railroads were not accepted nationally as an unmixed blessing. In "What's the Matter, Jamus?":

I'll tell you what's the matter,
Now listen Susie dear,
Another railroad's coming,
They say sometime this year.
From God knows where to whither,
But coming right this way,
And we're taxed all together,
Yes, taxed to make it pay.

Our farm is crossed with railroads,
Where busy engines fume,
And looks like your checked apron,
To the man up in the moon.
For a mess of potash, Susie,
We've sold the right of way,
For the nearest stopping station,
Is sixteen miles away.

Written a bit earlier, "Isn't It Exciting This Riding on the Rail?" still applies when vast numbers of well-traveled young people have never looked from a train's windows. "The Fast Line Galop" published in 1853 was respectfully dedicated to the "President and Directors of the Great Pennsylvania Central." In the 1870's "The Charming Young Widow—I met on the train" left the car with the narrator's watch and chain.

Acquisition instead of loss was the theme "On the Eastern Train." A "lovely maiden, bewitching and petite" sat beside a student. They chatted until a cinder blew into his eye. While she tried to remove it, the train swooped into a black tunnel. Back in the daylight, "Maiden is all blushes/ See what has appeared/Tiny little ear-ring/In the student's beard." The setting places the song as pre-Gillette. Today, beards and earrings are back, but the gathering of earrings and lipstick tracings relates to motorcars.

"In the Baggage Coach Ahead" typifies the conventional sad ballad of the 1890's and early 1900's. The verse introduced a young husband trying to quiet a crying baby. A passenger complained:

While the train rolled onward a husband sat in tears
Thinking of the happiness of just a few short years
For baby's face brings pictures of a cherished hope that's dead
But baby's cries can't waken her in the baggage coach ahead.

My copy shows on the cover "The Empire State Express—Fastest Train in the World," three passenger cars trailing behind the baggage coach and the smoke-belching choochoo. (Browsers among stacks of old sheet music in search of typical weepers pickled in pity will do well to look for titles by Gussie L. Davis, composer of the baggage coach song, Monroe H. Rosenfeld, Charles K. Harris, and Paul Dresser, all of whom plumbed the depths of sorrow, though not invariably or more thoroughly than several others, including S. B. Gray.) In "Please, Mr. Conductor, Don't Put Me Off the Train" a boy had boarded it without a ticket, taking the chance that he might get through to his mother "lieing so ill in pain."

In quite different motif, one of the last songs of the nineties about rail travel was the gay "I Want to Go to Morrow." Confusion reigned at the ticket window when a traveler said "I want to go to Morrow and I want to go today," to which the seller replied, "How can you go to Morrow when the train's a mile away?" Their misunderstanding was comparable to the impasse in "Two to Duluth":

"Two to Duluth" said the lady to the youth
Who was selling tickets for the train
"Tum-tiddle-tum" he replied, and then was mum
For he thought that she had water on the brain.

In 1911 water on the brain was the slang equivalent of today's hole in the head.

No one will question "I've Been Working on the Railroad" as the best-known rails song, with "Casey Jones" as runner-up. In the chapter about folk songs reference is made to "Casey" and the possibility that "Ingineer Joe," whose melody is published here for the first time, may have contributed to "Casey" lyrics, though the melodies of the two touch each other only in spots. Origins of true folk songs are always cloudy.

Selected from the many, folk and popular, here are a few more that record varying phases of travel by rail.

The Atchison, Topeka and the Sante Fe
Dapper Dan (the railroad man)
Down on the Lehigh Valley
Engineer's Child (The)
Fare Thee Well, Annabelle
Gandy Dancers' Ball
I'm Going Back to Caroline
I've Said My Last Farewell
(too toot, Goodbye)
On the Monon Line
On the N.Y., N.H. and Hartford
Pullman Porters on Parade
Put Me Off at Buffalo
Railroad Jack
Rocky Mountain Express
She's the Lily of the Lehigh Valley
Shuffle Off to Buffalo
So Long, Mary
Steaming Back to Dixieland
Sunset Limited
Toot Toot Tootsie (goodbye)
Wabash Cannon Ball
Western Flyer (The)
When the Midnight Choo Choo
Leaves for Alabam
Wreck of the Old '97 (The)

In the early 1900's novelties in transportation were in the making. Songwriters who were tuned to their times welcomed the electric cars, urban and interurban, that were replacing horsecars and also beginning to reach into areas untouched by the steam trains. Securities of the traction lines were believed by many to be among the safest investments for widows and orphans. "Look! We'll have a million more people in the state by 1915 and they'll need public transportation." Issues were floated in hamlets where one horsecar had easily handled all traffic between the depot and standpipe (water tower park), through the Square, of course.

Mark Twain was responsible for a city trolley car jingle with a fiendishly haunting line taken from "Punch in the presence of the passenger" as printed on the varicolored fare and transfer slips. It appeared originally in the *Atlantic Monthly*. Here is the first verse as reproduced in the music set to his poem:

Conductor, when you receive a fare
Punch in the presence of the passenjare
A blue trip slip for an eight-cent fare
A buff trip slip for a six-cent fare
A pink trip slip for a three-cent fare
Punch in the presence of the passenjare.

Other memories of streetcar riding are preserved in "The Last Three Seats for Smokers," "Waiting for the Street Car," "Ring the Bell and Let the Car Go On," and "You'll Have to Transfer." On the old Edison recording "Take a Car—it beats all your horses and automobiles" was paired with "On a Sunday Afternoon" and its invitation to take a trolley to Rockaway. Because our songs record almost everything in American life, "The Elevated Railroad" song accompanied technological developments that put mass transportation into the air. Its opposite was "Down in a Subway" by Jerome and Schwartz, the song-writing team whose ears were open perennially for news or names that could be converted into a song. A more recent one caught the atmosphere of the subway's molelike transportation in "Onions, Garlic and Fish."

When the electrics could no longer hold out against gasoline motors, the automobile put city trolley and interurban cars out of business, a repetition of the duel between riverboats and steam locomotives running along the rivers. In today's evolutionary phase the choochoo has, in turn, lost to the chugging diesel. The new autos provided personalized transportation at breathtaking speeds as high as 22.5 m.p.h. The sentimental streak in most songwriters showed in "Love in an Automobile." It was followed soon by "My Auto Lady" and "My Auto Girl." The natural corollary was "On an Automobile Honeymoon" and "Take Me on a Buick Honeymoon."

The vicissitudes of early motoring show in songs such as "Gasoline—Put it in a little tank/Then you swiftly turn the crank" and in "He'd Have to Get Under—and crank up his automobile." Many a broken arm testified to the auto's crankiness before the battery-operated starter. "It gets you there and it gets you(r) back" was a national quip about the most popular car. Nonetheless, "The Little Old Ford It Rambled Right Along." Engine speed determined the effectiveness of Model T's headlights. Creeping through a fog, they glowed with the brilliance of kitchen matches. But the car had hosts of loyal owners to whom it was, affectionately, the flivver or the Tin Lizzie. When Model A arrived with a gearshift, foot accelerator, 'n' everything, a popular song proclaimed, "Henry's Made a Lady Out of Lizzie." Only one name-brand song has outlived the economic storms that put hundreds of auto makers on the financial rocks. "Take Me Out in a Velie Car" recalls one of the many orphan makers, but "In My Merry Oldsmobile" sold on its own musical merits in millions of copies.

By association with the slang for a five-cent piece, in the free and easy teens of automobiling, a jitney was a privately owned car in which the owner carried passengers for a nickel. Running on irregular routes and schedules, most often during mass transit strikes, jitney operators would be forgotten today were it not for "I Didn't Raise My Ford to Be a Jitney," a play on the highly popular song of the same year, 1915, "I Didn't Raise My Boy to Be a Soldier."

The auto's perky beep-beep from a squeezed rubber bulb evolved into the raucous roar of hand-operated Klaxon horns, which in turn were eliminated by the electrically operated oo-oo-gah. The era of horn exhibitionism ended with "I'm Wild About Horns on Automobiles—that go ta-ta-ta-ta" which referred to a short-lived fad for musical horns. Each part and phase of the automobile and motoring was a symbol of the evolution that began with a rich man's toy. Along the way to daily use by multitudes, many industries allied to the auto's changes perished.

Social customs, as well as changes in mechanism and design, are apparent in "Get 'Em in a Rumble Seat" and "Parking in the Park with You." As early as 1912, girls had been warned to "Keep Away from the Fellow Who Owns an Automobile": "He'll take you far in his motor car . . . from your pa[r] and ma[r]." Customs as well as economics peep from "Fifteen Kisses on a Gallon of Gas." As time marched on, it led to "The Trailer Song" and "My Ten Ton Baby and Me" by Meredith Willson, the "Music Man." Perhaps someday we'll have one about the split personality that needs two traffic lanes.

Traditionally, writers of verse have their heads in the clouds, so songwriters would be expected to be unusually alert to a development that took men into the sky. In consequence, "Up in a Balloon" antedates "Around the World in Eighty Days" by about a century. Later songs about balloons are credited to such famous composers as David Reed and Jerome Kern. Referring to the Grosvenor bibliography, a song of 1894 titled "In Nineteen Hundred and Three" made a prophecy that ran counter to world experience and thought since primitive man gazed longingly but unavailingly at the flight of birds. The prophecy: "How people will stare . . . when aloft thro' a cloud we'll sail in their view in nineteen hundred and three. . . ." That was the year when the Wright brothers upset transportation precedent by flying a short hop successfully in the first heavier-than-air machine at Kittyhawk. Though our songs usually record events, that one was prophetic.

The theme of flying had everything needed for songs. Melodies could be in waltz time, ragtime ("The Aeroplane Rag"), or they could go "Hippity Hop" with a song of that name. The waltzy rhythms of Albert Van Tilzer's "Take Me Up with You, Dearie" when converted into shorter notes made it one of the best patter songs. The patter is inside the front cover of my 1909 edition. Its melody has sometimes been confused with the better known "Come Josephine in My Flying Machine" of 1910.

In 1927 Charles A. Lindbergh's solo flight eastward across the Atlantic, the first in history, sent ecstatic song writers to publishers in droves. Soon the presses worked overtime. Some of the Lindbergh flight songs were boastful, "American Did It Again" or "Lindbergh—the eagle of the U.S.A." Most of them were cozy, "Hello, Lindy," "Lindy Did It," "Lucky Lindy," and just "Lindy Lindy," which adult listeners projected into the better known "Lindy, Lindy, sweet as the sugar cane" of "Lindy Lou." The enormous number of Lindbergh songs rushed to the music counters must have caused acute discomfort to the modest young man whose trade was flying, not entertainment.

"The Wreck of the Shenandoah" near Cambridge, Ohio, in 1925 recalls the years of experimentation in big lighter-than-air craft. "Yep! The Zep Came Over" referred to the *Graf Zeppelins* that flew here from Germany until the holocaust at Lakehurst, New Jersey, when a giant burned at its mooring mast and became the subject of one of America's most published news photos. "When I Get Me a Helicopter" came out in 1943.

The sampling here of songs related to means of going places, as written into titles or lyrics, is comparable with a national poll of TV listeners' or voters' intentions. In each case the number in the sampling is small compared to the total number available for information. Songs related to mobility would fill a large volume even if merely listed without comment. However, enough have had their say to make it clear that they are the musical section of America's transportation history. History includes customs. Because the song record is all embracing, it even gives insights into changing social mores as in "You Can't Walk Back from an Aeroplane."

Oddities and Speculations

In thumbing through a stack of old music, the explorer's expectation of the unexpected keeps a curious person alert for oddities. They may be related to a specific interest, such as World War I, or to cover art that typifies a year or period or to any of the many other facets that gleam through the dust often found on old songs that someone has saved, usually for sentimental reasons. The oddity may have no relationship to a recognized interest, therefore it may strike without advance notice. Suppose, for example, that you're not particularly interested in old sad ballads, the weepers of the 1890's and early 1900's, but without warning you turn up "They Needed a Song Bird in Heaven So God Took Caruso Away," 1921. Or you might be surprised to find that Caruso himself wrote a popular song in 1912 entitled "Dreams of Long Ago" published by Leo Feist, Inc. Caruso's recording in Italian accent of his American ballad is worth searching for. In different vein, sports fans would find interest in "There Never Was a White Hope Whose Christian Name Was Cohen" (1916), published by Harold Rossiter Music Company.

The vast expanses of our popular songs have not been plowed and cross-harrowed as the field of literature and book collecting has been by research and bibliography. There are so many songs, far in excess of the number of books, and a popular song may have run into millions of printings. (More recently, popularity is measured by the number of recordings sold.) With so many copies of an old song in circulation and so few collectors compared with bibliophiles, real rarity lies only in first or early printings. In popular music, a searcher seldom shops for values that might be hidden in a stack bought for five or ten cents a copy at a Salvation Army secondhand store or an estate sale. He looks for oddities. A book collector may covet his first edition of *Huckleberry Finn* for itself and also because he picked it out of a pile of old books between trains (planes) in Kalamazoo, for sixty cents, excised and re-tipped page 283 and all, "and I've been offered a dollar for every cent I paid for it." A song collector wouldn't have a windfall like that in a long lifetime.

There's slight intrinsic value in a collection of old songs, but, like the "Rosary," the owner can count them over every one apart warmed by the glow of possession. Great numbers of books have been written by highbrows and lowbrows about our popular songs. Several autobiographies and commentaries are loaded with fascinating information, persons and incidents. In others, there's no barrier between memory and imagination, or, if one exists, it is so thin that osmosis has set in. Some of the books provide the sort of checklist that even a seasoned collector finds useful, while persons who have been newly introduced to the oddities of popular music read themselves into a pleasant state of nostalgia. A few suggestions are in Appendix F.

On a lucky day the wetting of a thumb may turn up an oddity that is as intrinsically valueless as the "Battle Hymn—Written by the Mikado of Japan" published in 1904 in the Sunday edition of the Chicago *American*. To a song addict, the artwork is beyond price and the song is also a record of the period when truth in advertising was itself a rarity. Obviously faked as to authorship, nevertheless it causes speculation about the real composer who wrote it to capitalize upon Japan's place in the news just then in its quarrel with Russia. Speculation's a form of mental rustproofing that costs nothing, is easy to apply, and adds luster to living, for curious persons who wonder about why and wherefore.

Recurrences or resemblances in musical sequences lead to speculation about the mathematical probability of a musical phrase occurring to two composers at the same time or at wider intervals. After all, music has only half as many notes for its expression as the alphabet offers for word formation. Sequences, tempo, and inversions of those few notes constitute the world's music. What would a computer tell us about a 1916 hit, "There's a Quaker Down in Quaker Town" and Albert Von Tilzer's "Give Me the Moonlight, Give Me the Girl" a year later? Play or sing the two simultaneously to hear musical phrases duplicated or approximated. (Repeat Quaker's ending twice to come out even.) Von Tilzer had attained national stature as a composer before he wrote the moonlight-girl song. Like any ethically-minded craftsman, he would shrink from plagiarism. I conclude that he wrote the moonlight ditty as unaware of duplication as a child would be in repeating a word or gesture with no memory of its source. It's quite possible that he'd not heard the Quaker song. Because of the gap in years, it is probable that the composers of "Music! Music! Music!" in 1950 never heard Joe Howard's "Goodbye, My Lady Love" of 1904.

Musical progressions that buzz in the head of a songwriter may be buzzing elsewhere at that same time or may rebuzz later. The haunting harmony progressions in the opening bars of Liszt's "Liebestraum" of the 1840's are duplicated wholly or partially, with varying tempos, in "Mandy Lee," 1899, "Best I Get Is Much Obliged to You," 1907, "When It's Darkness on the Delta," 1932, and probably more. It is impossible for one person to recall the melodies or lyrics of every song heard, and what has been heard is a mere splash in the ocean of published music. No one has heard them all and no one can recall fully the comparatively few that have been heard.

That applies also to repetitive titles. Without a personal query, I speculate that the writers of "Dearie" in 1950 had never heard of Clare Kummer's 1905 song of the same name. Nevin wrote "The Rosary" in 1898. Welles wrote another in 1903 and there are others. Nevin's is the one you recognize. Mention was made of H. Von Tilzer's "Summertime" and Gershwin's about thirty years later. Von Tilzer's "All Alone" of 1911 was pushed into the discard by Berlin's plaintive melody and lyrics in 1915. Even in the smallest type, a collection of duplicate titles would spill over pages. Surprises lurk in titles, as when "Heart of My Heart" is found to be, actually, "The Story of the Rose," exemplifying others that we commonly identify by a line or a word such as "Ida" 1903, whose title is "Ida! Sweet As Apple Cider!" or "Red Red Robin" for "When the Red, Red Robin Comes Bob, Bob, Bobbin' Along," 1926.

Dozens of songs, refer in the title or lyrics to older songs:

SONGS WITHIN SONGS

Casey Jones Went Down on the Robert E. Lee (double reference)
Goodbye, Sweet Marie
I Love You and the World Is Thine
That Old Gang of Mine (that sang "Sweet Adeline")
Alice, Where Art Thou Going? (referring to "Alice, Where Art Thou?")
I Ain't Got Nobody—and nobody cares for me (did better than the earlier "I Ain't Got Nobody")
I'm Looking for the Man that wrote the Merry Widow Waltz
I Wonder Why Bill Bailey Don't Come Home
When Alexander Takes His Rag Time Band to France
When the Last Rose of Summer Has Whispered "Goodbye"' (double reference)
When the Organ Played Oh Promise Me
When the Parson Hands the Wedding Ring from Me to Mandy Lee
Who Paid the Rent for Mrs. Rip Van Winkle When Rip Van Winkle Went Away?
I'm the Guy That Paid the Rent for Mrs. Rip Van Winkle (double reference)
The Daughter of Rosie O'Grady
Since Sally Left Our Alley (Sally in Our Alley—old English)
When Old Bill Bailey Played His Ukulele

and on and on—all of them flattery of an original.

Travesty songs can offer surprises, as when a schoolteacher said that her room was about to stage an "old-time vaudeville show." Could I tell her whether the master of ceremonies should be a boy or a girl? And would I suggest "several songs out of the Gay Nineties"? When informed that traditional vaudeville had no emcees, she asked, quite naturally, "How did the audience know about the next act?" Elementary, my dear Watson. A big card on an easel or an illuminated panel beside the stage introduced Katz's Dogs, The Flying Murillos, Will Mahoney, Joe Cook, or the Avon Comedy Four.

As to typical songs, she asked, what did I think of "No! No! A Thousand Times No" and "Heaven Will Protect the Working Girl" and "Don't Swat Your Mother, It's Mean" and might she use my "You Can't Convict the Mother of the Girl I Love"? Of them, only one was really related to old-time vaudeville, the working-girl song of 1909 as a travesty upon the sad ballads of that era. The rest of them were tongue in cheek, as recent as 1937 ("You Can't Convict . . . ") and quite untypical of the period she wanted to portray. "The Curse of an Aching Heart," "Take Back Your Gold," "The Moth and the Flame," "The Fatal Wedding," and "She's Only a Bird in a Gilded Cage" typify those that were sung seriously enough to make strong men weep.

Another working-girl song is set down here for posterity, as an example of the type of song *not* typical of the 1890's or early 1900's. "Luke McLuke," columnist of the Cincinnati *Enquirer,* published the lyrics in his column in the early 1920's. Maurice D. Sarbey of Cleveland sang them thus:

The Honest Working Girl *

One day an hon-est working girl was thirs-ty as could be. She
frisked her pock-ets and five cents was all that she could see. She
took her can to a sal-oon that stood close by her home, And
there a crool bar-ten-der, he filled that can with foam. The
work-ing girl looked at the can, a tear was in her eye---- She
saw that it was filled with foam, and she was ver-y dry-y-y. She

* From *A Handbook for Adeline Addicts,* 1932, out of print.

took the can and bowed her head, and home-ward went her way, But
to that crool bar-ten-der, these words she then did say---- Some
day you'll have a thirst, you brute. Some day you will be dry. And
peo-ple all will treat you then, as you have treated I. The
world will then des-pise you, sir, And home-less you shall roam. For
you have sold a work-ing girl, A bucket filled with
foam, A bucket filled with F-O-M-E Fo-o-oam.

While in the Cincinnati-Cleveland neighborhood, let's speculate a bit about "Beautiful Ohio," 1918, the one that most people recognize. It was written by Mary Earl. Mary was Robert A. Keiser (1862–1932), a prolific composer who changed his name to King. That is how it appears in ASCAP's biographical dictionary. It is likely that he wrote "While Strolling Through the Park One Day," 1884 (actually "The Fountain in the Park") under the name of Ed Haley. No one in the music trades ever knew Haley, but the song was dedicated to Robert A. Keiser. In 1903 he wrote "Anona," a very early song in the lengthy pseudo-American-Indian song cycle. The composer's name on the cover is "Vivian Gray (Miss Mabel McKinley)." In the publisher's ad on the back, the parenthesis marks are reversed—"by (Vivian Gray) Miss Mabel McKinley, niece of the late president." Did he write it for a fee so that she could appear as composer as well as vaudeville singer which she was? Was she actually the President's niece? Did he write it for Mabel as a gesture of friendship? Was Mary Earl of "Beautiful Ohio" fame another girl friend? During his long life he used more than twenty pseudonymns that included other feminine names, though others ("Moonlight on the Colorado," 1930, among them) were signed Robert A. King. Did he dislike Keiser or was he prompted by a quirky sense of humor? Did *noms de plume* pay better than Keiser?

Almost any adult recognizes "Just a Dream of You, Dear." I have two copies of it, one of them crediting Milton Weil for the words in 1910, the other naming Chas. F. McNamara as author of exactly the same words in 1912. Here they are:

Just a dream at sunset in the fading glow
Just a dream of you, dear, when the lights are low
Just a dream at twilight, ans'ring mem'ry's call
Just a dream of you, dear, just a dream that's all.

"But," you say, "that isn't the way *we* sing it." Nor does anyone else in my long acquaintance with off-the-cuff singers. Between 1910 and 1912 did Weil change his name to McNamara? And who wrote the words that you and I sing: "Just a dream of you, dear, when the lights are low/Just a dream of you, dear, in the fading glow/Just a dream of you, dear, when sweet mem'ries call/Just a dream of you, dear, just a dream that's all"? It's mystery like that that drives a song archaeologist to the bottle—aspirin, that is.

These and more speculations! Nobody at Witmark's who published the songs of Ernest R. Ball knows why several of that famous songwriter's opuses were credited to George Christie. There's little speculation as to why he signed his "Saloon" song as "E. R. Llab." He was gifted in ways that included personal charm, stage presence, and vocal ability that in combination with his pianistic skill captured audiences on his national vaudeville tours. His name must stand among the top dozen composers of our popular songs that last. The night life of the nation's Broadways cut his brilliant career short at age forty-nine.

Theodore F. Morse's songs such as "Dear Old Girl," "Down in Jungle Town," "M-o-t-h-e-r," and others that are still heard, as well as "Goodbye,

My Blue Bell," and other national hits which few recognize now, etch his name into any Hall of Fame list of America's popular-song writers. Few recognize Dorothy Terriss ("Three O'Clock in the Morning," "My Wonderful One," and others that are permanently fixed in the song record), as Theodora Morse, wife of Theodore. Until his death in 1924, she used the Terriss name and sometimes D. A. Esrom, reversed as in Llab. We speculate: did she use the pseudonym to avoid possible confusion of Theodora and Theodore? After his death she wrote under the name of Dolly Morse. More speculation: "Hail Hail the Gang's All Here," "Bobbin' Up and Down," "When Uncle Joe Plays a Rag on His Old Banjo," and others are commonly associated with Theodore. The ASCAP dictionary lists them under *both* names. Were they written by that gifted husband-wife team? Neither of them can answer. Speculations about puzzlers like that keep speculators awake while puzzling at three o'clock in the morning.

A 1918 song, "Home Coming Week in France," is an oddity because "America's Problem" is stated on the back as "Ships and Food—to Send the Most Food Possible in the Least Shipping Space." At the bottom, the solution: "Eat More Fish, Cheese, Eggs, Poultry and Save Beef, Pork and Mutton for Our Fighters." Between is an affidavit by composer Seneca G. Lewis that all royalties and profits from two other compositions are "in their entirety forwarded to the New York Sun Smoke Fund." As of September 6, 1918, the songs had earned $4,114.09.

By that time, the rise in the cost of living which dropped briefly in the financial panic of 1907, and would halt again during the Depression of the 1930's, was felt so widely that it affected more than living. With the permission of Leo Feist, Inc., the copyright owners, let's look at conditions in 1914 when World War I, limited then to Europe, started a sharp escalation of prices here at home.

The High Cost of Loving *

The high cost of loving, the high cost of loving
It's driving me mad, Yes, driving me mad
The high cost of living is only a joke
The high cost of loving is keeping me broke
You borrow from mother, from sister and brother
You try to keep up with the style
Ev'ry bricklayer's daughter drinks wine just like water
I'll have to stop loving a while.

A dollar was still a dollar twenty years before that (1893) when the New York Pork Store in Lynn, Massachusetts, gave away copies of "By the Sad Sea Waves" with prices on the back cover: Ham at 10¢ a pound, fresh pork 8½¢, sausage and frankforts 9¢, sirloin steak 15¢, chuck—three pounds for 25¢.

Popular music's archaeologists associate that year with "Good Morning to All" (Happy Birthday), "I Long to See the Girl I Left Behind," "Say 'Au Revoir' But Not 'Goodbye'," "When the Roll Is Called Up Yonder," and "Two Little Girls in Blue," among others that include "Sweet Marie," who developed into an oddity worthy of speculation. Adults recall her as the theme that was sung and hummed by Irene Dunne and William Powell in *Life with Father*. The movie depicted life in the 1880's, when bread was baked at home and affluent housewives ordered flour by the barrel. Remember? "Sweet Marie" came out frequently on the sound track of the picture depicting the 1880's. But the song wasn't *written* until 1893. Speculate upon that! Marie is still in circulation in recent stage revivals of the play. Anachronisms like that and others that have been mentioned contribute to that mental rustproofing process. Noting them, we conclude that high-powered research departments, scanning every detail for the desired authenticity of a play or movie, can trip up occasionally.

Oddities appear from all angles. "The Silvery Nishnabotna" is among them, for persons who've seen that stream with the Indian name alternate between dark chocolate floods and muddy trickles in southwestern Iowa. Composer Billy Wells, deceased editor of the Red Oak *Express,* wore rose-colored glasses. As yet, curiosity has not motivated a search among Carl Carmer's rivers of America to determine how far in popularity the Mississippi rolls on ahead of dear old Swanee or the Wabash where the candlelights are gleaming on the banks.

One of the oddest oddities was presented earlier in comment about "You're a Grand Old Flag" in which George M. Cohan wrote "rag" for "flag." What has been cited seems to provide ample reason for continuing a perennial search in the twists of the byways that proliferate from the main avenues of our popular music.

Folk Music in Evolution

In the 1950's violent quakes originating at the epicenters of hootnannies, folk sings and rock 'n' roll spread shock waves that jarred the realm of popular music. Music's seismologists report that the shocks are less violent in the late sixties and of shorter duration, though still stronger than any registered since ragtime's temblors cracked the crust of a placid musical world half a century earlier.

Phenomena such as these cannot be forecast, timed, or triggered like an atomic explosion. Internal pressures build slowly into unpredictable convulsions. The geomusical rumblings started early in America when waves of immigration from Europe washed our eastern coastlines. Each nationality contributed to the culture the folk music "made and handed down among the common people" in the mother countries. Nowadays, Americans who are removed by generations from Europe recognize the precious heritage brought here and bequeathed by their ancestors. The descendants of early settlers participate proudly in colorful folk festivals in which their forefathers would have been embarrassed to parade their own overseas origins.

Transplanted English folk music flourished best where local people were cut off from outside contacts as among the plainsmen and the hill people of the South, called hillbillies by their more prosperous lowland neighbors. "Barbara Allen" has been cited in the chapter "Memory Lame" to show how local color can tinge an ancient song over generations among remote people. Usually, their own folk compositions were sung to old held-over melodies that had been abraded by repetitions of those who sang unwritten songs by ear from memory only. The words of the lyrics had to be within the ken and the verbiage of isolated people of little or no formal education:

Squirrel, he's got a bushy tail
The raccoon and the bear
The rabbit's got no tail at all
Just a little bitty bunch of hair

Git along home, Sally gal
Git along home, I say
Git along home, Sally gal
Before the break of day.

Whether to an old traditional tune or to a new one sung to the accompaniment of a fiddle, gourd banjo, or homemade dulcimer, the traditions of Europe's medieval minstrels were Americanized. Songs were composed in praise of a person or to commemorate an incident. A celebrity murdered someone but eluded pursuit and, later, "two sheriffs he did slay," all to his credit in the opus of an unknown admiring hillbilly composer.

Folk music of the Eastern seaboard spread westward as naturally as sticktights attach themselves to persons or animals, get a long free ride to a new locale, then spring up where each generation takes on increasingly the local characteristics of soil, climate, and altitude. Some archaeologists believe that "Red River Valley," commonly considered a "western," originated in New York State, then migrated to the plains and beyond. "Springfield Mountain" became "Hoosac Mountain" in western Massachusetts' Berkshire Hills, though it was "Conway Town" or "Conway Mountain" in New Hampshire. Like all true folk music, it was buffeted severely by singers who almost remembered the words and by others who needed a tote bag to carry a tune. But, like "Frankie and Johnny," a clue to the identity is in all versions, a snake that bit a local citizen on the heel or toe, also the remedy for snakebite: "Samuel went and he did feel a pizen serpent bite his heel" or "Josey boy, when he did go down in the meadow for to mow was by a snake bit on the toe." In both cases and in other versions "the doctor gave him cal-o-mel" and he recovered quickly, probably to avoid another dose.

In the 1920's a few of the southern hill country's songs were recorded by Columbia at 78 by Craver, Dalhart, Stine, and others who sang them in authentic dialect with the simplest harmonica, fiddle, and guitar accompaniments. In the North, such selections were usually played by a host for friends whose music appreciations were above average. He and his guests recognized the hillbilly songs as samplings from unsophisticated folk music, bits of Americana from our varied cultural heritage.

That novelty of the 1920's, radio, brought sweeping changes to musicalizing. They affected listening habits and attitudes toward music. Radio brought *live* music into the home, music being played *at that moment* somewhere else. It was barely believable. In radio's earliest presentations of recorded music, the operator pointed the horn of his 78 player at the microphone. Even the Victor dog, the company trademark, had difficulty recognizing "his master's voice" as projected by the rudimentary broadcasting and receiving equipment.

Recordings were played largely as fill-ins. "By electrical transcription" carried with it an implied apology in pre-disc jockey days. Listeners had greater thrills from hearing a third-rate band live ("Just imagine—they're 'way out at Canobie Lake Park") than from recordings by better bands. The musical directors of great numbers of the new radio stations came there from the orchestra pits of waning local theaters or other more formal musical directions. They accepted Herbert and Friml, but some were inclined to look down their noses at Stephen Foster. At the mention of hillbilly music, their eyes crossed.

Nonetheless, by the late twenties a folk revival was under way, presented usually by entertainers proud of their authentic status and nomenclature as hillbillies. As the novelty spread, local combos agglutinated, patterned most often after the presentations of Nashville's Grand Old Opery, disseminating folk-type melodies with unadorned harmonies and artless words, such as "They Cut Down the Old Pine Tree." Cowboy songs were sung by urbanites who'd hardly recognize a horse at three paces. In his "Much Ado About Me," Fred Allen, our greatest comedian using self-created material, wrote about the personal appearance in vaudeville of a hillbilly radio troupe. "They sang sinus songs... they sweated through sets of square dances, gave barnyard imitations and exchanged rustic wheezes at which they laughed... there was no silo big enough to hold the corn those meadow minstrels dispensed." Later, *Newsweek* referred to the twang, wail, and howl division of the electronics industry. It was doing quite well, thank you, with "It Was Sad When That Great Ship Went Down," referring to the sinking of the *Titanic* on her maiden voyage in 1913, "Turkey in the Straw," and other traditional hillbilly songs, often announced by a consciously quaint Uncle Hez character.

By the 1930's city bands had discovered most of the previously unwritten folk tunes. Their orchestrations were generally in the mood of the originals since in those dark ages the intent was to re-create authentically. But the old numbers were worn out so fast by radio's countless mechanized repetitions that the composers for the burgeoning hillbilly music trade had to work nights to supply the demand for old authentic aged-in-the-woods folk music.

Scattered widely, a small army of resistance to all this fought a losing battle. The persons enlisted in it were individuals who worshipped at the altar of genuine folk music. Their thin ranks met sporadically to sing the traditional songs in the traditional harmonies—no populars allowed. When I commented to such a group that I considered "Casey Jones" a better folk song than "The Wreck of the Old '97," adapted from "The Ship That Never Returned," 1861, the group reactions reminded me of when a junior smashed the mirror on the open piano.* That crash was sustained by glassy tinklings, this *faux pas* by grim mutterings. I had been out of order. "Casey" was a popular (horrid word), written and published for profit. To them at that time, a folk song should be known only to limited consecrated groups. I didn't ask whether a folk song, tracked down in a mountain cove and written into a book on folkways, for the author's profit, became a mere popular after publishing.

"Sacrilege" was hurled at a later suggestion that all fences might well be removed between our folk and popular songs, though that process was already on its way. Both belong in a big pasture of musical Americana along with others branded as classical but as well known as the popular "Begin the Beguine" or "The Loveliest Night of the Year." Folk, popular, and classical music show cowlike tendencies to break down the fences. When that occurs and they mingle with each other, it is difficult to cut one of them out of the herd and identify it as belonging on a particular side of the fence. Brands are so easily erased, and new ones can be substituted.

For example, in the *Musicians' Handbook,* the reminder-selector for bands, the page of hillbilly tunes and cowboy songs has, for several years, included

* See Appendix G for comment about "Casey."

"Dear Hearts and Gentle People," "Buttons and Bows," "Darling Nellie Gray," "Listen to the Mocking Bird," "Sioux City Sue," and "The Trail of the Lonesome Pine" among others which, most of us thought, had composers, authors, and a profit motive back of them. Hillbilly applied originally to the hog 'n' hominy folks in the hills. Hillbilly music was largely folk music, "usually of anonymous authorship, often with many versions." So it would seem that the way a song is presented accounts for the *Handbook*'s classification. Otherwise, "Darling Nellie Gray," composed by Benjamin Hanby in pre-Civil War days, would not have jumped to the hillbilly-cowboy section. If played often enough with three chords on a guitar, it's possible that "Liebestraum" would filter through the fence to join "Sioux City Sue." Looking in the other direction of flow, we see "On Top of Old Smoky," "made and handed down among the common people" for generations before it began to earn profits for every hillbilly band and others as a "popular" (if national recognition of it by the populace is the criterion).

I have no convictions on these matters. In my mental quagmire shrouded by a thick fog, I grope toward the Great Truths which continue to be elusive.

By the 1940's, purveyors of hillbilly had become self-conscious. We began to hear it referred to as "country," often with a subclassification of "western." (As rendered then, several yip-ees inserted hither and yon made it western.) But its popularity in a new generation was being threatened. Simple melodies accompanied by three or four dissonant chords ("Hot Pastrami," "Great Balls of Fire," "Louie, Louie") were giving way to simple melodies accompanied by new and more sophisticated harmonies on the guitar. Since then, no shift in our popular-music history has been as apparent. The unprecedented resurgence in the 1950's and 1960's of folk-type songs, added to the rise of rock 'n' roll, launched an era of nylonese music that retains much of the balladry, storytelling, pathos, and bathos of folk music and the popular songs before World War I whose lyrics ran the gamut of human experience and emotions. But, as with other techniques in an electronic age, the weaving together of melodies, lyrics, and harmonies is quite different. Among the new generation of guitar pickers and pluckers, conventional harmonies and rhythms are as outmoded as limp leather postcards and bindings for "souvenir" books of 1905. In their revitalization, older songs are presented in modern styling in which arrangers often take liberties with the original melodies, but the harmonies reflect imaginative musicianship. Also, they demand highly skilled musical execution, often so intricate that they plunge old-style country guitar players into a dichotomy of admiration and despair.

As to old folk songs gone modern and new "folk" songs fresh from the busy production line, only music's archaeologists can state with authority whether some of the recordings are from early American music or from the 1860's or the 1960's. Of course, some of the newer ones are as falsely "folk" as an antique piece with fresh sawdust in its corners. The lyrics were written last Wednesday for immediate consumption. Some of the writers of lyrics for a few modern albums are afflicted by arrested development, therefore would find no meaning in "May the wind of humor blow the soot up the chimney."

The wind of popularity in popular music styles blows thisaway and thataway, from gale force to gentle zephyrs. Eventually, a younger clan of musicians will discover that our so-called populars carry Americana of all periods and sections—not limited to the pioneer era or to sections such as hillbilly and cowboy around which so much Americana folk music revolves—or did until it went modern in newly written song subjects and harmonies. They will find enormous numbers of populars that provide a much broader base for imaginative handling than do the folk types. Come that day, we'll hear Van Alstyne, Herbert, Romberg, and the roster of composers of the earlier 1900's presented with Loewe and Lerner as "early Americana" with a commentary upon the quaint folkways of that era. What that generation will do to the harmonies is unlikely to be more at variance from the originals than today's melodies, as performed by "interpreters," differ from the tunes set down by composers.

In rock circles, where beat had reigned over harmony and where dissonance was king, a new trend became audible about 1966. Dissonance is, of course, personal opinion whether of the performer or listener.

Guitarists and other accompanists seemed to be grasping for new musical dimensions. Oddly, the new were shaped upon modifications of the old pre-rock "square" harmonies. Critics, mostly adult (over forty), hearing sounds from the room to which the record player had been relegated, began to remark "Those Beatles aren't so bad." Beatles symbolizes other groups as well. Some of the musical passages in the newer presentations didn't rip and rend the sensitive quite as devastatingly as formerly. That trend continues more noticeably into the late 1960's, but it must not be mentioned hopefully in the presence of most juniors, whether they are composers, performers, or listeners.

Today, the definition of a folk song which I coined in the era of the dedicated aficionados—a song about which so few feel so strongly—doesn't apply. Hillbilly can be folk or country, western can be folk, while populars have also become folk. All of them spread joy to multitudes to whom a Mustang is not a horse nor a Rambler a bicycle but a hardtop. The current musical trends may evoke rude sounds from unappreciative diehards, but millions of record players do more than provide music in the home. They give incentive to great numbers of young people to learn to do for themselves what they hear. In many cases that incentive will lead to the greatest joy in music, self-expression.

PART THREE

Good Close Harmony

Born in the Barber's Shop

In popular music's annals since the 1930's, the resurgence of folk-type music and the revival of barbershop-quartet harmony singing relate them as kindred phenomena of the period. The relationship is that of separate entities, distant relatives, each slightly conscious of the other's existence but each with its own interests and preferences that are sufficient for its needs. Neither shows evidence of a desire to meet and mingle in One World even though their parents bore the old family name, popular music.

Both have common European ancestral ties. They present the music of the people and, as the two relatives developed into maturity, they shared similar experiences. Each represents restorations of what had been largely erased from the American scene. Both have burgeoned far beyond their near-moribund originals. Their popularity has taken both of them from tiny assemblages of small dedicated groups, as were touched upon in folk songs, into the concert halls of the States and Canada. Their evolutions from hobbies and their musical developments run almost parallel, each in its own avenue of interest, during this modern Restoration Period. Their kinship is one of chronology and evolutionary processes, not of the type of music which each represents. In that respect they differ as widely as they do in their organizational patterns.

One person's pleasure is another's poison ivy. That applies to any kind of music, folk songs, madrigals, rock 'n' roll, or barbershop (one word in modern practice). To a four-part *a capella* harmony fan, the word "barbershop" may mean the sweetest music this side of heaven. As used by another, it could indicate a sneer. As in calling a song old or new, it depends upon one's age and musical experiences. The meaning intended or received from barbershop might be the old conventional caricature of four drunks singing "Sweet Adeline" while supported by a lamppost or it may suggest the four commissioners singing "Lida Rose" in *Music Man*. Some of the most ardent symphony listeners of my acquaintance seldom miss a barbershop-quartet concert within forty miles of their homes.

The *Harvard Dictionary of Music* (13th printing) says that barbershop harmony is a colloquial term for a type of "highly chromatic, over-sweet harmony used in popular American part-singing." "Over-sweet? Says who?" challenge the aficionados as the argument starts. As a musical term, barbershop has logic and precedent back of it. Understanding of its background and evolutionary processes clarifies the reasons for the attendance at Carnegie Hall in New York, O'Keefe Center for the arts in Toronto, Severance Hall, home of the Cleveland Symphony Orchestra, the Masonic Auditorium perched on a San Francisco hilltop, and in comparable halls as well as churches and schools. in Canada and the States where the quartets and choruses sing for the public. Back of American precedents, there are others that were ancient before hair clippers learned to buzz.

As touched upon in "The Evolution of Barbershop Harmony" in *Music Journal* (anthology issue, July 1965), references to music in the barber's shop revert at least to Shakespeare's times. In 1583 the English writer Philip Stubbs made references: "You shall have your fragrant waters for your face, wherewith you shall be besprinkled; your musick again and pleasant harmony shall sound in your ears...." A character in Thomas Morley's *Plain and Easy Introduction to Practical Music* (1597) made reference to singing without musical notations. "You keep not time in your proportions; you sing them false.... It should seem that you came lately from a barber's shop." It applied in America to barbershop singers old-style. More about that later. In 1604 Cervantes referring in *Don Quixote* to Master Nicholas, the barber, said, "most all of that faculty are players on the guitar and song makers."

It was rare Ben Jonson (1573–1637), composer of "Drink to Me Only with Thine Eyes," who put angry words into the mouth of the barber's wife in *Silent Woman:* "That cursed barber! I have married his cittern [guitar]." In his famous diary, Samuel Pepys (1633–1703) wrote: "Musick is the thing of the world that I love most.... After supper my lord called for the lieutenant's cittern and with two candlesticks with money in them for symballs [cymbals], we made barber's music..."

Skipping across two centuries, in his *Oxford Companion to Music* (London, Oxford University Press, 1938) P. A. Scholes wrote: "One of the regular haunts of music in the 16th, 17th and early 18th centuries was the barber's shop. Here, customers awaiting their turn found simple instruments on which they could strum. The barbers themselves in their waiting time between customers took up the instruments and thus acquired some skill as performers." Mention of that skill recalls a comment in the early 1920's by the senior Steinert, piano manufacturer of Boston. His store on Boylston near Tremont was an actual "haunt of music." Mr. Steinert said that since once upon a time he had been a barber, he knew how to play the guitar.

American-born William Andrews commented upon old English customs in *At the Sign of the Barber's Pole.* "The barber-surgeon was a man of considerable importance. His shop was the gathering place of idle gallants.... The gittern, or guitar, lay on a counter and this was played by a customer to pass away the time until his turn came to have his hair trimmed, his beard starched, his mustachios curled, and his love-locks tied up." In principle, the practices in old England could apply in the early 1900's to a shop in Shelbyville or Jonesboro, U.S.A. Much earlier, I told how a guitar introduced me to the barber in Shelbyville, when I went only for a hair trim. That village shop, like countless others of pre-World War I days, qualified as a gathering place for the local gallants.*

* Thanks are due to an unknown in the National Recreation Association, New York City, whose undated *Bulletin* about some of the more ancient barber-music lore fell into my hands many years ago. The late Joseph E. Stern of Kansas City was another source.

Weaned in America

Obviously, "musick" in the barber's shop was born in Europe, but, most certainly, it was weaned and grew to adulthood many years ago in American shops where it took on the flavors of the new country and conditions. No one can pinpoint the year or place. Within my own experiences, as one opened the door the first sniff might be called vocational, a blend of the smells from the coal-oil (kerosene) water heater and the aromas of Pompeian Massage Cream, bay rum and other "fragrant waters for your face." In winter when the door of the heating stove was opened to add fuel, the sharp odor of coal smoke might permeate the room briefly. This could occur after a loafer reminded the boss, "It's gettin' chilly, Henry. Mind if I throw on another cob?" (A reference, intended as mild humor, to corncobs used to start fires in stoves, among other uses in rural and small-town America.)

As to the decor, on the mirror a fly-specked card read *Haircuts 25¢—Shaves 10¢*. At the rear, another sign above a partitioned cubicle said *Hot Baths 25¢*. At that time and place, only the finest homes had hot running water for the traditional hebdomadal bath. Rather than drag the washtub into the kitchen and heat kettles full for ablutions, some of the town's spendthrifts utilized the barber's zinc tub.

His shop was the only approximation of a men's club or youth center in a town where *The Flyer* made no scheduled stop at the depot or the railroad's dripping water tank. Instead, it seemed to speed through town faster as the whistle uttered a prolonged sneer in diminuendo, leaving only a whiff of sulfurous smoke and longings to be on one of the train's Pullman cars or even in the "smoker" attached to "the baggage coach ahead." Occupancy of that stuffy smoking car was exclusively male.

True to the literary traditions that have been cited, the barber in our town kept an instrument in good condition for cittern-gittern-playing customers and for the loafers who were welcome as long as they scored bull's-eyes in the brass spittoons, unknown to a cigarette-smoking generation. While the barber sheared, he could also hum a tune softly or pitch a harmony part to someone's hummed lead, the melody. If others could chime in with tenor or bass or baritone (bari), harmony reigned. Passersby smiled, "They're at it again," or entered to listen or perhaps demonstrate how to make the second down in "Way Down Yonder in the Cornfield."

Much earlier, I told of the broad-minded high-school music teacher who encouraged four shy boys to form a quartet. The barber welcomed rehearsals almost any evening except Saturday when the farm trade was in. He was capable of coaching in how to make the chords "ring." Also, he became the foursome's chief public-relations officer as he murmured into captive ears, "Those kids will be in tonight. Come in and listen." So usually, we had a small critically appreciative audience. Some of the drop-ins were out on the town, pub-crawling between the soda fountain at Yost's Drugstore and the depot to see *The Flyer* flash through.

While details differed nationally, these informal practices of catch-as-catch-can music in country towns and in urban neighborhood shops were back of the decision of the senior Oscar Hammerstein to stop work on a 1908 opus in which he had intended to use massive guitar effects. "I should have been obliged to engage all the barbers in New York."

We had but two barbers, the other a churlish fellow who, as in the Shakespearean accusation, had not music in himself nor was moved by a concord of sweet sounds. But the livery-stable office was available for singing on a Saturday night. However, the night man who slept in the office after midnight used horse blankets on his cot. Those blankets, carried right from sweating horses, and the potbellied stove that was often red hot in cold weather left minimal air and room in the tiny office. It reeked also of hand-rolled Bull Durham cigarettes and, less often, of more expensive Sweet Caporals, a penny each. Semioccasionally, the heavy odor of Turkish Trophies, smoked by a man about town, added a patrician character to the hot blue haze in which horse was predominant.

In such places, but particularly in barber shops of the nation, guitars, mandolins, and *a capella* singing were as widespread as they were informal. It was done strictly by ear and instinct for harmonizing. It was not predetermined singing. The typical barbershopper couldn't read notes, but most of his clan had their own ideas about the right chord and the possibility of adding a swipe at a spot where ecstasy was peering 'round the corner. For a swipe, the lead singer held the melody note while the other three parts revolved round it until the lead was blue in the face and threatened with syncope. A drummer (traveling man) who came in for a shave one evening taught us a four-chord swipe on the last "sweet" in "When You Were Sweet Sixteen" (1898) that had us groveling in gratitude. Often optimistically, this sort of harmonizing was called "close" harmony. About 1912, "Mr. Jefferson Lord—play that barbershop chord" became so popular that it replaced the older terminology.

Because songs lasted much longer then, when they were not worn out by mechanical repetitions, Mr. Jefferson Lord's popularity continued through World War I and well into the twenties. By then, hand-cranked record players had been sold in millions. So, great number of amateur singers had heard the Peerless Quartet, the Avon Comedy Four, or others of national reputation.

Nearly every professional quartet of high rank had earned its popularity on the vaudeville stage before cutting the 78 records. The members of famous ones included men with formal musical training and others whose skills were learned off-the-cuff in a barbershop atmosphere.

Among the songs that were favorites there until about the time of World War I were:

Some Barbershop Quartet Favorites Before World War I, 1917

Aura Lee	*1861*
Beautiful Isle of Somewhere	*1897*
Break the News to Mother	*1897*
Bring Back My Bonnie to Me	*1882*
By the Light of the Silvery Moon	*1908*
By the Watermelon Vine	*1903*
Comrades	*1887*
Cuddle Up a Little Closer	*1908*
Curse of an Aching Heart	*1913*
Daisy Bell (Bicycle for Two)	*1892*
Dear Old Girl	*1903*
Doan You Cry, Ma Honey	*1899*
Down Among the Sheltering Palms	*1915*
Down by the Old Mill Stream	*1910*
Down in Honky Tonky Town	*1916*
Down in Jungle Town	*1908*
Down in the Old Cherry Orchard	*1907*
Down Where the Cotton Blossoms Grow	*1901*
Give My Regards to Broadway	*1904*
Goodbye, My Lover, Goodbye	*1882*
Honey Boy	*1907*
Honey That I Love So Well	*1898*
I Can't Tell Why I Love You	*1900*
I'd Love to Live in Loveland	*1911*
I Long to See the Girl I Left Behind	*1893*
I Love You in the Same Old Way (modified into "Bright Was the Night")	*1896*
I Love You Truly	*1901*
I'm Wearing My Heart Away for You	*1902*
In the Evening by the Moon Light	*1880*
In the Good Old Summer Time	*1902*
In the Hills of Old Kentucky	*1914*
Is There Still Room for Me 'Neath the Old Apple Tree?	*1915*
It Looks Like a Big Night Tonight	*1908*
It's Always Fair Weather	*1898*
I've Got a Feeling for You (Way Down in My Heart)	*1904*
I Want a Girl	*1911*
I Wonder How the Old Folks Are at Home	*1909*
I Wonder If She's Waiting	*1909*
Just a Dream of You, Dear	*1910*
Just as the Sun Went Down	*1898*
Just a Wearying for You	*1901*
Just One Girl	*1898*
Just Tell Them That You Saw Me	*1895*
Keep the Home Fires Burning	*1915*
Kentucky Babe	*1896*
Last Night Was the End of the World	*1912*
Little Bit of Heaven (A)	*1914*
Long Long Trail (There's a)	*1915*
Love Me and the World Is Mine	*1906*
Love's Old Sweet Song	*1882*
Maiden with the Dreamy Eyes	*1901*
Mammy's Little Coal Black Rose	*1916*
Mandy Lee	*1898*
Meet Me Tonight in Dreamland	*1909*
Memories	*1915*
Moon Has His Eyes on You (The)	*1905*
Moonlight Bay	*1912*
M-o-t-h-e-r—a Word That Means the World to Me	*1915*
Mother Machree	*1910*
Mother Was Chasing Her Boy 'Round the Room (A)	*1900*
My Castle on the Nile	*1901*
My Little Girl	*1915*
My Old New Hampshire Home	*1898*
My Sweetheart's the Man in the Moon	*1892*
My Wild Irish Rose	*1899*
Not Because Your Hair Is Curly	*1906*
Oh, Didn't He Ramble	*1902*
Oh, You Beautiful Doll	*1911*
On the Banks of the Wabash Far Away	*1897*
Pride of the Prairie	*1907*
Put on Your Old Gray Bonnet	*1909*

Put Your Arms Around Me, Honey	*1910*
Rag Time Cow Boy Joe	*1912*
Red Wing	*1907*
Row, Row, Row	*1912*
Say "Au Revoir" But Not "Goodbye"	*1893*
School Days	*1907*
She May Have Seen Better Days	*1894*
She's More to be Pitied than Censored	*1898*
Shine on Harvest Moon	*1908*
Sidewalks of New York	*1894*
Silver Threads Among the Gold	*1873*
Somebody's Waiting for Me	*1902*
Stay in Your Own Back Yard	*1899*
Story of the Rose (Heart of My Heart)	*1899*
Summertime (Harry Von Tilzer)	*1907*
Sweet Adeline	*1903*
Sweet Cider Time When You Were Mine	*1916*
Sweet Genevieve	*1869*
Sweet Marie	*1893*
Sweet Rosie O'Grady	*1896*
That's How I Need You	*1912*
There'll Come a Time Someday	*1895*
There's a Girl in the Heart of Maryland	*1913*
Wait Till the Sun Shines, Nellie	*1905*
When I Leave the World Behind	*1915*
When Irish Eyes Are Smiling	*1912*
When the Bees Are in the Hive	*1904*
When the Harvest Days Are Over, Jessie Dear	*1900*
When the Harvest Moon Is Shining on the River	*1904*
When the Maple Leaves Were Falling	*1913*
When Uncle Joe Plays a Rag on his Old Banjo	*1911*
When You Were Sweet Sixteen	*1898*
When You Wore a Tulip	*1914*
Where the Morning Glories Twine	*1905*
Where the River Shannon Flows	*1906*
You're a Grand Old Flag	*1906*
You're a Great Big Blue Eyed Baby	*1913*
You're As Welcome As the Flowers in May	*1902*
You Tell Me Your Dream (I Had a Dream, Dear)	*1899*

By now it is evident that barbershop-quartet singing is actually related to the nation's small-town barbershops and those in many urban neighborhoods, though the singing was not confined to them exclusively. In cities, the amateurs often competed in local talent contests at neighborhood theaters. Some got the "hook," actually a hook on a pole used to pull a local artist off the stage if lack of audience applause or if catcalls warranted. Others went on to engagements on the vaudeville circuits. As the quality of quarteting improved, coincidentally with the number of quartets, the popularity of four men in a chord increased through the teens. Then came an era of misunderstanding and disrepute.

The Lean Years

Documentary research can be satisfying and resultful, but the flavors of an era and its songs and their associations are not in the findings. As documentation, the Eighteenth Amendment, often called the Volstead Act, was ratified by thirty-six states, January 29, 1919, and became law on January 16, 1920. It prohibited the manufacture, sale, transportation, importation, or exportation of alcoholic liquors for beverage purposes, though it did not prohibit drinking them. The number of businesses, including big ones, that banned drinking by employees increased steadily. Socially, to "show" your drinks had carried a stigma; then Prohibition made drinking so popular that adults who'd been bone dry took it up in order to be socially smart. Inexperienced in handling the weird concoctions, they smelled the cork, then presented still another of the sorry sights of that ugly era of illicit distilling, bootlegging, and organized criminal traffic in liquor.

On the bright side, the amendment helped to preserve participation in song. That included group participation in what, by that time, had become widely known as barbershop harmony. When Prohibition arrived, personal expression by amateurs was on its way out, pushed by that new wonder, the battery-operated radio. (Connection to the house-wiring came later.) When children had been put to bed, adults might fiddle with the novel dials until the small hours. At work, it was prestigious to announce "I got KMOX last night," or another station beyond the visible horizon. Appreciation of self-expression in the domestic art of singing was so low that a man was likely to hear a rap on the bathroom door and "Da-a-dy, you're drown-ding out the A.&P. Gypsies."

At social gatherings, bathtub gin provided courage for those who'd been accustomed to singing in the bathtub. At a reunion, when fortified by a beaker or two of Old Tiger, aged for a week by an honest bootlegger, a man who in past years had been content to listen to music might have to be restrained from conducting the gang in a third chorus of "Down by the Old Mill Stream." In his own or someone else's kitchen where the male section of a party had gathered, with courage produced by cloudy homebrew he might even attempt tenor in "There's a Girl in the Heart of Maryland" or others that had been so popular ahead of the recently ended (first) world war.

Hearing what came from those who were sampling 'round the crock in the kitchen, children were told by their mothers that it was "barbershop" singing, a term they'd heard somewhere. So, through the late 1920's and most of the 1930's, the word "barbershop," was, to the young and many adults, synonymous with any kind of gang-singing—good, terrible, or worse. Please hold that thought about a derogatory term. Hold it until we return from a bit of a snoop.

In those far away twenties and thirties a group of men were spotted throughout the States and Canada in about equal proportion to the population of any section where they lived. No census figures disclose whether there was one or as many as a dozen to each thousand adult male citizens. This is because census takers could not recognize any individual as belonging to the group, and hardly anyone in it realized that the others existed. It was possible for two or more of them to live on opposite sides of an apartment's wall, greet each other in passing, yet not recognize the other as a group member. This was because they kept their common mark of shame well hidden most of the time: they wanted to play or sing music *for themselves,* a condition directly opposed to dial-twisting trends. They wanted to participate in music that they liked best, not just sit back and listen to radio's variety. Only one common quality could have been recognized by a census. Their ages averaged in the forties. But they had no recognition apparatus. Few could read notes. They faked the three harmony parts instinctively.

Members of this underground might go for months without having opportunity to indulge in the self-expression that they craved. On rare occasions when the skeleton burst from the family closet, its presence was explained by a loving wife: "Yes, Bill does like to sing. But he's *all right.*" Broad-minded business associates could usually gloss over Bill's antisocial, perhaps neurotic, passion when promotions were being considered: "Bill's doing a good job. Sure he likes to sing, but let's not hold it against him."

As in other segments of the population, there were articulate Bills, but the great majority of them suffered in a void of silence. At a bridge party, an uninhibited dummy, sitting out, might wander to the piano and ripple through a few bars of "My Heart Stood Still" or "Among My Souvenirs." In consequence, the evening of a typical restrained Bill would be improved and ruined simultaneously: *Here I am, wasting time on cards. Probably that guy at the piano knows "Lady, Be Good" and "My Little Dream Girl" and "My Baby's Arms," too. Pardon? O-oh! I pass."* Too seldom, this might occur at a place where there was opportunity to musicalize. Bill wasn't the song leader type, and he was too rusty and unsure to more than hum softly while a group's volume covered his own halting notes. Then came that rare occasion when four newly discovered brothers, all late for the dinner party, took a little more time out. Bill might suggest courageously, '"Try it a note lower, Charley. Let's switch. I'll take tenor."

Back of those precious infrequent sessions there was much more than the enjoyment of harmonizing. What they sang represented a phase of life worth an attempt to recapture. It could be re-created momentarily in full color by music's magic. Old songs recalled incidents and persons and experiences. Bill didn't want to cancel the present and return to the peg-top pants era or more recent years when President Wilson had said that the war would make the world safe for democracy. "Gosh, no! The best part of life's ahead, not back of us, I always say."

But somehow the new music lacked something. "Now you take that new one, 'Let's All Sing Like the Birdies Sing,' that you hear on the radio all the time. It's pretty good but give me 'I Had a Dream, Dear' and 'Let the Rest of the World Go By' for harmony that you can really bust." Popular at that time, "Yearning" summed it up, though yearners had difficulty in putting identification tags on their nostalgic musical emotions.

In the 1960's, an account of such conditions of earlier years may evoke impassioned agreement, calmer understanding, scornful sneers, or dazed puzzlement in those who differ in age, attitude toward music, and discernment. In the November 1965 issue of *Music Journal,* Robert Cumming, editor, wrote: "Musicality is a hereditary disease. Those blessed with this communicable condition are uncomfortable without music in some form, expressed or understood. Partial immunity is induced by periodic inoculation (controlled exposure) to the germ of music itself. It resists most forms of sterilization. The average person may derive solely needed benefits from singing in a choral group, church choir or barbershop quartet. The germ is powerful, and many consider it a sign of weakness to show enthusiasm overtly—but that weakness is ever so strong and, with proper guidance, will blossom forth all the more eagerly for its long restraint."

That's how it was after those lean years, when in 1938 a musical bomb burst over Tulsa, Oklahoma.

SPEBSQSA Preserves a Tradition

Here I shall enlarge occasionally upon bits of personally recorded history of the ten years that followed the bursting of that musical bomb over Tulsa. When I wrote *Keep America Singing* (1948) as an eyewitness of the phenomena that followed, it was as a commentator twenty years closer to the explosion than now.

On April 17, 1938, the Tulsa *Sunday Tribune* asked in a headline, "Barber Shop Harmony a Thing of the Past?" It answered its own question by adding in a subhead: "S.P.P.B.S.Q.S.U.S. is Formed to Preserve It." At first look, that might indicate the scrambling of the symbols SPEBSQSA, which today mean "Those quartets—I love 'em" to millions throughout the States and Canada who've heard them in public concerts. But Virginia Burch's story disproves any mix up of letters. She wrote: "The Society for the Propagation of Barber Shop Quartet Singing in the United States—Yes, sir, that's what they call it." Then she told how the nucleus had formed when the trails of two Tulsa acquaintances, tax attorney Owen C. Cash's and investment executive Rupert I. Hall's, crossed by chance at the Hotel Muelbach in Kansas City, Missouri. (A plaque in the hotel lobby now commemorates that meeting.)

Their acquaintanceship led from travelers' talk about matters back home to more personal interests. Music was one of them. Each found that the other liked the kind of songs favored by men when four yearners able to sing four parts got together under conditions favorable to harmonizing. Such occasions were as rare in Tulsa as throughout the nation, and they were growing rarer as radio promoted listening instead of participation. Cash's personal recollections add color to the *Tribune's* account of the meeting of the two harmony-hungry Tulsans. "I ran into Rupert Hall, whom I knew slightly. I was lonesome that night and I asked if he could sing tenor. He said 'I suppose I'm the best barbershop tenor in the United States.' I tried him out on 'I Had a Dream, Dear' and he stayed on pitch." The results were so satisfying that they canvassed the lobby for a lead and a bass. "We picked up a couple and went to Rupe's room and developed a fairly good quartet."

The two talked late into the night about Cash's dream of organizing a barbershop-quartet club as he had discussed it with other Tulsans with whom he sang baritone infrequently. Hall promised to call Cash at the first opportunity "and get this thing started." He arranged for a meeting at the Tulsa Club. Cash drafted the invitation, dated April 8, 1938, to known Adeline addicts: "In this age of Dictators and Government control of everything, about the only privilege guaranteed by the Bill of Rights, not in some way supervised or directed, is the art of Barber Shop Singing. Without doubt we still have the right of 'peaceable assembly' which, I am advised by competent legal authority, includes quartet singing. The writers have for a long time thought that something should be done to encourage the enjoyment of this last remaining vestige of human liberty. Therefore, we have decided to hold a singfest on the Roof Garden of the Tulsa Club on Monday, April 11, at six-thirty P.M." The invitation continued in that light vein. "We will have a private room and so will not be embarrassed by the curiosity of the vulgar public. You may bring a fellow singer, if you desire." It was signed "Harmoniously yours, THE SOCIETY FOR THE PRESERVATION AND PROPAGATION OF BARBER SHOP QUARTET SINGING IN THE UNITED STATES—Rupert Hall, Royal Keeper of the Minor Keys, Braniff Investment Co. —O. C. Cash, Third Ass't. Temporary Vice-Chairman, Stanolind Companies."

They could think of only about a dozen who might be interested. Actually, fourteen received the invitation and twenty-five men turned out for that first meeting. Continuing Cash's narration, "Rupe Hall got there first. Donnie O'Donovan of Station KVOO, Elmer Lawyer of the Tulsa Paper Co. and I were next." The three were standing 'round when S. M. (Puny) Blevens, well over six feet, arrived and asked, "What are we waiting for?" Blevens sang lead, O'Donovan tenor, Cash bari, and Lawyer bass. The first song sung under society auspices was "Down Mobile," an oldie even then in 1938.

No one took time to eat much at that meeting. Hall, who has lived to see his local singing club grow to international proportions, says: "After an hour or so of catch-as-catch-can singing, someone suggested the organization of a permanent club. Someone else asked 'When do we meet again?' An enthusiast yelled 'Tomorrow night!' " Actually, they delayed the next meeting until the following week. As the word got about, more than seventy harmony-hungry men came to that second one.

It didn't occur to anyone, while making up for time lost in the lean years, that they were also making news. But, as reports were relayed from one singer to another, chain reactions set in. Hall reminisces: "Owen Cash, who originated the idea of the singing club, and I were busy answering 'phone calls and letters and visiting with those who hadn't been at either meeting but were practically crying to meet in harmony."

The third meeting was the one that really started the rush to the Cherokee Strip, so called when in 1893 for the second time the government opened Indian Territory lands to settlers in land "rushes" which were races from a starting point. (Those who reached a desired piece of land first were entitled to "stake a claim" on it. Sometimes a "sooner" jumped the gun by sneaking in and staking in advance. Bloody fights resulted. When a man had staked, it was up to him to hold off interlopers with his shooting irons until a friend or member of his family could ride hell for leather to the land office to register the claim.) Cash's family had gone by covered wagon from Missouri to the Territory at about the time when it became Oklahoma, the Sooner State, in 1907. By then, the headlong races for land and battles with squatters had given way to a peaceful governmental lottery.

Cash said later about the third meeting: "About a hundred and fifty men showed up at the Alvin Hotel. Someone looked out the window and called my attention to the traffic jam. We paid no more attention to it until a reporter, Ralph Martin, of the Tulsa *World* came in and said he'd seen the cars jammed and had asked the cops 'Where's the wreck?' An officer said 'That's no wreck. It's just some damn fools singing up there in the Alvin." The reporter sought the source on the hotel's second floor.

Next Sunday morning, June 1, 1938, the *World* reported: "No, No, Folks—You're Wrong. That Was Musical History in the Making." Martin's feature story led off: "A little yellow moon as thin as a finger nail paring was hanging in the sky Tuesday night as certain astonished citizens coagulated at the base of the Alvin Hotel. They were listening to musical history in the making. The mighty sounds caused one staid and settled taxpayer to voice the consensus fermenting in the group—'Hell,' he muttered in a tone compounded of equal parts of alarm, astonishment and admiration, 'has broke loose in the henhouse!' "

Most of the readers were close enough to rural life to appreciate a squawking hell of flying dust, loose feathers, and confusion. His story presented such colorful handling of the fourth human need (in order: food, shelter, clothing, and *music*) that the wire services which send material to newspapers throughout the country picked it up, and the society was national news. When the reporter had asked Cash whether other singing clubs were being formed elsewhere, "I thought fast," Cash said, "and I remembered my old friend, Everett Baker, vice-president of the Frisco Railroad in St. Louis. I'd busted a few chords with him. So I said that Baker was organizing a chapter in St. Louis."

By wire service, Cash's statement appeared in the St. Louis morning papers. About ten o'clock Baker called Cash to tell him that the phone had been ringing all morning, "But it's all right. My secretary is taking names and addresses—more than seventy-five already—and I'll get a group together in a few days." By that time, Judge Edgar Shook of Kansas City had a vision, like St. Paul's in which the Macedonians called, "come over and help us."

He invited the Tulsans to come to Kansas City to help organize a western Missouri branch of that society with the long name. The judge's gesture had precedent. He and Cash had previously tried a case in Jefferson City. After hours, feeling the need for four-sided harmony, the judge "gave a bellboy four bits to go through the lobby calling, 'Call for a barbershop tenor and bass.' In a few minutes we had calls, all certifying that they were the best bass or tenor in Missouri." That too had precedent, since Cash frequently admitted modestly that he was the best baritone in the world. About forty men from Tulsa went to Kansas City by special railroad car. The meeting there on June 18, 1938, was such a success that several, urged by their newfound friends to sing just one more, missed the special when it pulled out for Tulsa. But K.C. was organized, the second chapter in the society. St. Louis and Oklahoma City, the latter sparked by oilman I. S. (Hank) Wright, were soon in the huddle.

By its nature, in the early stages the society was a big laugh. Before the arrival of the Tulsa delegation, a Kansas City paper carried an advance notice: "K.C.

Will Be the Sounding Board in Noble Drive to Rescue Cherished Privileges" and afterward "Male Divas of Tulsa Barber Shops Invade K.C." But Lowell Lawrence, drama editor of the *Journal-Post* wrote: "Professional entertainers better look to their laurels." He referred to the barbershoppers as a choral group that could compete with credit against professionals. "The society nobly fills a need in American life." The organization was a reporter's dream. It had color, local names, and a new twist that lent itself to humorous handling. As groups were formed in other cities during those first months, typical headlines read: "Quartets Gargle Tonight," "Harmonist to Wail," "Harmonizers Plan Tulsa Reprisals," "Gag Organization May Spread," "In Tones Nasal," "Bawl Game."

Uninhibited as the broncos of the Cherokee Strip, the Tulsans spent the rest of 1938 in a maze of surprise that "Doing What Comes Natur'lly" had focused national attention upon them. Rupert Hall recalls that he and Cash were swamped by mail, telegrams, and long-distance calls. "It got so bad that our stenographers threatened to quit unless we cut down the letters on harmonizing, so Cash and I chipped in and had some printing done. Soon we were spending too much time and too much of our own money answering mail. We had invitations from all over the United States to tell about the movement. We both traveled a lot, so we did our best to take care of inquiries, but it wasn't long before we had to decide whether we were going to devote our lives to harmony or to feeding our families." Cash said, "We had a bull by the tail and we couldn't let go."

Oklahoma City's *Legal News* had recorded the incorporation of the society, July 6. 1938, "just in case" according to the founders. In Cash's scrapbook, one of the original invitations to attend the first meeting shows "Encouragement" penciled in to replace "Propagation" and a line drawn through "United States," with "America" scribbled above it. So it was incorporated as the Society for the Preservation and Encouragement of Barber Shop Quartet Singing in America. In usage "barber shop" became a unit: barbershop. Later, Cash added "Founder" and "Permanent" to his title on the invitation to the first meeting. The additions made him Founder and Permanent Third Assistant Temporary Vice-Chairman.

As a lawyer for an oil pipeline company, he had neither training nor experience as a publicist. Nor did his associates. But Cash recognized a fundamental of the public-relations trade, that public actions make news and names make news. The news of the society, spreading like a dust storm blowing in all directions from Tulsa, invited continued action. Like Koko in *The Mikado,* he might have sung "my brain it teems with endless schemes." Owen Cash could have dropped his law career, gone into press agentry, and outdone the feats of the recognized giants in that field. He was a natural publicist.

Hard-up one time for something to say to an interviewer, he said that neither he nor anyone else knew the verse of "Sweet Adeline." It was printed nationally in newspapers, often with a side-bar local story to supplement the statement. When he suggested that owners of old shaving mugs donate them to the society, it made front pages across the country and editorial humor. He announced that SPEBSQSA would petition WPA, the temporary government agency, for $9,999,999.99 to finance a survey of the vocal range of American males. (My own correspondence with him includes the suggestion that, instead of cereal, we feed birdseed to babies in order to develop more needed tenors. That brought the counter thought that we might provide canaries to all pregnant women, to exert prenatal influence upon voices forthcoming. In the society's thirtieth year it is apparent that there's no accounting for heredity. A son of a bass may become a natural tenor, though vice virtuoso is more likely, after the offspring's voice changes.)

Cash invited nationally known Alfred E. Smith, ex-governor of New York, to judge at a "national quartet contest to be held sometime soon." Then he said that Herbert Hoover, presidential candidate Alfred Landon, Al Smith, and James E. Farley, all in the top of the news, would be asked to form a quartet at the contest. "Cash also hopes that the Duke of Windsor and the Archbishop of Canterbury may attend and sing 'Dear Old Girl' as a duet," it was reported. This referred to the abdication of England's King Edward VIII and the rift between church and state because of the former King's marriage to a divorced American commoner. Cash recognized the value of names. Bing Crosby had been invited to attend that first meeting in Kansas City. He wired his regrets but dedicated a song to the society on his radio program. Walter Winchell and other national columnists of the period took note of the quartets, sometimes with tongue in cheek, often with the hope expressed that it might become national in membership, organization, and activities.

Organization in terms of orderly procedures does not describe the society in its early stages. Its incorporation had brought a nine-page questionnaire from the U. S. Department of Commerce. The reply to the questions were to determine the society's status in case a bill pending to license corporations doing interstate business passed. This one was totally without organized finance. Starting in 1939, Hall and Cash spread membership cards and chapter certificates gratis throughout the country. The cards were displayed by many who thought that the barbershop quartet movement was in the same category as the Guild of Former Pipe Organ Pumpers and others with humorous intent. No dues were asked by SPEBSQSA, hence none were received. Hall says that it was a hobby and they wanted the world to share their interest.

Without dues, planned effort, direction—all that goes into organization—the society was an easy mark for a promoter to stage a barbershop quartet contest by simply implying that he represented the group becoming increasingly well-known. As in the case of the original club, locals elsewhere were organized around the enthusiasm of an individual, sometimes two. Where they met, how they were run, what was sung, conformed to whatever pattern was most pleasing to the organizers. In St. Paul, the *Dispatch-Pioneer Press* and radio station WTCN issued membership coupons to anyone—"No Fees, No Dues." Hundreds received coupons, but the momentum provided by numbers could not carry the so-called "chapter" through the doldrums of unorganization that followed the initial wind of enthusiasm. Each chapter was a self-contained unit without direction beyond a local man's idea and without connection to any central guiding body. How could Tulsa guide when it had no experience as precedent? Most of its members wanted only to make up for lost time in personal singing while basking altruistically in the thought that, far beyond the Oklahoma horizons, others were doing the same.

It was as if the flight of spring's robins had arrived, ready to burst out with suppressed morning trills and vesper song. But, due to unavoidable delays, the flight faced the busyness of immediate search for nesting materials and suitable locations. Eggs were laid hither, yon, and helter-skelter as others hatched in widely dispersed places. The newly-hatched twittered and squawked for parental guidance toward a happy and songful robinhood. "Incorporated in the State of Oklahoma, the Society was operating in various states of confusion," says *Keep America Singing,* the history of those early years.

The frustration, endured during the Lean Years, explains why the new singing club was hailed so enthusiastically by men everywhere whose vocations ran the gamut of variety but who voted avocationally as a solid bloc in favor of self-expression in song. More than enthusiasm would be needed to advance the front beyond Tulsa and consolidate the gains. How this was accomplished necessitates following SPEBSQSA's course through early obstacles that made its national survival chancy despite favorable conditions at the start. The obstructions were often high, tough, and well entangled with barbs.

Heading for the First Roundup

It was stated earlier that unserious musicians need no audience and that they may resent direction of their spontaneous efforts. The early worshipers at the altar of Adeline felt no need for listeners. As to direction, the self-confessed world's greatest baritone and his counterparts needed no guidance in off-the-cuff harmonizing. The majority of them, being duly sworn, would have deposed that they invented barbershop harmony. J. Frank Rice, who sang lead with Cash, declared himself "the sweetest lead this side of heaven." Hank Wright, who helped get the Oklahoma City club off the ground, was willing to knock off work at any hour of any day to demonstrate to anyone anywhere how to sing a real bass. Like scores of others in the budding society, these were conservative business and professional men to whom exaggeration was as foreign vocationally as it was natural in after-hours buffoonery.

No, they didn't need an audience or a song leader. But one characteristic common to all of them, altruism, kept them from out-and-out *resentment* of listeners. Altruistically, they wanted to share the joys inherent to ringing a four-part chord. "Locking" one is synonymous with ringing. A chord that was rung or locked produced chromatic overtones that brought sheer ecstasy to its singers. "Oh, boy! Let's sing that again!" (and again and again). No audience was needed in that harmony heaven, but, out of pure generosity, they might feel obligated to call a barbershopper friend in St. Louis or Little Rock, long-distance prepaid, at 1:15 A.M. so that he too could revel in the tinny telephonic effect of a newly discovered chord or swipe in "Way Down Home." Their benevolence, they knew, would be received with gratitude unless his wife answered the phone located remotely from the bedroom. Wives were unpredictable.

The society's progress across the country was not entirely unopposed. Without music in her soul, or specifically barbershop music, a wife could put the brakes upon her husband's long-repressed desire to journey into harmony land instead of playing bridge or fixing that faucet. Also some general dissenters tried to throw monkey wrenches into the singers' pitchpipes. One such Tulsan wrote to the editor: "The whole is a vituperative affront to the memory of Jenny Lind [1820–87], the Swedish Nightingale who trilled the notes into an hypnotic lullaby of the soft susurrus, a rank indignity to the Mesdames Eames, Melba, and Schumann-Heink, the De Reskes, Pugna, Caruso, et al. Let the disciples of would-be coloratura vocal artistry be led away by an infuriated mob to some lagoon where they may chortle to the bullfrogs the intoxicating strains and dulcet cadenzas of Sweet Adeline." Only Eames was living, in retirement, so comparisons of whispered *sussurandos* seemed impractical to the boys in Tulsa. Furthermore, they were more interested in busting a solid ringing chord than in hypnotic lullabies. No infuriated mobs appeared to lead them to the frog pond.

Always with the thought of sharing, the Tulsans began to talk in late 1938 about staging a quartet contest and a "national" convention the next year. It would not be for the ignorant, the often amazed, and the unappreciative. It would be limited to devotees of the art who might be induced to display their wares before their own kind. Again Cash took up his whimsical pen to announce "Why You Should Come to Tulsa." By that time he and others in the Tulsa singing group had contacts, spottily, throughout the country. Slightly abridged: "In the first place, you need a vacation. You haven't been looking so well lately. You have attended conventions before. What did you get? You listened to a mess of dry speeches, reports of committees, and heard meaningless resolutions read: then reached your room exhausted and tried to organize a quartet. The only thing about a convention quartet that is 'organized' is the singers.

"Have you ever participated with 2,000 men in busting 'I Want A Girl' wide open? So get three or four of your cronies together, come by plane, train or covered wagon—but come. Be extremely nice to the little woman from now until June but if she doesn't soften up, do as I do. Just give her a good stiff punch in the jaw and come anyway.

"When you get to Tulsa, I want to show you the baritone to 'Mandy Lee.' I am the only baritone in the United States who can do it correctly. Now if you mugs don't come to this party, the next time I see you I am going to kick your britches right up between your ears."

As carelessly optimistic about barbershop harmony as he was conservative in handling legalities for Stanolind pipelines, his 2,000 estimate shrunk to about a hundred from out of town when the recipients of his invitation arrived. No national officers greeted them nor were there any judging rules to grade the quartets who came from as far away as Illinois. The schedule of events, labeled *For men only,* said in part: "Friday—Barber shoppers will be vaccinated, ear-tagged and tattooed so they can be returned to the herd if lost, strayed or stolen." The winning quartet would be crowned World Champion with "emoluments, gratuities, appurtenances and benefits, along with commission as Colonel on the Oklahoma Governor's staff." The second-place winner would be adopted by the Pawnee Indian Tribe. "Also rans—a box of throat lozenges."

On the morning of June 2, before the afternoon contest, those who were willing to take time off from singing in the lobby or washrooms and corridors of Hotel Tulsa attended the first "national" meeting. There were no delegates since no regulations for their appointment or election existed in Tulsa or anywhere else. It was a barbershoppers' town meeting. Rupert I. Hall, co-organizer, was elected National President. Cash retained his title of Founder and Permanent Third Assistant Temporary Vice-Chairman. Since none present were willing to consider an officer lower than vice-president, seven were elected. Their duty: to disseminate the Word to the uninformed in remote provinces, even as far away as the wilds of distant Ohio. Crass details, such as paying dues to the national committee or to chapters, yet to be organized officially, were not presented to the assemblage in the brief meeting. On adjournment, it broke immediately into splinter groups, each singing something different in the hotel's small parlor.

The eligibility rules for quartets in the afternoon contest stated merely that they must be nonprofessional. As to judging rules, there weren't any. Six judges listened for what each liked best in barbershop harmony presented by twenty-three foursomes. In the finals next day, the Bartlesville Barflies were crowned World Champions and winners of the grand prize, fifty dollars, with the understanding that it would not affect their amateur status. Their "My Own Cabin Home Among the Hills" was adjudged the outstanding number sung. About a hundred and fifty men, including the competing quartets, were in the audience.

The Tulsa *World* reported that more than half of the delegates were from out of town, "many from out of the state." Most of the "delegates" had traveled to the Tulsa roundup from places where no chapter existed. They were there to listen, learn, rub elbows with their kind, and inspect their tonsils. (One singing competitor, Glenn Howard of Cisco, Illinois, was the only member there who, since then, has attended every annual convention-contest.) The faithful from out of town returned home as fired-up as ardent revivalists. Yearners who had not gone to Tulsa read the account, sent by wire services to their local papers, and vowed to become evangelists.

By far the great majority in the nation still smiled tolerantly at the antic news about grown men getting together to harmonize old songs. Some were skeptical. "In *my* opinion, it's an excuse for a night out." At least, the national meeting attended by men from seven states demonstrated that the movement was more than a reporter's dream of wishful thinking by oddballs. Solid citizens had spent their money on expenses to Oklahoma in an attempt to recapture what had seemed lost forever. They reported widely that the investment was worthwhile. The *Reader's Digest* published a half page about the society. Between that and the returned conventioneers and the newspapers' reports of the gathering, "We were swamped again," Hall recalls. "We had no true organization." They continued to dip into their own pockets for postage, printing, visitations, and all that went with the notoriety. "But we had a glorious time."

The Souls of Artists

When President Hall called for a winter meeting of the national board in St. Louis, it was largely to provide uninterrupted opportunity for the directors to get acquainted and to find out who sang which part and how well. A few minor considerations of policy and operation might intrude, but the board was assured of time and a place for more important (musical) matters. Even though the permanent third assistant temporary vice-chairman recognized the drawing power of such an incentive, he was really surprised when three national officers and five regional vice-presidents answered roll call on January 20, 1940. They came from as far away as Cleveland.

The business meeting dealt with offers from several cities that wanted the society's second national convention and contest. New York City promised publicity for the newborn organization as a feature of the World's Fair that year. The names of nationally known Al Smith, former governor, and Mayor Fiorello La Guardia carried such conviction that the newly hatched society decided to try a pinfeather flight to Manhattan on July 22.

St. Louis, where they were gathered, had one of the few chapters with organization, direction, and financial stability. Dues of five dollars a year were payable to the chapter for its running expenses. In other cities, some of the so-called chapters met in schools, churches, almost anyplace that was rent free. Those not so fortunate tried to finance their meetings by the unsatisfactory kitty method. In some instances where members were not called upon to ante up, the expense accounts of a few swelled disproportionally under "customer entertainment." Usually, the local secretary was allowed to foot the bills for postage as evidence of his loyalty.

By the time of the St. Louis winter meeting, the boys in Tulsa realized that they constituted the nucleus of a national phenomenon that could have enormous outgo with no income. With the intention of reversing that flow somewhat, they invested additional dollars in stationery, lapel pins, and certificates. Hopefully, they might receive enough return from the markup, above their cost, to tip the financial scales. The certificates stated that its recipient would be entitled to harmonize at any time, day or night, "to his heart's content subject to the by-laws and rules and regulations of the order [there were none] and conforming always to the applicable state laws relating to the preservation of the public peace," obviously another Cash whimsy. Board members and the many others to whom he sent membership cards were surprised and pleased to find that they were paid up until December 31, 1999. Few members who received these documents could take the time from harmonizing to send the three dollars covering the kit.

That was the happy condition of unorganization in January 1940 when the national board held its first meeting in St. Louis. After business hours, one event stood out above all others. They heard about thirty local members sing barbershop harmony with such precision that it sounded "like a single foursome." The precisionist was Dr. Norman F. Rathert who had done work professionally as a musician and was a patron of any worthwhile musical effort. He led that first barbershop harmony chorus through a dream medley, an Irish medley, "Little Sir Echo" and "Tittle Tattle Tale." The board's members were used to hearing each foursome, usually a pickup four, give its own interpretation of any number sung. It might vary between singings, since all harmonizing was by ear with no record of how they sang it previously. Here, they heard agreement between voices singing the same harmony part, and total agreement between the parts, drilled into them by Rathert. Added to the unprecedented volume, that multiple harmony raised goose pimples. The echoes were rerung in July when the St. Louis delegation arrived in Manhattan.

Living up to their promises, the Fair people had sent Sigmund Spaeth on tour to supervise preliminary contests in several cities. No one in the country was as well qualified as Spaeth. By training and early experience, he was a musical highbrow, but if he favored one type of music over another, it didn't show. His doctoral dissertation at Princeton had been on Milton's knowledge of music and its significance in his works. He was concert master of the classical Orphic Order orchestra which, he said later, was often called the Orful Odor. Because his "voice could never make up its mind," he sang each of four parts in choral societies.

In New York he was music critic of the *Evening Mail* and he was the New York correspondent for Boston's famous H. T. Parker of the *Transcript*. Spaeth's book, *Barber Shop Ballads,* 1925, so far as is known, contains the first published barbershop-style harmonizations. The little book included recordings of the arrangements in it, but they were brittle, so hardly anyone heard Spaeth's recorded baritone. These are a few of the many qualifications that made him the natural selection for organizing preliminaries in several cities ahead of the contest at New York's World's Fair.

If payment of dues was the qualification, it is probable that the St. Louis group there outnumbered the combined bona fide members present. The event had been ballyhooed as a national contest sponsored by SPEBSQSA but no Manhattan members greeted the visitors, because no chapter existed in New York or its environs. Parks Commissioner Robert Moses was on the judging panel that included Mayor La Guardia, the city's official greeter Grover Whalen, and Harry Armstrong of "Sweet Adeline" fame.

The mayor told the audience that the fifty quartets chosen in the national preliminaries had the souls of artists. He said that the judges were as "infallible, uncertain and unpredictable" as those in any other court. Spaeth was master of ceremonies. When the infallibles emerged from their huddle after the last chord had been rung, the Flatfoot Four, Oklahoma City, was declared the national champion quartet. They were policemen who'd utilized their vacation time to visit New York.

The greatest benefit of the meeting came from the national news that identified SPEBSQSA as something that really existed and functioned. It was no longer a whimsical jest from the Southwest. Manhattanites had seen men on the streets wearing costumes of the West, which they wore at home only on special occasions. They looked like cattle rustlers in a movie. New Yorkers had seen the traffic jam when four singing cops in strange uniforms "directed" traffic at Broadway and Forty-fourth Street, the Flatfoot Four, of course, in connivance with the New York Police Quartet. Great numbers of pictures of colorful incidents were published in the nation's newspapers. The Flatfoots sang on two radio networks. In faraway Tulsa, stay-at-homes were thrilled. "Imagine that! Our little quartet society being introduced by Ben Grauer on a national hookup!"

Many of the visiting singers were seeing New York for the first time, and in consequence, the cowhands had to scour the plains of Flatbush and the canyons of the city to round up a quorum for the board's business meeting. They found enough directors to elect Dr. Rathert national president for the next year and award the 1941 convention to St. Louis. It was quite a day for him. He had sung with his "Chromatic Canaries" and made the finals of the contest. The exalted seven vice-presidents joined in demoting themselves to mere directorships—and the meeting adjourned, sung out.

When the board reconvened at its winter meeting in St. Louis in January of 1941, it had for consideration a document that laid the foundation of regulations and rulings for the society, the first draft of a constitution prepared by Vice-President Carroll P. Adams of Detroit. It allowed chartering of local groups by the national president when he was convinced that the applicant groups were "properly organized and worthy. All such groups must agree to be bound by the constitution and rules." It called for annual dues of fifty cents per member of each chapter chartered. To some, half a dollar a year seemed too big an outlay for those who'd joined just to sing. Who ever heard of paying out cash for that privilege and right? But the board approved Adams' constitution with hardly any revisions. Joseph P. Wolff, also of Detroit, was appointed chairman of a committee to prepare a code of ethics.

The year between adjournment in New York and convocation in St. Louis, July 3, 1941, was a busy one for second president Rathert and his right-hand man, Joseph E. Wodicka. No national secretarial records existed until that year when Joseph E. Stern, a Kansas City realtor, was elected secretary-treasurer. Provisions to charter chapters existed constitutionally, but no charters were printed until March. One hundred of them went out to individuals in cities where known interest existed. A bill for three dollars was enclosed. Payment of it would make the charter official. When the convention convened in July, seventeen cities had replied and Stern had $51 to add to $106.47 in the national treasury to clean up deficits and finance the convention. The income from the kits of society stationery, lapel pins, and the rest, sent earlier, had been less than the postage required to send them. If the good times in the society were to continue, it must have organization and income beyond what came from the pockets of the faithful.

The 1941 convention and contest in St. Louis was a principal crossroad on the trail from notoriety as a freak club to recognition by the American public and by music educators. Later, decisions had to be made at other crossroads farther along, but the society wouldn't have reached them if it hadn't taken the right turns at St. Louis. The fork to the right can't be identified by any single act of general membership, quartets or administrators. They chalked up several firsts, but the most important one was an awareness that became apparent as members met and board and committee meetings progressed—the talk about the serious work that must be done at the grass roots of the chapters if they were to survive and provide future enjoyment in their hometowns. Many of the visiting firemen had seen local groups rocket under SPEBSQSA power, sizzle a few sparks for the home folks, fizzle out, and drop into obscurity like a rocket's stick. But those who came had hope, and some faith, for continuation.

How many chapters were functioning with how many members? The answer was conjecture. Not even the founders would make an uneducated guess, except for publication. Then, of course, membership was never reported in less than thousands. Years later, Carroll P. Adams, by then international secretary, said that to give accurate charter dates of chapters and their membership during the first two or three years was as impossible as for him to jump over the moon. That would have applied also to what was going on in the chapters. Some so-called, had no connection with the parent society other than the SPEBSQSA name which they used free and freely.

The known chapters had members to whom harmonizing was as natural as the affinity of a four-year-old for screen doors in flytime. Their idea of a perfect chapter meeting was to select three others who knew the old songs without coaching, then go into a huddle. Others, not so sure of melody, words, or harmony, liked gang singing where they could park in a chorus beside a proved practitioner as a guide and stay. How to find what the organization had—and what to do with it in guidance?

Several months before the 1941 convention, Rathert and Wodicka prepared a little booklet designed to eliminate part of the flood of personal correspondence with outsiders who wanted information. It included facts about the genesis, constitution, ethics, and names and addresses of officers, directors, and chapters. By that time, they ranged nominally from Northampton, Massachusetts, to Los Angeles. The compilers included suggestions for the conduct of meetings that still apply: "Choose a meeting place where no one would hesitate to attend . . . ask members to bring friends . . . tactfully invite guests to become members . . . devote the first part of the meeting to teaching one new song [strictly by ear at that time] . . . call on quartets. If no units volunteer, pick a quartet at random."

In some chapters, the man who arranged for that suitable meeting place might be stuck with the entire bill. It was well that the St. Louisans had given a preconvention minstrel show and dance to help defray some of the expense. Income from the affair, added to that from 309 all-event coupon books bought by those registered, plus the $51 in the national treasury, resulted in a deficit of only $150. When the last quartet had sung, Rathert and Wodicka paid for twenty cups awarded to the contestants, but several promised sponsorships had not materialized. "The convention nearly busted Joe and me physically and financially," Rathert recalls fondly.

Among the other firsts in St. Louis, an attempt was made to judge the quartets by categories. Each judge was given an instruction sheet. Barbershop harmony and blending would be rated at 50 percent, song selection and originality, 25 percent, stage presentation, 25 percent. It was the start toward present-day practice in which each judge listens for a particular phase, such as harmony accuracy. One item in the instructions to the quartets was shattered time after time. "Each quartet must be prepared to furnish the National body with one of its arrangements for the purpose of preservation."

In the interest of preservation and encouragement that was an excellent idea, but how could a quartet preserve on paper when hardly any contestant could write or read musical notes? The first-place Chordbusters from Oklahoma City rehearsed from arrangements prepared by a professional musician, Lem Childers, of their city. When news of that dark fact was spread during the preliminaries, the protests by veterans of song in the barber's shop were not always muttered in their beards. "It ain't barbershop when you sing it from notes." The Chordbusters in "Bye Bye Blues" introduced the amazed audience to "bell" chords in which each singer sounds his note in succession with such precision and so rapidly that they pile upon each other with a bell-like peal. It had such appeal to listeners that many jumped up to cheer. The judges, who by then were all society members, had to maintain judicious attitudes. Only their eyes could show their appreciations. Some confessed later that they'd never heard the likes o' that. Those "Blues" can be heard today from Decca's album, "The Best of Barbershop Harmony," DXB-180 (M).* It records the SPEBSQSA champions over the society's first twenty-five years.

For reasons that have been touched upon, also matters of organization, regulation, and other live issues, the business sessions of the society bulked more importantly at St. Louis than formerly. Vice-President Carroll P. Adams was elected the third national president. Returning home by train, some members tried to catch up on lost sleep. In dreams they sang in quartets such as they'd heard for three days and nights. Others who'd driven to St. Louis got through on coffee—barely.

* M for monaural. If not at dealers, write SPEBSQSA, Inc., 6315 Third Avenue, Kenosha, Wisconsin 53141 about this or other barbershop quartet recordings.

Annoted

From the beginning, these notes have been presented as a tour conducted among the fields of popular music and the facts, fancies, and speculations associated with it. Viewed from the field where the permanent third assistant temporary vice-chairman delved so earnestly with his husbandmen and recruits, the panorama has included the conditions that made a small club in Tulsa national news which attracted men from every economic, social, national origin, religious, and political level. We've seen the local developments that followed colonization and the national conventions. But we haven't pulled off the road to look at the *res,* which in law means a particular thing. The thing itself is a particular kind of harmony now in musical dictionaries.

The urge to mortgage the old homestead to attend a convention or to tunnel under walls to harmonize with three others is no more identifiable than the invisible magnet that draws victims into collecting stamps or enjoying sunrises or garlic or playing a mandolin backward as was described earlier. So, we bypass compulsive urges and focus upon the *res* itself, barbershop harmony.

After the St. Louis meeting, a committee wrestled with the undefined. Its findings were presented "with the hope that it will be improved upon." The definition: "Barbershop harmony is produced by four voices (tenor, lead, baritone, and bass) unaccompanied—when the melody is consistently sung below the tenor—when rules of time, expression, and word theme are sacrificed to obtain blending harmony satisfaction—usually with at least one harmonizing chord on each melody note." That left several areas untouched. Item: Though characterized by a four-part chord on each melody note, the lead sometimes sings a note, even three or four, at the beginning of a phrase as a "pickup" unaccompanied. It is done so quickly and in rhythm that the chain is not broken. The tenor may touch infrequently upon a melody note in order to avoid awkward voicing or to give aid and comfort to a lead whose range does not reach the stratosphere. Fans of barbershop harmony who, themselves, don't sing harmony parts may not recognize such components. A bird watcher may not be able to tell a chickadee from a titmouse or nuthatch, although enjoying their antics as thoroughly as does the informed ornithologist.

The outstanding characteristic of barbershop is the dominance of the resolving dominant (barbershop seventh) chords as recognized by musicians. In sequences, they are resolved on the circle of fifths attributed to Bach. Because of their "coincidence of harmonics," so termed by physicists, the harmonic tones are in a ratio which in combination best produces the "ring" of overtones characteristic of well-sung barbershop harmony. Other chords are harder to ring. Elsewhere, in much vocal ensemble work today, the sixth chord is used in sequence after sequence. In such profusion it cloys upon barbershoppers' ears. Strawberries with cream and sugar are delicious to most, but not three times every day. Sixth, ninth, augmented fifths, and others have definite use in barbershop harmony. Less can be said for the major-seventh, though there are times when its clash of tones can't be avoided. A characteristic of much folk-type singing, genuinely old or synthetically new, sets it and barbershop harmony at opposite poles. Much folk-type music is in minors. Barbershoppers hardly ever use them when they can be avoided, since a minor is a three-note chord and barbershoppers don't enjoy doubling. They reach for that fourth note to fill their sense of harmony.

A Grade-A quartet has still another characteristic, recognized if four voices have a familylike blend. Call it voice quality in the absence of a better term. It does not refer to volume uttered by a single voice, since one voice may hold back or put out an increased volume to give the desired effect on a certain chord. Voice quality may be expressed best by a comparison. Imagine the blend, or lack of it, in an instrumental quartet made up of a buzzing oboe, slithering Hawaiian guitar, shrilling flute, and booming tuba. Each has a distinctive recognizable tone quality that doesn't melt into the three others. Or visualize a chest that glows with the rich tones of matched light and dark walnut, into which a strip or two of hemlock-crating lumber was inserted. In barbershop singing the most obvious enemies of blend are a voice with wide zigzag vibrato (the other parts can't zig or zag with it so the chord becomes muddy), a wire-edge tenor, a bass that booms roughly, or a baritone whose voice quality projects that unharmonious part too strongly. Again, none of these refers to volume but to an undefinable quality that makes one speaking or singing voice distinguishable from another.

Lest a sensitive bari be offended by "unharmonious," let me interject at once that the baritone part is the cream in the coffee, the topping for the parfait, the indispensable part. It fills in to produce the ultimate in four-part harmony satisfactions. Sung alone, a bari part seems as unrelated as the parts of a small snake that have just traveled through a power mower. When blandly inserted with restraint into three other singing parts, bari crowns the chord structure. In Pittsburgh one time I told a member that he sang the best bari I never heard. He still repeats that compliment. It was not backhanded as the uninitiated might infer.

The late Arthur Christian of Jackson, Mississippi, characterized the singers themselves in "All Quartets Are Divided Into Four Parts" (in the society, that is —outside, any number is permissible).

In a quartet somebody must carry the tune, and this job is tossed to the lead. *He usually can't sing anything else, and would have to be called the "load," which he sometimes is anyway. Some lead singers are broken-down tenors.*

The main requirements for a lead are a good pair of bellows and memory for words. He should also be able to hit the melody note right on the schnozzle, but this point doesn't seem to bother him too much. To keep him happy, the lead is given most of the solo parts (he's the only one who knows the words). There are usually more leads in a Society chapter than pimples on a duck. The melody carrier is considered the key Joe in any quartet, except by the tenor, baritone and bass.

The tenor *is frequently referred to as the "top" tenor because he so frequently blows his top. Tenors add lightness and counteract the coarse rumble of the other three voices. Good tenors are as hard to locate as a quart of Old Crow at a church convention. They have to be handled with silk gloves (a stout two-by-four will do also). Tenors come in two sizes, either very fat or very skinny. You have to be born a tenor—they can't be developed from common stock.*

Every quartet needs a bass *to give a deep mellow body to the brew. Many basses are too old to sing baritone. Others are too smart to try. Some basses sing awful low, and others just sing awful. You can generally spot a bass by his roving Adam's apple. Bass singing shouldn't be encouraged. It doesn't have to be.*

When some character discovered that a well rounded fully packed chord contained four notes, the baritone *entered the picture. Being the last one in, he was handed the missing note that nobody else could sing. It may lie between a low gurgle and a high squeak. A bari must have vocal chords with a hydromatic shift.*

Most baritones are patient and self-effacing citizens, with a far away look. The bari keeps on only by the realization that the quartet would sound incomplete without him. He is sustained by the thought that, when he loses his grip, he can always become a bass.

Science has never been able to determine how or why anyone starts singing baritone. Some believe that it's because he fell out of his cradle—to a concrete floor—on his head. The name baritone is derived from the Latin "baro tonum," meaning "bats in the belfry." You don't have to be crackpot to sing bari, but it helps.

A successful bari must be a consistent optimist with faith that he'll be able to fit into the next measure, a songbird in search of a perch, a regional shepherd in search of the lost or strayed. He's in charge of the missing-notes department and, usually, he's jealous of anyone who finds that missing note before he does. Now that we've seen a sort of oscillograph of the *res* itself and its singers, let's get back on the road.

The fledgling society rode high on the early waves of enthusiasm. A few members recognized the need for better organization for continuance. When Carroll P. Adams of Detroit became president at St. Louis in 1941, he brought a rare and invaluable combination of abilities to the less-than-adolescent musical upstart that hoped for a place eventually in the American scene. He had a good musical background and experience in directing affairs of musical organizations as president and secretary of Detroit's Orpheus Club and secretary of the Michigan Male Chorus Association. He had headed the Midwestern Conference of Male Choruses and served as vice-president of the Associated

Male Choruses of America. Added to these practicalities, he had been secretary of the Michigan Alumni Club in Detroit and was an executive in that city's Board of Commerce at the time of his election.

He took the presidency with the understanding that a primary responsibility would be an attempt to uncover the length and breadth of SPEBSQSA. He would be lucky, he said, if that could be accomplished during his one-year term. The society was supposed to have about a hundred chapters. It didn't take Adams a year to find that only twenty-four actually functioned. Great numbers of the arrows shot into the air from Tulsa had disappeared. As uncontrolled missiles, the majority were duds. A few carried delayed fuses that functioned later.

His vision of the society's future stability included revision of its constitution which he had written. Conditions were changing from week to week. Changes demanded a broader pattern for operations than he, or anyone else, could have conceived in January of that year. He saw the new document as a binder that could draw loosely connected pieces into a compact unit. Other national musical societies with which he was familiar had amalgamated existing groups. But no precedent existed for this society. SPEBSQSA lived largely in hopes rather than in tangible records. Field research might make a roster possible. The vision included local and national articles about the society and preparation of a quarterly publication to bring a semblance of uniformity into the scattered chapters. A new constitution would contribute to clarification of problems ranging from finance to ethics.

Even those who sang entirely by ear, and who had protested that it wasn't barbershop harmony if learned from notes, realized that Adams' call for written arrangements had logic. How else could a Chicagoan haunted by the harmonies of "Sweet Roses of Morn," ever since he'd heard it sung by the Mound City Four of St. Louis, teach three harmony parts to his own Windy City foursome? Relief was near. Phil W. Embury of Warsaw, New York, had been charmed also. He was one of the few who could write as well as read music. In St. Louis at 2 A.M. he induced the Mound City boys to repeat "Sweet Roses" while he wrote the spots on the back of an envelope. It was published by mimeo duplication during Adams' year, the first written arrangement under society auspices. Joseph E. Stern, the secretary-treasurer, contributed a barbershop harmony arrangement of "Daddy, Get Your Baby out of Jail" as he'd sung it in pre-society days.

In 1941 there was another reason for written harmonizations. Dr. Rathert's barbershop chorus, mentioned previously, made such an impact upon the officers and directors who'd heard it at the winter meeting that, back home, they talked up choruses to their own chapters.

Four members of a quartet might have, were likely to have, four concepts of a chord that might bear rapturous fruition or could bring them to a halt and an accusing "Who blew that one?" (An example is the next-to-last Lee in "Mandy Lee.") Stretch four concepts to thirty or forty in a chorus, each singer a ragged individualist or uncertain about his harmony note. Unless agreement was reached by long-drawn-out repetitions by ear, the output of the gang when singing a slightly known or unknown song could resemble the effect of ringing pigs. (In only one respect is ringing a pig comparable with ringing bells: on a still, windless day both can be heard from a mile away. A pig's nose is made of tough gristle. He uses it for rooting [shovelling] earth when he searches for buried acorns, seeds or roots that might be to a pig's taste. His excavations sometimes tear out the roots of crops, like clover or winter wheat, which the farmer wants to achieve further growth. So, before turning the pigs into such a field, it became standard practice among farmers to clamp one or more copper wire "rings" into each pig's nose to make rooting uncomfortable to him. From the instant when he's caught for ringing until the ear-piercing shriek signalling that the ring has been clamped in, the pig emits a series of grunts, squeals and ululations which defy description to one who hasn't heard a pig-ringing. Neighboring farm folk would merely comment: "Sounds like the Martins are ringing pigs this morning.")

Though few members could read music, a written note that went up meant higher, down meant lower. How high or low might be a puzzler. Despite that possibility, the notes of an arrangement provided a crutch for those trying to follow a rocky harmony route which they hadn't traveled before.

One project that came before the board during Adams' administration was shelved—the publishing of a society songbook. The permanent and so forth vice-chairman spoke feelingly about that one. In 1940 a "publication committee" in Tulsa issued a booklet, *Let's Harmonize,* with the society's first armorial shield on the cover and, inside, facts about the infant organization. Forty pages were filled with the words, no music, of well-known songs. "There's a Gold Mine in the Sky" led, followed by "School Days" and "When Day Is Done." The last of 161 lyrics was "It Looks Like Rain in Cherry Blossom Lane." Copyrights on the great majority were live and valid. They'd been printed without requests for the permission of the copyright owners or credit to them as publishers.

Fortunately, Sigmund Spaeth received a copy in New York. (Mine is No. 24 signed by the vice-chairman before he prefixed "permanent" to his title.) Spaeth called ASCAP, of which he'd been a member since 1925, and made calls to friends at publishing houses whose songs he recognized. His explanations, followed by others, saved the boys in Tulsa from the miseries of colossal lawsuits in which, obviously, they'd have been found guilty of breaking the copyright law. Most of the songs they'd reproduced were such natural parts of their environments, like "Happy Birthday" mentioned earlier, that it hadn't occurred to them that anyone owned or cared about copyrights.

The trials, errors, starts in one direction, stops and quick changes when a course proved wrong, have an analogy today in the gropings of the world's newly emerged nations. "There is no substitute for experience." President Adams had no precedent for the right or wrong way to preserve and encourage. He did know what had been good or bad for other national musical associations, and he guided study committees. Contest judging needed attention. The decisions of judges at the St. Louis (third) national contest when each tried to weigh the merits of quartets by a few categories had brought reactions that ranged from compliments to Bronx cheers.

Some members had dark suspicions that a judge would favor any sort of quartet from his hometown or vicinity. This judge had been seen talking to a quartet before the contest. "It's in the bag!" That judge smiled at a quartet when it came on stage. "He didn't smile at us." An eager beaver in the audience had seen another shake his head in disapproval of a chord. Feeling ran high in chapters outside the "axis" that no quartet had a chance unless it came from the mother state of Oklahoma, as the first three winners had been. Scuttlebutt was rife. As to favoring the hometown, later experience proved the opposite. Knowing the feeling that existed among some members, the judges became so intent upon being fair to all that they were inclined to penalize the boys from home more severely than the unknowns from beyond the horizon. That led to accusations and arguments within chapters.

Adams appointed Harold B. Staab of Northampton, Massachusetts, to head a committee to study judging procedures. He submitted a questionnaire to membership. The returns showed that stage presence was relatively low in importance. Song selection even lower. In consequence, judging procedures and their categories received the first of the many modifications that would come as experience accrued. At the forthcoming contest at Grand Rapids, Michigan, judges would be assigned to harmony accuracy, 25 percent, arrangements, 25 percent, voice expression, 30 percent, song selection, 10 percent, stage presence, 10 percent. Staab said: "The basis of grading is not as important as the selection of competent judges."

As 1941 went out, the founder honored with certificates those who had substituted at widely separated places and hours for a member of his Okie Four, "world's foremost exponents of barber shop harmony," it said. That and a line in the certificate reveals the flavor throughout: "Deems Taylor, outstanding musical critic, heard Brother J. Frank Rice [the Okie's lead] sound off with 'Don't Cry, Little Girl, Don't Cry.' He managed to gasp "'It is like a voice from heaven, hyperstatic, transcendental and disembodied'—which it should be!" Taylor's broadcast commentaries from New York about opera and symphony were on a level several notches removed from the free and easy hyperbole of the barbershopping pioneers. On the last day of the year, Adams sent his order of business for the midwinter meeting. The directors had thirty-seven items to consider on the agenda. The society was in transition from hope-and-pray. It was growing into long pants.

The Changing Image

Keep America Singing, the history of the society's first decade, records that the fourth convention-contest at Grand Rapids in 1942 marked the upward turn, when the hopeful organization realized its potentials and moved into consolidation and utilization of what it had learned by hunt-and-poke methods.

Growth had followed the prehistoric pattern established by a troglodyte who craved a back door. A friend helped him to develop one. Then the local housing committee went into action and spread the word. Each convert reached others ripe for exploration of possibilities. The evangelistic group took embryonic form. A movement was launched and, as it touched at ports beyond the original horizon, more sympathizers rallied 'round. The barbershop society's early advances were comparable with those of Christianity, votes for women, communism, the W.C.T.U., and democracy. All such have a common experience of temporary confusion as to direction, controls, representation, and methods. Charter members may keep iron-fisted control, or it may pass to those with the ability and desire to lead or direct or command. They rise from the ranks like walnuts above beans when shaken in a jar. Original concepts are modified. Splinter groups may conform and be absorbed or they may take over, as in the formation of our major political parties.

The public's memory of conventional patterns, whether of a quartet society or other, lingers until it is replaced by current developments. When SPEBSQSA came into being, a reference to four men singing for their own pleasure flashed an impression that had been common to an earlier era: a highly saturated four singing at 2 A.M. beside a lamppost. Just as the public's impression of the Negro in the North, presented earlier, came from stage caricatures, joke books, illustrations, and comparable media, the majority of cartoonists, and illustrators and some reporters held to the old clichés in depicting the society in its early stages.

When founders Owen Cash and Rupert Hall went forth to sow, much of their seed landed among thorns and on rocks. But enough took root and reproduced increasingly over four growing seasons to bear bountiful crops. For the fourth convention-contest, more members and better quartets (sixty in all), appeared at Grand Rapids. For the finals, an audience of almost five thousand filed into the Civic Auditorium. Some were members who had traveled long distances, but the majority were local people who came from curiosity or earlier knowledge of what four matched voices can produce in harmony.

World War II had started. Of the Grand Rapids meeting, George W. Stark, columnist of the Detroit *News,* wrote: "This is a curious manifestation of the American way, the industrialist, the banker, the baker, the factory worker, the soldier and sailor running the scale of human emotions . . . the token of the essence of our country, the four corners of America each worshipping God in its own way. That's another thing we fight for."

The beloved permanent temporary vice-chairman told the press that the quartet restoration movement had started at about the time when Hitler began to mess up Europe, "If it hadn't been for him, we'd have 25,000 members today instead of only 10,000." That second figure brought wry smiles from President Adams and Secretary-Treasurer Stern. When the latter took office a year before, he wrote to the twenty-four chapters that seemed to be functioning and asked them for the fifty-cent dues of the national organization. "In some cases I got no money, in others I got no answer at all and in too many others I got nasty letters. One chapter secretary asked why his group should pay *anything* to the National."

Few chapters had vision beyond the walls of their meeting places. Some weren't sure that other chapters existed. Several functioned under the name which, they felt, had been forced upon them. Others appropriated the name in order to launch a local singing club, but felt neither compunction nor responsibility for thievery from the parent organization. Though the number was low, as in other organizations, a few members were by nature suspicious of just about everything that went on. Rumor had it that dues went largely to pay the expenses of the directors at the best hotels where they lived off "the fat of the land." Echoes of the Depression still lingered and several board members wondered whether they should continue to be targets of criticism, sometimes abusive, while they could ill afford to spend their own money in the interest of growth, improvement, and unification. In that respect, their experiences paralleled those of the judges of contests. Too often, the latter were the targets of soapbox oratory.

A pioneer was asked "What's the lowdown?" and with a knowing look, "You fellows are making a nice thing out of this. What strings do I have to pull to get on the board?" Others, oriented entirely to their own localities, asserted that the National isn't going to tell us how to run our chapters. Some resented that their chapters weren't represented on the national directorate. They had no specific gripes or criticism but were sure that something phony was going on. "If I were a director, I'd do something about it." Self-perpetuation was one criticism heard by board members from a few to whom criticism and intrigue was more important than the joy of singing.

In these respects, the society experienced the pains that have been common to all organizational growth, though fewer than most. The pains were discussed in clinical sessions that kept the directors in smoke-filled rooms. Members without such responsibilities were free to do what came natur'lly. They had joined to sing and had come to sing. Other guests marveled at the sight and sound of solid citizens from far places who colonized by fours in corridors and washrooms of Grand Rapids' Pantlind Hotel just to harmonize "without any music or accompaniment."

The grapevine telegraph kept busy. Mills Music Company, cognizant of the potentials, was about to bring out a book of barbershop-style songs.* Composer Geoffrey O'Hara's "The Old Songs" would be the official theme song of the society. A resolution urged members to refrain from the use of Spebsqua or "dear old Speebsqua," as a raucous West Coast radio announcer enunciated it. (Because of the penultimate *S*, the initials can hardly be pronounced.) Related to that, the advance notices of the Grand Rapids meeting set a precedent by dropping the ultimate *t* and *e* from quartette. They've never been replaced in reference to a male foursome. The elision has saved the society tons of paper. Members heard for the first time about the possibility of district associations. President Adams had started one that year in Michigan, and the blueprint and record of its performance were available to all sections.

The judging of quartets started on Friday morning and continued into Saturday until fans had heard everything that barbershop harmony had to offer. So, that night, they went to the finals to hear more. Those who claimed that no quartet had a chance to win top place unless it was from Oklahoma changed their tune when the Elastic Four of Chicago won. Dyed-in-the-wool critics said it was still in the bag. "The judges had to spread the honors around the country." Without cynicism, Chairman of Judges Maurice E. Reagan, electrical engineering consultant of Pittsburgh, said, "The only ones who agree with the judges are the winners, and they're outnumbered."

The Elastics brought something new to the roster of champion quartets. They used several numbers that had been favorites of the barbershop cult for years, such as "Down by the Old Millstream," but the introduction of "Up a Lazy River" into their cycle provided a novelty without precedent. It wasn't the kind of song on which veteran quartetists had been reared. The melody was intricate, so intricate that today most guitar-strumming vocalists eliminate many high-low jumps and sing it in near monotone. The conventional tiering of the three harmony parts—tenor above melody, baritone below it, and bass on the bottom—would have kept the three hopping 'round into difficult intervals. So, Frank H. Thorne, the Elastic arranger, forward-passed several normally bari notes to himself, the bass, and lateraled a melody note occasionally to another harmony part. It was all in barbershop style, moving so fast that keen ears in the audience could hardly tell which Elastic hopped to another part.

The Elastics' "Tell Me You'll Forgive Me" introduced a number that is a standard today when a pickup four faces "What'll we sing?" They set another precedent. They wore natty summer sports attire. Their predecessors had worn the garb of the Southwest and, in the case of the Flatfoot Four, working uniforms.

The directors elected Harold B. Staab to the 1942–43 presidency and induced President Adams to accept part-time secretarial duties of the society, to be handled at his Detroit home. That relieved Joe Stern of Kansas City of his

* *Barber Shop Harmonies,* Mills Music Company, Inc., 1942. Several arrangements provided by quartets, as sung in contests.

dual duties as secretary-treasurer. He had been following precedent by paying most of the expenses of his office from his own pocket. Some criticism was directed at one item charged to the society, five dollars a month for a girl to help, after working hours, with the society's growing correspondence.

Chaos Declines

Men who worked with President Hal Staab from 1942 into 1944 agree that he had the ability and will to focus upon details as fine as petunia seed while his peripheral vision swept widely over his duties as chief executive. He had a business background, principally in sales. Before learning about SPEBSQSA, much of his avocational time and effort was in administrative duties for the northeastern section of the Kiwanis Club. As he drove between cities, he composed songs and jotted them down between stops.

The team of Staab and part-time Secretary Adams, experienced in other musical societies and immediate past president of this one, was aided by officers and directors whose judgment was as sound as their appraisal of the sound of a quartet. The 1942 president envisioned the unification of the thirty-five chapters he had inherited and the rehabilitation of several that had not paid their dues. Bolstered by association with each other, all of them would have more fun and would provide launching pads for extension.

His first move was to familiarize the chapters with his vision of unified operation. (To some officers in them, to spend time on that sort of thing was a waste of singing time.) He promised a quarterly publication and made his promise good in September with the first issue of *Re-Chordings,* changed later to *The Harmonizer*. Song arrangements, over which a committee had sweated, argued, and compromised, went out to the chapters that year. Skeptics or recalcitrants began to see tangible returns from their dues which were increased from fifty cents to two dollars annually.

Hammering away to drive home to locals the advantages to them of multiplicity and unification, he gave such impetus that all but nine states came into the fold during the society's first decade. He put a burr under the tail of a committee chairman who failed to work nights and weekends toward extension, interchapter relations, community service, or promotion of membership by publicity and personal effort. One committee's duty was to develop ways and means for chapters to raise funds to carry on their activities. Out of dire necessity, several had sold raffle tickets.

Chaos declined and new recruits came into a society that had the beginnings of order. Harmonyland's population center was shifting eastward. Michigan alone had thirteen active chapters visiting each other songfully. Three were in the Detroit area. Floods of letters, postmarked Northampton, Massachusetts, urging action, were hardly exceeded in volume by the correspondence from Secretary Adams' home. Since the society's treasury didn't warrant buying a typewriter, the Adams' Underwood seldom cooled. It was a rare evening when members from one or more of the Detroit or neighboring chapters failed to drop in at the home office with suggestions, questions, or gripes. If the secretary wasn't there, it was because he'd gone on a visitation where he was needed to advise, encourage, cajole, or lay down the law.

Chicago's Elastic Four was much nearer to the shifting center of membership than the champions' predecessors had been. Illinois and Michigan led the country in membership. The champs spent most weekends and many other nights in visiting chapters, singing for chartering parties, and appearing frequently before civic, charitable, and war activity groups. They stretched their appearances so far and often that, collectively, they lost forty-six pounds during their championship year. Other quartets did not match the Chicagoans' schedule but they were in frequent demand, particularly on request from towns where a small nucleus had heard about the society and wanted a quartet to fire up a group of local citizens by demonstration.

The West Coast, as a whole, made a slow start, then set a fast pace later. Some eastern units approached stability, but great numbers of the public still looked askance at the antics of those singing fellows. It was about this time when one of the original seven vice-presidents appointed in 1939 by the founder learned about the stature of his society in Ohio. He had spent two years in convincing musically inclined friends that the singing group with the incredible name was not a gag. A chapter was organized in January 1940, and it had started several others. An industrialist queried Cleveland's Chamber of Commerce about a firm competent to do some special work. A chamber executive, conservative, exact, and truthful, gave him the name of the former vice-president's firm. (By then, he was the society's historian.) He gave the name but with a cautionary warning uttered *sotto voce:* "I must tell you that this man is active in that quartet singing society." There was no mention, as earlier in Tulsa, of an affront to the memory of the Swedish Nightingale and Caruso or of infuriated mobs and frog ponds. Later, the industrialist recounted the incident gleefully to the quartet-oriented historian.

Barbershoppers are tolerant of the avocational oddities of others. They know that some persons relax under the soothing stares of home-raised guppies, or they play croquet or puzzle over crosswords. Quartetists see nothing odd when amateur lapidaries shape and polish a beautiful gem from the splinter of a Coke bottle. Let them also take to the hills in November, if they feel the urge, to revel in the pale yellow witch-hazel blooms while pondering its off-beat cycle. Let them take chances too if they want to climb a leafless tree to salvage a deserted high-swinging Baltimore oriole's nest woven of last year's gray silk from milkweed stalks. Barbershoppers will agree that chess is probably harmless: Let addicts enjoy it or the assembling of hi-fi kits, reading

Emerson or Mailer, shooting Rocky Mountain sheep or carrying a flintlock in a PTA pageant. 'They like it. It's good for 'em. Now, give us a B natural, Harry. It'll go better half a note higher." That's the view through their end of the pitchpipe.

"Why do they need a pitchpipe? Why don't they just sing?" My friend, you're tampering with disaster. A tenor can soar just so high, some higher than others, and that goes also for a bass in the opposite direction. Few singers are gifted with a sense of perfect pitch, meaning the ability to sound off on any note named. Some scientists believe that no one has perfect pitch but that is niggling and trivial, carrying the weight of a pinfeather. A person with perfect pitch might utter a given tone a few cycles off true pitch as measured by physicists, but the human ear could not pick out the error.

The late George Scarbo, NEA cartoonist, had perfect pitch as near as the ear can judge sound. Even in an area where other musical sounds dominated, when George was asked for a B flat, or any other, he'd hit it, to the surprised admiration of anyone checking him by pitchpipe.

Pitchpipes were a novelty to many in the audience that filled Chicago's Medina Temple in June 1943 to hear the fifth national quartet contest. Also, most of them heard for the first time an enormous chorus singing barbershop harmony—150 in the Cornbelt Chorus of Illinois. The 900 members present were familiar with the routine when a quartet member blows the pipe to sound the pitch, usually the keynote. Cases are on record where the three others missed the pitch as if it were a knuckler. It is calamitous if they muff it, after all have pranced on stage, radiating confidence as they huddle slightly to catch the note thrown by the pitcher. Sympathizers barely restrain themselves from sobs.

Nothing of that sort occurred among the fifteen quartets in the Temple, the survivors of forty-eight starters. But the public address system had low fidelity and there were dead spots in the great auditorium. Because everyone wasn't hearing alike, the deviations produced misunderstandings, complaints, and a few recriminations directed at the "tone-deaf" judges. The society's record of the previous year was repeated when a Chicago quartet, the Four Harmonizers, won. Walking back to headquarters at Hotel Morrison, founder Cash commented on the basis of his observation of five national contests: "You can't rate a quartet by what you heard last night. You have to call 'em as you hear 'em in just two songs tonight. Maybe they're on the beam during those six minutes, maybe not."

Chicago's chapters had promised to sell enough tickets to outsiders to raise $1,500 against the expenses of the convention. They exceeded that by $43.79. The national board was so elated that it approved a $5,900 budget for the ensuing year. Of that, all but $530 was earmarked for supplies, postage, printing, and secretarial work. That budgeted allowance to part-time Secretary Adams, whose hours in the society's interest exceeded full-time, meant that it was no longer necessary for him to pay secretarial help out of his own pocket. Also typewriter ribbons for his personal machine came under "supplies."

Though a few changes were made in the society's directorate, the same leadership continued into 1943–44 when Staab accepted the mandate of the board that he continue for another term. He accepted after Secretary Adams refused to serve another year unless Staab would stay. Together they'd add impetus to what had been started during their first year as a team. From the beginning, board meetings had been opened with songs; a candid entry in the official minutes of its 1943 meeting in Chicago read: "The singing of the Board was lousier than usual."

A Successful Shakedown Cruise

In the ancient days of song in the American barber's shop, and even when the Four Harmonizers won at Chicago, the harmony of a typical amateur foursome singing by ear was almost as unpredictable as the pattern on a pancake. It may be approximated again, but it is never duplicated. That absence of uniformity characterized the harmony output of men meeting socially and infrequently, or perhaps for the first time. By telepathy or through a chance remark they became aware of the other's interest in searching for the lost chord, perhaps dropped by Sir Arthur Sullivan. It was most likely to be found in the kitchen.

Singing in the breakfast nook, the three members responsible for carrying the harmony parts tried to read the eyes and minds of the others in order to anticipate the notes that would fit best when integrated with the lead's melody. When by accident or intent they uttered a soul-satisfying combination of tones, it was natural to give themselves an encore. Listen to them from the living room: "Sing it again so we'll have it nailed down." On the fourth repetition, the tenor gets another idea about refurbishing that tumbledown shack in Athlone. "Hey, Bill. Let's try this. I'll drop on 'stone'—'sto-own'—like that and you go up a note."

If the stone doesn't resonate quite as he hoped, the tenor goes up again and Bill drops as before. They decide that it's the perfect version. "That is *it*. Let's remember that." Five months later, that same group meets again by fortuitous circumstances. They recall the thrill but the sequential chord changes have been crowded from their memories. So they start again on the road that leads back. Tolerant wives wouldn't discourage them by cringing openly. "They're enjoying themselves. Henry needs this change. Hey, boys, would you mind singing that *all the way through just once?* It's beautiful, but."

Nobody told the baritone what to do. In fact nobody paid any attention to the bari unless he called a signal occasionally. The others took for granted that at the right split second he'd join the harmony huddle from his inconspicuous safety position. By intuition or something he'd find his parking spot on that stone. Natural baris were a race apart. They were seldom temperamental like tenors, many of whom had to be handled like high explosives, which might detonate at the slightest jar. Or they might play dud and sulk if they couldn't win an argument. A bari was flexible. He'd bend in the wind but he seldom broke. When a bari said, "That sounds right," that's how they usually repeated it if they could remember how they'd hit upon the chord so joyously. "Let's do it again. Now, remember, Bill, drop a whole note on that second half of 'stone.'" Bill didn't read music but he could count to one.

In principle, that is how the Four Harmonizers, winners in 1943, and also two others among the society's first five national champions as well as several others later, approached agreement where thrilling success or dismal failure depended upon going up a note, dropping a half, or holding it straight across—"like that." The trial-and-error methods that applied to harmony learned by ear were slow as compared with those of later quartets. Nowadays some of them read music as easily as a newspaper. But among most of the pioneers, notes might just as well have been Assyrian cuneiform. The Harmony Kings of Springfield, Illinois, provide a good illustration. They had been close to the top in competition for four years but never made the peak. When Mills Music, Inc., decided to bring out the first barbershop folio, mentioned earlier, it would include numbers "as sung by" the society's quartets. The committee agreed at once that the Harmony Kings' "'Way Down Home" must be included. Frank Dragoo, their bari whose word was law to the other three, was asked to submit their arrangement of that old favorite. By ear, he could create chords or rectify them, and he recognized the notes that were inside the staff of the treble clef, but above or below it he was lost in the forest. He had no acquaintance with the bass clef, though half of a quartet's contribution originates down there. He had never attempted to write music.

After two months of arduous effort, he submitted the arrangement. All the notes were there but they looked funny, he said, with some of the stems facing east and other west, and several tails dragging. Phil Embury of Warsaw, New York, who had written down "Sweet Roses of Morn" from hearsay after the St. Louis contest, changed the arrangement into standard form. That's how "'Way Down Home" evolved to provide to posterity the Harmony Kings' example of barbershop harmony as sung in presociety days and in its early years. It exemplifies the struggles of others attempting to make visual what was so clear by ear.*

A quartet that jelled into definite, though perhaps temporary, members had the advantage over a pickup four that met semi-occasionally. Usually, a Grade-A quartet had gone through a period of guesswork, estimating and trying out potential members. Most often, two men had the urge to form their own foursome. They listened here and there, invited and tentatively selected two members for their troupe. By trial and propinquity, the four decided that the combination wasn't right or that it might be a good one, not only in the matching of voices but because, happily, they got along well together. Also their wives were *simpático* with each other and, more importantly, with barbershopping and its impacts upon the domestic scene. Quartet rehearsal after the children went to bed, or when a social engagement must be canceled because a husband "had to practice" that night, could set up hurdles in

* The foreword to *Barber Shop Harmony* by Sigmund Spaeth says in part that the collection is meant for "all those singers who love to agree or even disagree on chords and progressions that every devotee of this unique art will recognize by instinct.... The notes are merely a guide. Barbershop harmony at its best is sung by ear, extemporaneously."
In my note which was the second part of that foreword, I wrote, "those of us who can't read Sigmund's little black dots will find someone who can, someone with endurance."

the path of true love. They met in the homes where they were most welcome.

Flaws in voices or temperaments or the attitude of the little woman could be cause for a member to drop out or be replaced. One or more might split off into another partly organized four. This is in answer to a question asked by interested persons who presumed that SPEBSQSA quartets are formed by appointment or other form of regimentation. Their servitude to Adeline was and is voluntary. Today, when conjugal attachments come unstuck increasingly, their perennial devotion to Dear Old Girl is a pretty sight indeed, a heartening example of fidelity.

Over the years since the first arrangement committee committed the simple harmonies of "Down Our Way" to paper, the constant flow from the society's headquarters of "standards," in the terminology of the music trades, provides a musical Esperanto. It takes time to learn a new universal language and, as every educator knows, receptiveness varies among pupils. ("The hell with notes! Let's sing it off-the-cuff.") Styles in arranging the standard songs change over succeeding generations though not as much so as modes in skirt lengths, double- versus single-breasted suits for men, auto design, and other mutations that make us so dissatisfied that we'll buy out of embarrassment. (If new-and-amazing were stricken from the vocabularies of ad copy writers, the national product would nose-dive.) The harmonies of the pioneers who learned them by ear and by trial and repetition linger in the more modern versions of the oldies.

President Staab's second term, with Adams continuing as national secretary, developed into a year of high tides in accomplishments. The society became international when the Windsor, Ontario, chapter received its charter. That was a natural result of hands across the river. Per capita, Windsor had as many harmony-minded men as Detroit. They'd been exchanging skylines via ferry, tunnel, and bridge. Their nationality origins and traditions paralleled—family names, Mother Goose rhymes, hymns, sports (bowling on the green excepted), independent attitudes, educational systems, self-government, and songs. Detroit's "America" was lifted from "God Save the King/Queen" and "Star-Spangled Banner's" melody from an old English song. The Canadians were familiar with traditional barbershop and popular music which was the same as their neighbor's across the river. The accession of Windsor brought the chapters to ninety-six. None of them were ghosts as formerly. Secretary Adams was on part time, but he had no time for phantom chapters.

During Staab's second term, moves were made to make the society collegiate as well as international. Several groups in universities and colleges did well for a semester or two while the original enthusiasts were still on campus. Due to the shifting population, college chapters have not shown permanency. Their value as nurseries where the twig can be bent toward permanent grafting into another chapter later is a nice theory. As yet, it has not been tested by statistical study of twigs that took root elsewhere after college.

The administrations of the first four presidents (1939–44) were comparable to a shakedown cruise, a testing period. It was evident to all on the cruise that minor adjustments would be needed to correct compass deviations; the steering gear dragged a bit; power leaks must be stopped; extra rivets would do no harm at several places—yet, the craft was seaworthy. The skills of the crew improved daily with experience. It would be an overstatement to compare conditions to those on "The Capital Ship," where no wind that blew dismayed her crew nor troubled the captain's mind. The harmony crew had often been dismayed by winds that threatened to blow it and the troubled captains on the rocks.

In the beginning, so many men outside Tulsa felt cravings for comparable clubs that the climate for quick extension beyond Oklahoma's horizons was unusually salubrious. But it must be evident by now that during those years the chances for survival of the few scattered chapters, run haphazardly, put them on the short end of any betting odds. Everyone concerned recognized the potentials in preserving and encouraging barbershop harmony, and all saw proof of vitality and widespread acceptance of an idea. The worry that was ever present concerned holding the chapters together until pooled experiences could provide a preliminary blueprint of this unprecedented edifice they proposed to build. Had the central core of the society with the grandiloquent name disintegrated during those early times, it is likely that the initial impetus would have carried just a few chapters along, for a short time, under the aegis of a defunct SPEBSQSA. Because of experience within their own chapters and from observation of others, everyone working toward stability recognized that it could be found only through a strong central organization.

For understanding of the society's rise, it has been necessary to portray the problems along with the joyous musical phenomena. The evolutionary processes that began when the original singing club became news shaped the course that the society follows generally today. The shakedown cruise ended when skipper Staab left the bridge at the end of his second term in 1944, the fifth year of converting chaos to order.

Turbulences Ease

The turbulent years of the early 1940's have been recorded in principal details in order to show the climate in which the unprecedented singing society took root and the spirit of the many who nurtured it through the doubtful years. Its survival is proof of a vast longing for musical self-expression and evidence of the conviction of early planners that they might be able to connect dispersed links into a national chain of chapters. That same urge among Canadians made the bond an international one when in 1944 Windsor, Ontario, became the first link across the borders. Since the beginning of the quartet society, more than 250 members have been called from the chapters to serve on the international board which determines the course and speed of the Good Ship Barbershop.

As their terms end, they become eligible for membership in *The Association of Discarded and Decrepit Past Members of the Board of the Society for the Preservation and Encouragement of Barber Shop Quartet Singing in America Without Voice and Without Portfolio, not inc.,* mercifully known as *The Decrepits*. It was conceived in the early 1940's by R. H. Sturgess of Atlanta, Georgia, funster, composer, and the artist who designed the society's first lapel pin and the cover design of *The Harmonizer* magazine, "Devoted to the Interests of Barbershop Quartet Harmony."

At the Decrepits' annual, and only, meeting of the year at convention-contest time, the Most Antique Relic's call to order signals mirthful disorder, Rabelaisian witticisms and robust merriment such as is unlikely elsewhere. Founder Cash always faced a question and standing vote as to whether he should be seated among the august. No record of his admission to the society existed and his term as Temporary Etc. had not expired. Co-founder Hall has not suffered that indignity, since records prove that he was the first president. Nevertheless, just in case, he always brings documentary evidence. Other official titles include the Keeper of the Wampum and the Chief Custodian of the Wheeled Chair. In their more sedate moments, members of the Decrepits may totter into sessions of the Executive Committee or of committees on contest and judging, ethics, finance, laws and regulations, long range planning, nominating, service, harmony foundation, employees' pensions, or other working groups that keep the society on the road.

Obviously, the full nomenclature of the Decrepits was intended to be in keeping with the society's name, arrived at to out-alphabet the sprouting alphabetical agencies of the 1930's whose matured leaf growth now blankets the nation. A sampling of the names that quartets choose shows a projection of that spirit of levity exemplified by the first champions, The Bartlesville Barflies. Titles include the Buzz Saws, Four Flushers, Crow-Matix, Atomic Bums, Harmony Hounds, Village Idiots, Show Boats, and Scale Tippers. Others turn to the ramifications of music for names, such as, The Keynotes, Four Chorders, Clef Dwellers, Four-in-a-Chord, Hi-Los, Hi-Chords, Calling Chords, and Four Naturals. Throughout the society, the presiding officer's "All in favor give the usual sign" is often the signal for a four-part chord. Without a pitchpipe, they've been known to miss the sign.

The Harmonizer, bearing the Sturgess masthead, has grown from an original printing of 1,200, half for promotion, as President Staab's *Barber Shop Re-Chordings,* to a standard run of 32,000, typically twenty-eight pages with covers in color. It was intended to draw the few chapters into a semblance of uniformity through understanding of objectives and chapter potentials for personal enjoyment and the community services in which Staab believed. Page one of the September 1942 issue carried a message from him: "We have suffered from growing pains . . . it is imperative that we create order out of chaos." His objectives: "To institute a system of national records . . . make the national office a clearing house for all kinds of information and ideas that will be of assistance to each chapter . . . stimulate the right kind of publicity, cultivate a desire to render altruistic services and promote extension. . . ."

With reference to Staab's last two items, between 1965 and the end of the decade, the society's chapters had contributed almost half a million dollars to the Institute of Logopedics, Wichita, Kansas, where children who suffer handicaps in speech communication receive treatment. Music is important in the institute's therapy. A special education department has made it possible for little ones who have such speech handicaps or with aphasoid (unable to associate words with meaning) difficulties to participate as singers, bell ringers, percussion instrumentalists, or even as performers on simple wind instruments. Longtime SPEBSQSA member Fred Waring is on the institute's board. This is the society's unified international project, but almost from its beginnings the chapters have engaged in all sorts of local civic and charitable musical activities.

In addition to the original intents, *The Harmonizer* also serves as a forum of opinion for members from Nova Scotia to San Diego and Miami to Vancouver. Their views may express experience limited to a chapter and its nearby area, or, more broadly, to the district, of which there are fifteen, each with its officers, responsibilities, and district publication. Other opinions stem from international service and thinking. The subjects that provoke the most letters to the editor are those that affirm, challenge, or criticize. An article that touches sensitive nerves is certain to live again in letters to the Mail Call column.

Published, they prove that the membership has one common meeting ground, the desire to sing. What, where, and how to do that has sometimes raised the column's temperature to near boiling. Great numbers of young members and even recently indoctrinated neophytes express strong attachment to the musical form stated in the society's name. They resent suggestions that "we ought to go modern." A well-meaning member suggested in *The Harmonizer:* "Give the people what they want—not the addicts, not the fans who rarely fill an auditorium but the people outside who simply want to sing and listen to the old songs . . . as we push toward 500,000 membership gleaned from groups like the millions of Mitch Miller fans." He suggested that the mastery of barbershop harmony be confined to "very short periods" in chapter meetings.

One of the less scathing replies suggested that the author drop out and join the Miller millions who think that a "bass sings melody an octave low." Bundles of letters disagreed with the suggestion of soft-pedaling harmony techniques in order to attract that half-million new members, whose musical appreciations are seldom above "two-part harmony," one said. From another, "I don't want to belong to a big organization" expressed the fervency of more whose chief interests center upon the preservation and encouragement of traditional barbershop harmony and improvement in singing it.

Quite naturally, membership includes a few enthusiasts whose eyes are upon size, in the American tradition that what is bigger is better. It has even been suggested that the name of SPEBSQSA be changed to The Men's Singing Society without reference to its origins and specificity of purpose. This suggestion ignores the fact that in combination these account for the society's gladsome reception and its growth into the largest autonomous organization of male singers in the States and Canada. Without its individuality of purpose it would have been just another undistinguished musical group among the many. It would have about the same chances of winning friends, members and status as a car in competition at the Indianapolis 500 without gears or a steering wheel.

Opinions aired by publication in *The Harmonizer* on almost every phase of the society's operation indicate that in the main the membership is progressive as long as it can progress within its own line fences. That excludes duets, trios, and instrumental accompaniment. The members show no evidence of an urge to bring them in from the fields of sin exemplified by jazz, folk music, harmonicas, and stringed instruments. Nonetheless, subtle infiltrations into the enormously varied repertoire are apparent to the society's veterans. Increasing stress upon public performance and contests directs attention increasingly to vocal refinements foreign to the freewheeling days. Then, the typical member craved primarily to let the rest of the world go by while, with the door locked against intrusion, four guys could nurse harmony swipes just born in those few precious fleeting minutes. The love light in their eyes for their newborn had a Madonna-like quality beautiful to behold, had beholders been allowed.

The trend toward public performance and listening rather than a personal wooing of the Lee sisters, Aura and Mandy, is exemplified by the changes since the first Woodshed came into being when Buffalo, New York, hosted the 1949 international convention. The Woodshed was conceived to provide a place where a man who was not a member of an organized quartet would have a place to meet others also unattached. It was just possible that in such a place the loner might find three others who could be induced to sing. A photo, snapped at Buffalo, shows how men from Birmingham, Michigan, Northampton, Massachusetts, Pittsburgh and Cleveland found a common meeting ground as well as interest in the Woodshed. Later, Sturgess of Atlanta made up a kit of props commonly found in the nation's woodsheds (rusty axes, broken bucksaws and sawbucks, wedges for splitting elm chunks from the pre-petroleum-gas era). It traveled to several conventions where it was received so joyfully that donations to Woodshed memorabilia presented a serious problem in storage, transportation, and assembly. The name lingers, but today's Woodshed is an auditorium in the headquarters hotel where organized quartets entertain an audience.*

Much of the older era remained when Carroll P. Adams became full-time international secretary. Membership had reached a size that demanded headquarters facilities larger than the Adams spare bedroom in Detroit. Also, life at headquarters had become quite complicated during his part-time secretaryship over two years. Several chapters were within half an hour's drive. Members flocked in to air their views, get information and advice, or to register protests. Too often, temporarily dissident members who came to scoff remained to bray. This could occur several nights a week. In the headquarters at home, Adams lost weight but not his aplomb nor zeal for his pivotal job. The first full-time command post was in a store building in northwest Detroit, soon abandoned for a larger one.

During those middle years, with Adams as coordinator and the link that connected succeeding administrations, the growing membership continued to reverse Horace Greeley's advice by moving easterly from the mother city, Tulsa. Growth gave increasing confidence that even larger headquarters would be needed for services envisioned by each new group of administrators. In 1949 President O. H. King Cole wrote in the *Harmonizer* his vision of a headquarters building to be the "permanent international shrine of barbershop harmony."

When Adams resigned in 1953 after burning the midnight lights at headquarters for ten years, he was succeeded by his trainee Robert G. Hafer under a new title of Executive Director. Hafer instituted a survey to locate the society's center of population. It was found only a few miles south of Chicago. As need for more space continued in Detroit, a committee and independent scouts searched for a new location nearer the center. Lady Luck smiled and guided them to a mansion at Kenosha, Wisconsin, near Chicago. In the 1930's, it had taken five years to complete the home at a cost of more than half a million pre-inflation dollars.

An appraisal showed the replacement cost of land and structure of Belgian stone, built to the specifications of an exacting industrialist, to be above $650,000. As the Lady smiled more broadly, the society acquired the property for $75,000 to settle the former owner's estate, "for a song" in two ways. On four levels, the building on Third Avenue, Kenosha's old Gold Coast, provides space for future office requirements, for the Old Songs Library of popular music, a Founder's Room, a President's Room where board meetings convene, a printing plant and distributive facilities for the enormous volume of mail

* See Appendix H.

exchanged between the fifteen districts, chapters, and headquarters. All earlier dreams came true in Harmony Hall.

When President Jerry E. Beeler, who had worked on the acquisition, burned the mortgage on stage at the nineteenth annual convention, he said: "We can't make it more beautiful outside. Inside, it can fulfill all our dreams for the right service headquarters, while fulfilling more than we had hoped for as a hall of harmony." Even so, in the 1960's the society's broadening activities such as the Harmony Education Program (HEP) drew several hundred eager participants, too many for Harmony Hall. In consequence, meetings are usually held during the summer sessions at colleges in several cities.

In the society's thirtieth year, the musical barbers of literature would be puzzled by references to HEP or to a paper, "Problems of a Choral Director," presented by Robert D. Johnson, director of the society's musical activities, to a seminar of the National Music Council. The meeting was attended by the dean of a university's music school, a symphony's chorus director, and others to whom music means vocation. It was conducted by Dr. Howard Hanson, of the Eastman School of Music, who had cheered the barbershoppers' intent and accomplishments since the first chapter was formed in Rochester, New York. Several champion quartets have demonstrated the art before meetings of the country's music educators.

All this points to quite an evolution since the days of Elizabethan barber's musick and since the days of chords-by-guess known to today's rapidly dwindling corps of veterans. They recall music in the barbers' shops and the days when a haircut cost only a quarter for more hairs cut (this inverse ratio illustrates a law recognized by economists—a diminished supply usually means a price increase).

By Arrangement

The changes in the Woodshed at conventions, from come-all-ye participation to a place where organized quartets entertain an audience, symbolize other changes. Two of the most apparent relate to choruses and written arrangements, neither of which was in existence when four early birds at the first meeting in Tulsa (1938) introduced themselves and immediately woodshedded "Down Mobile" while other guests were arriving. The quartet society might not have advanced beyond that stage of singing spontaneous and individualistic harmonies had it not been for the early development of choruses. This included love's labor by those who supplied published arrangements as guidelines for uniformity and by others who directed the choral singing, often without previous experience.

Since then, a new generation of singers has been reared on a different kind of music and the average age of members has dropped. About half are below age forty. The quavering notes of those of age sixty-five or older come from only 6 percent of the total international membership. In recent years the importance of music in grade and high schools has risen and teaching methods have been improved steadily. So it is no surprise to see a high-school choir read the music of Haydn's *Creation* or Vivaldi's forty-page *Gloria.* With such experience, many quartet and chorus singers find meaning in pages that in the 1940's were mere blurs of dancing dots and cabalistic symbols.

Many members lose the older ones with the songs of the 1940's, '50's, and '60's. Conversely, most of the melodies that were so familiar, Howard's "Hello, My Baby" as example, are unknown to most until the published arrangement is dealt out to the choristers.

In some chapters the quartets are overshadowed by a chorus. In the often quaint miscellany that makes *The Old Farmer's Almanac* a perennial delight, the 175th edition (1967) includes an item about vocal sounds, dated 1865: "The range of the human voice is quite outstanding, there being nine perfect tones but 17,592,186,044,515 different sounds... these independently of different degrees of intensity." A century later, a chapter's chorus director says that those trillions represent only a few of the sounds he hears from forty or more voices in the first run-through, *a capella,* of a song unknown to the members.

The use of published music is like the evolutions in folk music during recent years, though the reasons for the parallel are different. There were few folk songs in comparison with the thousands of populars written since Stephen Foster's time that lend themselves naturally to barbershop harmony. Folk music had no Tin Pan Alley production lines nor the prolificacy of composers who, in the first half of this century, wrote melodies that stick in the memory like burrs to a Bedlington. Van Alstyne, Sterling, Luders, Herbert, Kern, Morse, Ball, the Von Tilzers, Donaldson and Fischer and their colleagues were, in many cases, composers of musical comedies that ran for years. That applies also to composers of music for the movies (*The Wizard of Oz* and *Snow White,* as examples), and their hit tunes that continued into the era of "Around the World in Eighty Days."

Because of the shortage of established folk tunes, composers for the new folk trade of the 1940's and 1950's could hardly keep up with the demand of performers specializing in hillbilly-folk-country-western musical naïveté. In those fields, when an entertainer can't find a song suitable to his public image, he's been known to write his own. Many folk-type presentations are as fresh as new-laid eggs, not in the theatrical sense. Whether the song is traditional or new and synthetic, the sophisticated instrumentations are quite different from the original simple folk accompaniments.

Quartets face no dearth of musical material. Theirs is a problem of selection from a vast supply of new and old. (To many of today's society members a song of the 1950's is an oldie.) Most songs have been arranged for four voices by arrangers within the society, and every quartet that attains popularity beyond its chapter is sure to receive suggestions about songs that, well-wishers claim, are "naturals for barbershop." But the foursomes may face a major difficulty in building a repertoire. The perennial search for "good ones," usually with the avowed intention of finding something that's "different" calls for 400 percent approval. If one member doesn't like the mood or the lyrics or the harmony sequences, it is seldom a good song for his quartet. It's possible that familiarity may breed content, but it's unlikely.

Despite the enormous treasury of popular music available, there is a tendency among many quartets to settle upon a song that has been popularized by another quartet. After the Elastic Four used "Tell Me You'll Forgive Me" to win a championship in 1942, it swept through the few chapters like a brush fire, and it is still a standard throughout the society. When the former champion Buffalo Bills (now disbanded) sang in the stage and moving-picture productions of *Music Man,* "Lida Rose" insinuated herself into the repertoires of dozens of other quartets. In the mid-1950's, "I Believe" was sung at almost every public concert. Much earlier, "Daddy, Get Your Baby out of Jail," introduced by the Kansas City Barberpole Cats, and the Flatfoot Four's "Shine" were heard wherever society members gathered. Published arrangements disseminated them.

Written arrangements carry a song to faraway places, and they are essential for chorus work. Two disadvantages are minor compared with their merits in providing a visible trail to follow. The first is the tendency to accept the published harmony as the *only proper way* to sing a certain song, and second, through dependency upon the published notes, some hesitate to sing without that crutch. In the first case, in singing standards such as "Tell Me Why," "Aura Lee," "Let Me Call You Sweetheart," or "If I Had My Way" there are spots where the three harmony parts might park harmoniously on either of two, even three, chords. The following opening bars of 'Kentucky Babe" demonstrate briefly that freedom of choice.

As Commonly Sung

Skee-ters am a- hum-min' on de hon-ey- suck-le vine....

Now Try This

Note the Change in Sound When the Baritone Drops on Two notes—and the Bass Moves a half-tone on "vine"

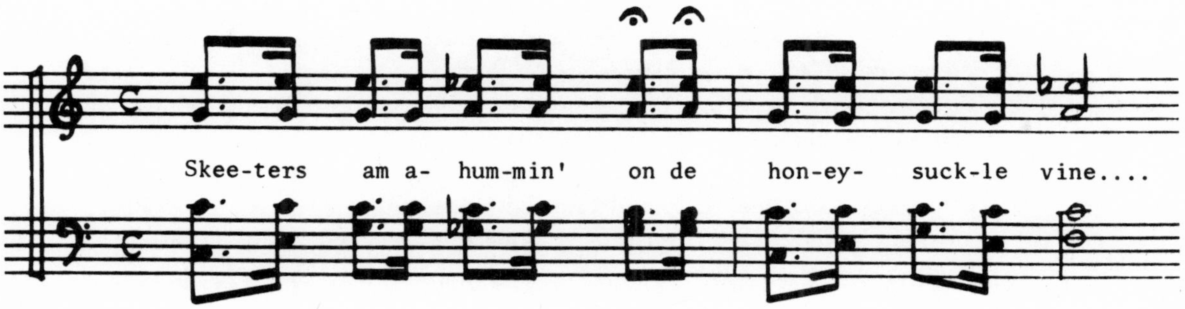
Skee-ters am a- hum-min' on de hon-ey- suck-le vine....

A quartet may make a choice or re-embroider it to another design.

As to the second point, dependence upon written arrangements, deceased preservers of free and loose barbershopping must have stirred uneasily at the comment made when a conclave gathered to discuss chapter matters. While a dozen or so waited for latecomers, an irrepressible piped up, "We're wasting time. Let's sing." "We can't," another countered, "we haven't got any music." His comment reverts also to the first point made. To him the written note is no more changeable than the laws of the Medes and Persians were allowed to be. Yet this respect and increasing understanding of published music is responsible for the growth and stability of the society today. They promote chorus effort, and without choruses it is doubtful that SPEBSQSA would have survived its growing pains.

Experienced foursomes recognize the fact that no two quartets have exactly the same range or quality or sound. One may include a tenor who can outsoar the thrush at eve. They're likely to feature him for their own and listeners' enjoyment by modifying a written arrangement. That can happen at the other end of the musical spectrum when a quartet is blessed by a bass whose mother was frightened by a foghorn. In his case it isn't a matter of depth in range but the natural bass *sound* he utters. It isn't necessary for him to bellow to prove he's a bass. In the absence of such a one, a bari whose voice has slipped because of age or too many cigarettes, is cast as the understander in the harmony pyramid. But he's still a baritone simulating bass, often quite acceptably.

It is natural that harmonies in a thirty-two-year-old singing society have experienced evolutions comparable with folk music. The society's published arrangements are excellent in encouragement of a new generation of singers. Sometimes preservation suffers a bit. As in the serious modern music referred to earlier "composed for art's sake rather than the listeners'," a few of the society's arrangers have considered their harmonization as proof of personal virtuosity rather than preservation of a traditional musical form.

As in folk music, any tendency to over-arrange is part of the evolution that brings to public performance what was originally played or sung for personal satisfaction. The society's seminars on arranging are attended by old hands at roping four voices into accord, and they are particularly valuable to others who've been reared in the boogie, rock 'n' roll era. It would be natural for these younger men to try to transfer to barbershop harmony the kinds of music to which they've been accustomed. (Asked to define barbershop harmony, four eager young enthusiasts hesitated, then one spoke for the four, "I guess it's four guys singing together.") The seminars are invaluable in the interest of preserving a traditional American art. Without preservation, it could have gone the way of hand weaving, pegged furniture, and the cornstalk fiddles that still delight little folks.

The society's membership is from that typical cross section, so dear to demographers of the States and Canada. In consequence, its views on what's good in harmony are as diverse as American life, right-wing to would-be builders of a great new society (at either extreme or between, a Progressive is one who agrees with *you*).

These conditions are fruitful of discussions between those who hold that the role of preservation of barbershop harmony is stated as a mandate in the society's name and others who consider the name and its traditions less important than getting a big hand at a public concert. Evolutions such as have been touched upon are inevitable. Criteria exist in every social grouping, starting with the family. Just as some members of a family have changed the inherited name, some members of the society would discard a title that symbolizes colorful Americana, increasingly vivid over the past thirty years of SPEBSQSA administrations. The initials themselves have become an international tradition.

Current Ideologies

In 1935, three years before SPEBSQSA was conceived, *Esquire* magazine published an article, "Ewer Sixteen, My Villidchkween." For some, the title seemed to pluck upon a vague, muted, distant chord, perhaps related to an old mill stream, down by the, or something. Other readers searched for meaning in the cryptic cipher. Adults who'd kept alert read the code at a glance. That article provided links between the ancient days of song in the barber's shop, the genesis of the quartet society, and the present. An excerpt is borrowed from what I wrote before the events at Tulsa in 1938 and subsequent developments which enlarged the opportunities for informal four-part vocal participation.

In 1935: "The typical catch-as-catch-can quartette [note archaic spelling], consisting of a decisive individual who thinks he can sing tenor, assisted by several shaky leads trying to sing bass and bari, doesn't worry about minor details of words. It's the harmony swipe that counts . . . except in barber shopping, human nature likes a little appreciation of individual effort. But these harmonists need neither approbation nor listeners. Deaf mutes make the perfect audience for all concerned."

In 1935, not even in delirium could a participator of that era dream of a time when several thousand listeners would pack an auditorium to hear men sing barbershop harmony, as is common now. Because today's members present their wares to the public, their relations with audiences and the public as a whole become increasingly important. As director of communications, Hugh A. Ingraham must keep Harmony Hall in Kenosha tuned to what goes on in cities and towns throughout two nations for awareness of public reactions to the society's actions. In mid-1969, he commented:

As SPEBSQSA has grown, so have its public relations problems. When Owen Cash, Rupert Hall and their friends got together in April 1938, they knew exactly what they wanted: to harmonize the old songs to their mutual satisfaction. Today, there are more than 30,000 members, and few would be satisfied to spent fifty-two weeks of the year doing only what Cash and his friends did in 1938.

Somewhere along the line, a barbershopper realized that we had a product that people wanted to hear, the harmonizing that the boys did for their own amusement at chapter meetings. And so, in the early 1940's we had our first public show. We called it a "Parade of Quartets." Suddenly, we were performers, with a responsibility toward the public to which we had sold tickets.

The transition from the informal meeting hall to the public arena, be it a PTA meeting, a chapter show, or an international convention-contest, has for the most part been a smooth one. Our shows are generally well produced and well attended because they are among the few that are suitable for the whole family. Our convention reputation can best be summed up by the comment of a manager of a large hotel chain: "You sure make a lot of noise, but you're always too busy singing to cause trouble."

Not that our record is without blemish. Sometimes a quartet mars an otherwise fine performance by attempting to bring nightclub material to a family show, or sometimes four overly enthusiastic harmonizers make pests of themselves by using public space for what should be a private rehearsal, if it could be called a rehearsal.

But most of our members are keenly aware of our Code of Ethics, and try to abide by it. Indeed, the Society's public relations program is based upon two sections of the Code: "We shall deport ourselves and conduct the Society's functions in such a manner as to reflect credit upon the Society and its membership; and we shall refrain from forcing our songs upon unsympathetic ears."

The nightclub material to which he referred is minimal. A large majority of the membership is dedicated as strongly to Keep It Clean as to Keep It Barbershop in harmony to preserve the American art. To hold those two lines against the encroachments of the kind of music on which most of today's members were reared and to avoid embarrassment to a chapter and its hometown audience by off-color songs or stories told between songs by a visiting quartet's spokesman calls for alertness as the price of good repute. Because of the variance in opinions as to what is suitable for public performance to a "family" audience, the Ethics Chairman in the society's fifteen districts must be judicial as well as alert.

Anecdotes came into the public performances early when a member of a quartet told a quickie to give the singers a break of a few seconds between numbers. Anecdotes became stories, and new quartets began to think them obligatory. Unskilled in stage techniques, a few narrators reached into the garbage can, and defended the intrusion of off-color monologue into a quartet concert by "They laughed, didn't they?" The attitude of the membership as a whole: Sing more and talk less in a singing society's performance. Ingraham sums up that majority's belief by telling quartets: "If there's any question about offending anyone by a song or story, don't use it." That recalls a comment by the late C. B. Larrabee, editor of *Printers Ink,* that those who laugh at a story in the club car may resent it in a public performance.

Members of the Ethics Committee are not bluenosed, sourpuss policemen averse to fun and frolic. A typical meeting of this committee at the International was titled "Pride in the Chapter and Society." It was unanimously agreed that most failures in good conduct within the chapters or in the behavior of a few quartets that got out of line in public performance stem from ignorance or thoughtlessness of the society's aims and objectives.

The relations between a singer and his family are hardly public relations but they can bulk just as importantly, sometimes more so. In the main, wives and families have approved father's nights out at meetings and have attended his public concerts pridefully. For full enjoyment of these activities, a husband needs clearance that's given ungrudgingly. That applies particularly when he says he'd like to have a few of the boys in, next Tuesday night, for a little harmonizing. If he sings regularly in a quartet, there will be rehearsal nights, too. That calls for understanding and loving tolerance. In Tulsa during the society's very early stages, some members wanted to follow the precedent of other organizations and form a women's auxiliary, a singing one, to bridge a gap that sometimes existed between his and her concept of a constructive avocation. Also, some wives had a lively interest in personalized harmony singing.

Out of that desire for personal participation, a women's group called Sweet Adelines emerged. Most of its members had licit wives' shares in the society, and some felt that they had earned additional rights by allowing, even encouraging, their husbands' pursuit of lost chords. ("Lost, strayed or stolen" was the terminology in the cattle country's advertisements for stock that had disappeared.) Related to that, an early movie taken at a society contest shows founder Cash busily and conspicuously jotting down chords as he "steals" them for his Okie Four. Good comedy!

As to Sweet Adelines' affiliations, the founder's invitation to the first Tulsa meeting had declared that the society would preserve "the last remaining vestige of human liberty." The implication throughout the sprouting chapters was that pursuit of happiness applied to men. Caught between the clamor of those who demanded women's rights and some of his own members who dissented, he suffered, as did others, as the news of Sweet Adelines was spread by the society's grapevine.

In part the disquietude may be traceable to the feeling of masculine insecurity crystallized in a song from *The Red Mill,* 1906. Two characters, the Burgomaster and Willem, in a duet to Victor Herbert's music, drew upon personal experience and observation as they sang their version of the feminine ethos:

You can tell about the weather, if it's going to rain or shine!
You can figure on the market and you're apt to get a line!
You may handicap the horses and perhaps you'll "dope 'em out,"
But to figure on a woman is to always be in doubt!
For you never can tell about a woman
Perhaps that's why we think them all so nice
You never find two alike any one time and you never find one alike twice
You're never very certain that they love you
You're often very certain that they don't
The men may fancy still that they have the strongest will
But the women have the strongest "wont"!

The possibility that members might, at "any one time," face a demand for a women's auxiliary spread consternation through segments of the society, but, wisely, no decision was affirmed immediately. As the growing Sweet Adelines put roots down in other cities, it became apparent to both women and men that pitfalls would be avoided if each group progressed under its own power and direction. Eventually, a statement of policy, approved by both, cleared the way for friendly cooperation under full autonomy as each thrived.

The broad-minded tolerance of most members of the society toward the hobby interests of others has already been cited as a phenomenon in such a single-minded group. Its concentration upon the preservation of barbershop-style harmony was summed up as far back as 1950 when "The Ohio Story" radio series dramatized events in the Buckeye State from pioneer times. One broadcast was written around SPEBSQSA's entrance into the state, ten years earlier (1940). Script writer William D. Ellis, author of the *Bounty Land* books on early Ohio history and others on later events, introduced the advent this way:

There is, mixed with the normal population, a species which looks like other people so much so that its members are allowed to vote, hold jobs and live in houses. It is known that they eat food and have about the same life span as normal humans, though slightly longer. To them, there are no rich people, poor people, Republicans, Democrats, Christians, or Mohammedans. To this species, mankind is divided into those who sing four-part harmony and those who do not. Members believe that music expresses that which cannot be said, and upon which it is impossible to be silent.

A comment by "Music Man" Meredith Willson gives a clue to the reason for addiction to this kind of self-expression. Asked why he wrote a barbershop quartet, the four commissioners, into *Music Man,* he said that impromptu quarteting was characteristic of small-town life in the era portrayed, and "barbershop harmonizing tastes the essence" when four well-matched voices come into "complete musical agreement." That essence was cited in terms of the "ring" of certain chords because of the coincidence of harmonics, as stated by physicists. So *that's* why you still like "Lida Rose" and why crowds continue to turn out when invited to hear the barbershop quartets and choruses. The nostalgia and complete musical agreement keeps the typical audience alternating between joyous applause and emotions that make tears a joy.

A reason for the unusual growth of the society in its early stages, a reason that continues though it has never been a main one, is that there was and is no necessity to own or buy a musical instrument, have instrumental skill, voice training, or the ability to read music, though that helps in these more mature days that have been sketched. Basically, all that's needed is a love affair with a melody waiting lone and lorn for three harmony parts to rally 'round and keep it happy.

Happy rallying dominated the thinking of founders Cash and Hall when, in 1938, they "talked late into the night" at Hotel Muelbach in Kansas City about the possibilities of revitalizing the fading art of impromptu quartet singing. None could have been more surprised than they when their invitation to the harmony revival ignited a train of fuses. After the rush to the Oklahoma country swamped the founders, they were grateful when others took the burden of organization from the early standard bearers. Cash thrilled at SPEBSQSA's past and pondered its future; his ground rules covered an association that ended after fifteen years. He died on August 15, 1953.

Though he was committed personally to social, carefree, spontaneous harmony singing, Cash recognized its limitations when applied to widely separated chapters whose members were younger and less familiar with singing harmony off-the-cuff. In his fifteen years of participation, it became obvious that the newer membership included many who knew music and whose views and attitudes were diverse because of their musical experience and sectional distribution. At all times the founders supported any change that would strengthen the society's international structure. Nowadays, cofounder Rupert Hall enjoys the organization, much as a beaming grandparent dotes, from the sidelines, upon the youngsters' play as he leaves base-running and basket-shooting to them.

As the second fifteen-year span neared its end, the period had not produced major revisions. The earlier era is remembered for fortuitous decisions, for errors corrected during consolidation and for refinements that were a part of evolution. At Harmony Hall in Kenosha, Executive Director Barrie Best is quite aware that the society in its international status is not what Cash and Hall envisioned.

Both he and Ingraham recognize that theirs is no longer a society of a few socially oriented, informal singing clubs. "At Kenosha," he says, "our duties are to a multifaceted collection of chapters. In evolution the 'preservation of barber shop *quartet* singing' rests increasingly upon the chapters' *choruses*."

Though it is apparent to him, as it is to veterans, that the backbone of many chapters is the chorus, he is concerned at the shortage of quartets in a society for the encouragement of quartet singing. "Even pickup quartets are not in evidence often enough in our chapter meetings. Woodshedding, in which three wrestle with the harmony parts of a song that a melody-carrying lead is trying to teach them, fades in the older chapters and just doesn't exist among too many of the newer ones."

In his belief, the rise in importance of the chorus is because large numbers haven't the time, inclination, or talent to go along with the discipline obligatory in a quartet that sings regularly. "In many cases the chorus singing satisfies the desire to lift one's voice in song in the aura of congeniality that's typical of chapter meetings where the objective is harmony." He knows too that members are influenced by their exposure to contests, entered by the selected few, and by recordings of medalist foursomes that have attained near perfection. The attitude that was apparent when a member volunteered at the drop of a song title to sing the best bass, bari, or tenor ever heard in harmonyland, whether he knew the song or not, is replaced by self-conscious respect for precision singing to please the public.

Best forecasts that chapter activities will be geared more closely to members' families. "Community and local philanthropic services will continue to play more important roles, in addition to the society's international logopedics project." He accepts the growing challenge of keener competition for men's leisure time. "It's formidable now and will become more so. Some chapters that started with a bang heard throughout a community are being muted. The original head of enthusiasm has declined because of lack of fuel under the boiler as members are drained away by other hobbies." As in some sports, a chapter's sophomore year can be the most trying one. "Programming to hold old members and attract new ones to the chapter is the answer, of course. Its importance increases when, nowadays, traditional concepts, practices, and nuances of singing barbershop harmony are unknown to many in our chapters."

If there is an international saturation point for membership in SPEBSQSA, few members, young or old, recognize it. Most communities continue to ask, "When's your next show?" and the typical concert is a sellout. As in the ancient days of vaudeville, four men singing familiar popular songs in harmony are crowd pleasers.

This applies equally to singing for their own amusement. Recently in a family-type tavern, two members chanced upon two others from nearby. The spontaneous harmony that developed evoked a query from a fascinated listener: "Are you fellows professional singers?" "No" was the reply, "we're acrobats, the only act on the circuit that sings without a net."

Old-timers bewail the death of vaudeville. Maybe a spark of life remains. If so, perhaps SPEBSQSA offers an elixir for its revival. Open with a good loud quartet ahead of the trained seals or Katzes' Performing Dogs, insert another foursome in the middle to offset the quiet of the Living Statues, and close with the big feature—what else but a male quartet?

It is possible that such a suggestion indicates favoritism coming from one who has participated in quartets as they introduced, and as they now preserve, musical Americana which a new generation continues to encourage.

PART FOUR

Musical Friendships— Priceless & Enduring

References for Preferences

Perennially, groups throughout the States and Canada present revivals of Old Times, and this will continue. It may be for a centennial celebration, an Old Settlers' Picnic, other civic activities, a minstrel-type or variety show, or whatever. Usually, the committee tries to add authenticity and color by including the music of the period to be revived. As has been pointed out, the designation of a song as an oldie depends upon one's age, so, the search for period material can be arduous and sometimes acrimonious. Quite naturally, younger members of the music committee consider any song of ten years ago as very old. Others may have World War II as their gauge. A small number remembers the First World War. An ancient on the committee may poo-poo such verdancy.

In addition to the dated pontifical selection here of the one thousand most *used* songs from the so-called "gay" '90's into the 1950's, there are shorter notations on such categories as transportation, songs of prohibition, drinking songs, and hymns as examples of others. Of course, in some cases this results in duplication, not too often I hope; also I hope that any who disagree with my selection of the most used group will have taken tranquilizers before knocking at my door.

"But," you say, "there's the song title, but—but where can I find the words and music? The festival's coming up next month." W-e-l-l, if you're lucky, you know someone or know someone who knows someone who has a stack of old pop music in the attic. You may not find the song you have in mind but you may discover one whose copyright date, at the bottom of the first page, is in the year or era you want (after, as I do, getting an erudite person to translate Roman numerals of the copyright year).

Collectors of old sheet music watch the newspapers for notices of estate sales. Very often, among the furniture and various items offered, there's a stack of old music. Collectors are also sharers. A notice in your newspaper about the need of period music for the festival is likely to set your phone ringing. Also, it's probable that a local radio station will be glad to cooperate.

Musical Friendships — Priceless and Enduring

Depending upon the interests of librarians, past and present, some libraries house collections that are treasuries for research. The county library at Buffalo was mentioned in the "Going Places" chapter, but its colossal content is not limited to songs about transportation. Though it's unlikely that your library has a comparable collection, it might have some of the books mentioned in Appendix F, with dates and song publishers' names. Usually, a publisher will reply to a request. Enclose with your letter a self-addressed stamped envelope as an accelerator.

Suppose that you need songs which antedate this century. Here are a few tested ones culled from the thousands.

1840's INTO 1890's

Erie Canal
Sweet Betsy from Pike
Grandma's Advice
Green Grow the Rushes
A Hunter Did a Hunting Go (among the leaves so green-o)
The Gypsy's Warning
Don't You Go, Tommy
The Sweet By and By
Sleep, Baby, Sleep
Her Golden Hair Was Hanging Down Her Back
Champagne Charlie
Where Is My Wandering Boy Tonight?
Golden Years Are Passing By
Nancy Lee
Paddle Your Own Canoe
Drunkard's Doom
A Hunting We Will Go
In Old Madrid
Santa Lucia
Take Back Your Gold
Just One Girl
Moth and the Flame
My Wild Irish Rose
Story of the Rose (Heart of My Heart)
Daisy Bell (Bicycle Built for Two)
Ta-ra-ra-boom-de-re
Fatal Wedding
Two Little Girls in Blue
Sunshine of Paradise Alley
Sweet Rosie O'Grady
Wedding March (Mendelssohn)
Ave Maria (Gounod)
Forgotten
Alice, Where Art Thou?
Church Across the Way
Annie Rooney
Won't You Come to My Tea Party?
I Don't Want to Play in Your Yard
Lass from the County Mayo
Girl I Loved in Sunny Tennessee
Maryland! My Maryland!
Whispering Hope
Sing Me a Song of the South
She'll Be Comin' 'Round the Mountain
Oh, Susanna
Old Folks at Home (Swanee River)
Jeannie With the Light Brown Hair
Little Brown Jug
I'll Take You Home Again, Kathleen
In the Gloaming
White Wings
After the Ball
America the Beautiful
Band Played On
Abide with Me
Battle Hymn of the Republic
When Johnny Comes Marching Home
When You and I Were Young, Maggie
Sweet Genevieve
Kerry Dance
There Is a Tavern in the Town
Drill, Ye Tarriers, Drill
Reuben and Rachel
Carry Me Back to Old Virginny
Still as the Night
Passing By
* *A Pretty Girl*

It seems appropriate to end with a girl song, since so many of those songs are about her. I'd like to write a book of comment, a thick one, confined entirely to that list. Many of these songs appear, by dates, in books mentioned in

* Sung by Della Fox in *Wang,* 1891, with DeWolfe Hopper, best known for his later spoken recording of "Casey at the Bat."

Appendix F here. That carries over, of course, to songs published in the first decade of this century, which will end the listing by dates. Scan the one thousand most *used* list of songs for those later than 1910.

1900 INTO 1910

Bird in a Gilded Cage
Goodbye, Dolly Gray
Just a-Wearying for You
Maiden with the Dreamy Eyes
Mighty Lak a Rose
Bill Bailey
In the Good Old Summertime
Mansion of Aching Hearts
Under the Bamboo Tree
Bedelia
Dear Old Girl
Hiawatha
Sweet Adeline
Toyland
Under the Anheuser Bush
Blue Bell
Give My Regards to Broadway
Meet Me in St. Louis, Louis
Yankee Doodle Boy
Put on Your Old Gray Bonnet
By the Light of the Silvery Moon
I Remember You
Yip-I-Addy-I-Ay
I Wish I Had a Girl
Red Wing
Napanee
Always in the Way
On a Sunday Afternoon
So Long, Mary
Ah, Sweet Mystery of Life
Sugar Moon
Under the Yum Yum Tree
Cheyenne
Everybody Works But Father
In My Merry Oldsmobile
In the Shade of the Old Apple Tree
My Gal Sal
Rufus Rastus Johnson Brown
Wait Till the Sun Shines, Nellie
Love Me, and the World Is Mine
Waltz Me Around Again, Willie
Where the River Shannon Flows
You're a Grand Old Flag
Glow Worm
School Days
Cuddle Up a Little Closer
Down in Jungle Town
Shine On, Harvest Moon
Take Me Out to the Ball Game
Casey Jones
I Wonder Who's Kissing Her Now
My Pony Boy
Meet Me Tonight in Dreamland
Don't Take Me Home
Rainbow
Be Sweet to Me, Kid
Pride of the Prairie
San Antonio
Sing Me to Sleep
Hello, Central, Give Me Heaven
Moon Has His Eyes on You
Call Me Up Some Rainy Afternoon
Two Little Love Bees
Let Me Call You Sweetheart

It's necessary to stop the little sampling of that incomparable musical decade somewhere; so why not on the song that, in my opinion, is the common denominator, popular-musically, to the most persons age twenty-five to ninety? It's sure-fire for audience participation, both words (approximately) and music, from a beach party to our largest auditoriums anywhere in the States or Canada.

Except to those who are really interested in our older songs or those who search the unknown for songs of a certain date or type, lists can be boring. To the rememberer, songs fascinate as they recall occasions, incidents, persons, and flavors of a year or an era. Since "References" is here primarily in an attempt to help those looking for period songs or songs related to classifications, we turn to song subjects. Our songs record almost every phase of living, so a compilation of all categories is impossible. Therefore, what follows is selective, with a few suggestions in each selection. In some cases the reference is within the lyrics rather than the title. Because the music committee is likely to recall most readily the songs of the 1940's, '50's, and '60's, the songs cited by category range from old to ancient, depending upon the viewer. The following are for concentrated reference. Some of them may have already popped up elsewhere here.

ANATOMICAL Let's start with anatomy: Hot Lips—Hair of Gold, Eyes of Blue—Heartaches—In the Garden of Your Heart—I Can't Forget Your Eyes—Your Eyes Have Told Me So—You've Got Your Mother's Big Blue Eyes—Ten Little Fingers and Ten Little Toes—All of Me—Body and Soul (totally)—Heart Bowed Down—Heart—There Goes My Heart.

ANIMALS Animals and a few birds and insects: Be My Little Baby Bumblebee—Old MacDonald Had a Farm—Twenty Froggies Went to School—Birdies' Ball—Brown Bird Singing—Who's Afraid of the Big Bad Wolf?—Three Little Pigs—Big Brown Bear—Monkey Doodle Dandy—Tale of the Kangaroo (a roo also appears in "Moonlight in Jungle Land," with a monkey maid, turtle dove, and chimpanzee)—Tale of the Bumblebee.

COLLEGIATE Collegiate songs: Sweetheart of Sigma Chi—Heidelberg—Betty Co-ed—Collegiate Sam—On Wisconsin—College Life—All American Girl—College Rhythm—Hail to Thee, Cornell (By Cayuga's . . .).

CHILDHOOD Children: Slumber Boat—His Lullaby—Rock-a-bye, Baby—Babes in the Wood—Jolly Old St. Nicholas—My Shadow—London Bridge—Kentucky Babe—Irish Lullaby—Drowsy Babe—All Aboard for Blanket Bay—Toyland—Sun Bonnet Sue—Won't You Come Over to My House?—Huckleberry Finn—Yama Yama Man (with Bessie McCoy in her clown suit).

DANCING About Dancing: Too Much Mustard—Everybody Two Step—Grizzly Bear—Dancing Around—Everybody's Doing It Now—Waltz You Saved for Me—Yiddisher Rag—Dancing with Tears in My Eyes—Charleston—Gaby Glide—Continental—Carioca—Cubanola Glide (When you do the).

DOWN Now *down* we go: Down Among the Sugar Cane—Down South—Down Among the Sheltering Palms—Down Home in Tennessee—Down on the Farm—'Way Down Yonder in the Cornfield—Down in the Old Cherry Orchard—Down Where: the Wurzburger Flows, the Cotton Blossoms Grow, the Swanee River Flows, the Blue Bells Grow, the Daisies Grow, It's Always June—and Down in the Coal Mine underneath the sod . . . That's far enough down.

DREAMS The dream songs could fill a page: Day Dreams—Bartlett's Dream—Dreaming—Beautiful Dreamer—When I Was a Dreamer—Did You Ever See a Dream Walking?—You Tell Me Your Dream—I'm Not Lazy I'm Just Dreamin'—Dream a Little Dream of Me—My Isle of Golden Dreams—Meet Me Tonight in Dreamland—Dream Days—Day Dreams, Visions of Bliss. Even Enrico Caruso wrote and recorded "Dreams of Long Ago."

Quite a group of songs related to Drinking appears earlier in the book. That applies also to foreign-language songs sung in English translation and to songs about Ireland. Here are a few non-Irish that need no translating.

FOREIGN Blue Bells of Scotland—Songs My Mother Taught Me—The Maple Leaf Forever—Men of Harlech—Sally in Our Alley—Loch Lomond—Campbells Are Comin'—Japanese Sandman—Chinatown—Hawaiian Butterfly—On the Shores of Italy—and the Chinese and the Russian Lullaby.

FLOWERS Now, with flower songs coming up (not down) we face a crisis. Your compiler would like to include at least thirty rose songs, some of them girl's names. But even roses could be cloying in such profusion. So every alternate title will be rosy: Jeannine I Dream in Lilac Time—Garland of Old Fashioned Roses—Tulip Time in Holland—Only a Rose—That's What the Daisies Say—Rose of No Man's Land—Poor Little Buttercup—My Baby Rose—Violet (Chin-Chin) and Violets of S.A.E., also Every Morn I Bring Thee and The Message of the—Rose, Fairest Rose—Where the Morning Glories Grow—Mighty Lak a Rose—Daisies Won't Tell—Beautiful Garden of Roses—Apple Blossom Time in Normandy—Belgian Rose—Lily of the Valley—Red Roses Bring Dreams of You—Tiptoe Through the Tulips—My Little Persian Rose—and two-in-one: When You Wore a Tulip (and I Wore a Big Red Rose), closing with the portmanteau Honeysuckle Rose.

G follows F for flowers, and G stands for girls' names in our popular songs. That way lies madness if we attempt to sample from "Annie Doesn't Live Here Any More" and "Anona" and "Aura Lee" through the feminine ranks that stretch beyond the horizon to "Zula Zong." Pick your own dozen or twenty or more. It'll take most adults only a minute or so.

HAPPINESS What about happy songs? Let's start with "Ain't We Got Fun" and a "Cheerful Little Earful" to introduce: Smiles—Singin' in the Rain—I Wake Up Smiling—Happy Days Are Here Again—When My Baby Smiles at Me—I've Got a Rainbow 'Round My Shoulder—Blue Skies—Save Your Sorrow for Tomorrow—Learn to Smile—Watch for the Silver Lining—Sing Hallelujah—all of which are "Painting the Clouds with Sunshine," or trying to.

We don't need any more hymns after that sentimental list that appeared 'way back there. And there was also quite a listing of the "I'm going back to" classification, including the yearning to be returning and learning about conditions down south.

LAZY S'pose you need a song for some character in the pageant. You might try any of these for fit: Please Go 'Way and Let Me Sleep—Lazy Bones—Oh, How I Hate to Get Up in the Morning—Lazy Mary, Will You Get Up—Don't Wake Me Up, I'm Dreaming—Lazy—I'm Not Lazy I'm Just Dreamin'.

LOVE NESTS Love nests dot the scenery everywhere in harmonyland—from a Tumble Down Shack in Athlone to Home Sweet Home. There's a Cottage Small by a Waterfall—here's a Little Gray Home in the West—the Bungalow Where the Red Red Roses Grow—an unidentified Little Bungalow an hour or so from anywhere—Little House o' Dreams—the Little Log Cabin in the Lane (some might say they prefer A Small Hotel)—the Little House Upon the Hill—all of them related to Feather Your Nest.

MEN'S There's nothing epicene about these songs for men: On the Road to Mandalay—Brown October Ale and the Armorer's Song from *Robin Hood*—Old Man River—Asleep in the Deep—Gentlemen Rankers (Kipling) which became We're Poor Little Lambs—When the Bell in the Lighthouse Rings Ding Dong—Your Land and My Land—Sunshine of Your Smile—Love Me, and the World Is Mine—I Love Life—In a Shanty in Old Shanty Town—and Give Me All of You, one of the best.

MOON My computer staff's latest report indicates that to sing all the moon and star songs requires about the time of flight, landing, and return by rocket, computed on Moon Light Saving Time. It's the Same Silv'ry Moon, Underneath the Stars, wooed by poets and songwriters for centuries. Look: Every Star Falls in Love with Its Mate—If All Moons Were Honeymoons—June Moon—Once in a Blue Moon—Lazy Moon—The Moon Has His Eyes on You —When the Harvest Moon Is Shining—Moonglow—Silver Moon—Shy Moon —When the Moon Comes over the Mountain—Carolina Moon—Stars of a Summer Night—Indiana Moon—Give Me the Moonlight, Give Me the Girl—Shine On, Harvest Moon—Moonbeams—Under the Harlem Moon—Stardust—Twinkle, Twinkle, Little Star—When the Moon Plays Peek-a-Boo—and, and, and...

RURAL If you want a song stemming from farm life, here are a few in rural settings: Mornin', Cy—Sweet Hortense—Farmer in the Dell—Down on the Farm—Reuben Tango Huskin' Bee—Suckin' Cider Through a Straw—When the Bees Are in the Hive—How Ya' Gonna Keep 'Em Down on the Farm?—Ioway—Wagon Wheel—Daisies in the Meadow—When the Harvest Days Are Over—Wal I Swan—I Want to Go Back to Michigan—and, of course, 'Way Down Yonder in the Cornfield.

TIMED And finally, what time is it, which day or month or season? When Day Is Done—At Sundown—All Alone Monday—Summertime—Three O'Clock in the Morning—At Dawning—On a Sunday Afternoon—When It's Springtime in the Rockies—World Is Waiting for the Sunrise—When the Sunset Turns the Ocean's Blue to Gold—Nighttime Down in Burgundy—Nights of Gladness—When the Angelus Is Ringing—The Hour That Gave Me You—June Night—Mine (in the lyrics)—September Song and September in the Rain—April Showers—Maytime—When the Leaves Begin to Turn—Five Minutes More—When It's Darkness on the Delta—Apple Blossom Time —and Now the Day Is Over, night is drawing nigh.

Success to the festival, with a hope that it won't rain.

The Way I See It*

"I disagree, but I shall defend to the death your right to your opinion."
—attributed to Voltaire

Genuine appreciation of the classical need not hinder nor end a love affair with the populars, or vice versa. Coexistence can be more rewarding than isolation within either sphere. A city dweller may leave his steam heat or air conditioning, electrical conveniences, and twice-daily newspapers to canoe or packsack into temporary discomforts and joys that make the city and his homecoming the more inviting.

Analogously, in the rarer atmosphere that nurtures the sequoia trees on the Sierras, visitors are likely to linger fascinated by the grandeur. Association with those world-famous sequoias doesn't lessen by a millimeasure one's admiration of the crewel work on a dwarf fern's frond. Few people will, or can, climb or drive to the mile-high remoteness of the sequoia forest. But millions can, and do, revel in the splashed colors wherever frost touches hard maples nearby and turns the ash's green to purple. Great trees have great beauty. So does a tiny pink arbutus. In nature, music, or elsewhere, true comparison is like-to-like. Sports cars are judged within their own class. It is incongruous to compare feather-light "Nola" to a Wagnerian truck.

Disagreements among musicians and music critics about the merits of a composition or its presentation show that, as yet, no calculator has been invented to evaluate music. A series of trials, carried to the highest courts, would prove only that each judge and panel has individual opinions. The evidence that a musical selection is worthwhile lies in the continuity of its repetition because of public preference. When a second and a third generation want it repeated, it's good music regardless of who wrote it, when or where, or performed or reviewed it originally.

Vocational association with music and study of its anatomy can increase understanding and sharpen perceptions. In any field, the outsider who belittles the professional's conclusions is likely to do so out of ignorance. But despite his training and experience, the musician's only tangible evidence of the musical merit of a composition lies in its repetition because of public preference or amateurs' use by free will. The professional may be called upon to perform

* Title of a column of comment started by the author in the *Harmonizer* in the early 1940's.

what he doesn't particularly like; others are free to play, replay, sing, or whistle what they prefer.

The baseball umpire has opportunity to invoke visual evidence. But, even there, photographs have shown a runner nipped, as the grandstands roared "safe," or the opposite. A music critic may call a strike while those in the audience continue to believe that it was a ball. Hence the flops in musical history, or vice versa. Majorities in the nation's grandstands decide eventually whether "Finlandia" or a Stephen Foster song or any other, classical or popular, old-style or new-style, will continue as Liszt's "Rhapsody," "Tea for Two," and "April Showers" have continued because each is good in its class.

In the 1700's, the importance of listeners and avocationists (whose appreciations can be as great as their virtuosities are limited) gave Joseph Addison a theme for comment in his *Spectator*. He wrote that a song that is "the delight of the common people" cannot fail to "please all as are not unqualified by their affectations or ignorance." Continuing in the double negative that was the affectation of his era, he added: "It is impossible that anything that be universally tested and approved by the multitude ... hath not in it some aptness to please the mind of man." Affectation among the few who insist upon maintaining a stout fence between classical and popular may be proof of their ignorance of what lies beyond the self-imposed boundary line. I am not unsure that Addison would be unappreciative of lack of disagreement with him, two centuries later.

The way I see it, I shall continue to disregard the dictum of any who dismiss the delightful "I Could Have Danced All Night" or Lehar's "Melody of Love" as merely popular, with the implication that all popular music is trash. I shall also deplore the ignorance of one who says that Grieg is just another one of those highbrows, though once this commentator had to be dragged to a concert. Those who dislike dogs are likely to be in the small minority whose knowledge of canines is limited to observation through thermopane of the pillar-to-post urban dog patrol. Many musical prejudices are just that, prejudgments, jumping to conclusions without acquaintanceship, condemning Puccini's *Butterfly* or barbershop harmony by name or class without a hearing. We can miss a horde of musical treasure by depending upon others' approval before investigating. Great numbers of us evaluate musical worth by report or association. As to the first, we like a composition but hesitate to say so after someone, whose comment we respect, has turned thumbs down. Or we get nothing from an opus, yet we feel that we should because so many others say they like it. It's beautifully correct to them, but so's your old multiplication table. Ought ain't is.*

Association can also help to make up our minds for us. The fact that a song is from Opera, with the big O, may place it upon a pedestal. Yet in some cases, it could be the aura of association rather than melodious qualities back of the high repute. I shall defend to the death your right to your opinion that McCormack's popular "Macushla" excels the trite "Home to Our Mountains" as sung by Caruso in the opera *Il Trovatore,* both as music and in its execution. Other defenders may communicate with this commentator c/o The Dog House.

Association can influence more than the public's opinion. A few years ago,

* "Songs We Like—Or Ought to Like?" *Music Journal,* September 1955.

soprano Helen Traubel was reprimanded by Metropolitan Opera's management for singing in a nightclub. According to the press, she replied that artistic dignity is not a matter of where one sings. She said that in other countries our wealth of popular music would be called "folk," and highly regarded. This American popular, or folk, she believed, was as much in the province of American artists as Beethoven. She added: "To assert that art can be found in the Metropolitan but not in a nightclub is rank snobbery that underrates both the taste of the public and the talents of the composers."

Theorizing upon association and report, here is an opinion about probability. More than a half century ago, "Oh, Dry Those Tears," 1901, wasn't a national hit but it was on great numbers of pianos and was heard often in public, usually sung by a contralto, with violin or mellow'cello obligato. If the song had been translated then into Italian or French and interpolated into an opera, as DeKoven inserted "Oh, Promise Me" into the light opera *Robin Hood*—and if during the succeeding years it had been glamourized by opera stars, their orchestras, and stage settings, and by famous concert artists—the song would be included today among the Classics approved by the Right People and hummed by the multitudes, as "Barcarolle" and the "Toreador Song" are recognized. Many others have had the same potential as "Oh, Dry Those Tears," but lacked a press agent (an archaic term for an image-making public-relations counselor). Of course, they would be square currently among the juniors. But rock 'n' roll and folk fans constitute special groupings, as in ragtime, jazz and its subdivisions, rather than recurring national cross sections.

Music's medical record includes poxes that have afflicted it from time to time. Antibodies, developing within the musical systems of listeners, subdued the diseases that, at times, have been endemic. No musical serum can provide permanent immunity, but the patient always recovers. After recovery, the victim may retain traces of the infection, and perhaps that is good. George Bernard Shaw, who was music critic for two London newspapers before attaining dramatic and literary fame, said that the development of modern harmony in any generation is a history of growth of the ear's tolerance of chords that sounded discordant and senseless to most musicians when first heard. That is borne out by the experience of Bach and later composers. During Bach's lifetime, he was as far out as Arnold Schönberg was to his generation, two hundred years later, and still is to most.*

The physics of musical sounds are well understood: as example, the physicist's co-incidence of harmonics that makes a barbershop chord "ring." But why one sequence of sounds appeals to one but repels another remains a mystery. There's more than G.B.S.'s ear accommodation. Of course the listener's mood has some bearing, usually temporarily. However, a sustained national mood can influence musical output and acceptance. The fireworks that sizzle from a million record players today are related to national conditions, as we follow the news. Some of our current music's roots were planted as far back as World War I and nourished by its aftermath.

In *The Greek Way* (Norton), Edith Hamilton wrote that the direction in which a nation goes affects its arts. The musical arts offer proof, particularly in the segment of popular music. Songs of our own Model T era prolonged much of the conventional music and the thought and attitudes, customs and

* Recommended: Peter Paul Fuchs, "In Defense of Modern Music," *Music Journal,* November–December issue, 1959.

environment of horse-and-buggy days. After World War I, our national tempo accelerated like our newer cars and single-winged planes, and since World War II our total tempo has sped furiously into the current jet era. The popular music of both periods shows the effects of impacts made upon it by our national life. Today's furious speeds of change, without certainty that the nation travels in the right direction, affect melodies and harmonies but particularly instrumentation and lyrics. The changes are apparent to adults who accept TV and radio as a way of life. I commented earlier that much of the music heard, and that includes some interpretations of longtime classics in today's concerts, is disturbed music, and I repeat, "So are we."

Apart from that, it must be taken for granted that in every generation impatient and angry young men protest conventional concepts of order, and that includes the dry-as-dust musical modes of their predecessors. It has always been so, and it will continue. The last three words constitute the only gem of wisdom between these covers.

Inevitably, there will be revivals and partial throwbacks to some of our earlier musical patterns. The late 1960's provide an example of the influence of older square harmonies, apparent in advanced rock circles where harmony sounds quite different from the 1940's, 1950's, and even early 1960's when rock 'n' roll gave the effects of a busy bulldozer operating with sticking valves and cracked gears and faulty ignition. (Rock fans will resent that—*not* the reference to the bulldozer, but to the influence and acceptance of any musical form older than yesterday.)

It is good to have musical preferences. Sincere selectivity doesn't necessarily indicate snobbishness or ignorance. We like certain sounds so well that faced by a one-way rocket trip to the moon, we'd select the few recordings allowed to the moon manifest, instead of leaving selection to a federal office of American Culture and Enforcement of Music We Ought to Like. After sampling most kinds and liking them in varying degrees over three quarters of a century, it's probable that I'd take as many carefully selected discs of Berlin, Chopin, and Herbert as clearance would allow. But because personal participation is more important than supine listening, a musical instrument would take precedence over any recordings. (The Thousand Tops in Their Times and more thousands take up no space whatever stowed away in the memory locker.) "Which instrument would you choose?" All I know is that on that trip it wouldn't be a grand piano.

The selection of music with which we'd be willing to spend the rest of our lives on the moon may be as illogical as some friendships. Who can define all the qualities, values, and sometimes incongruities covered by "friend"? Lasting allegiances to musical sequences that are carried as regularly and easily as a wristwatch are just as indefinable. They are opinions, and sometimes incongruous ones. But there they are, personal friendships beyond price and musical friendships that endure for reasons beyond factual explanation.

Appendices

Avalon to Zanzibar

As a result of World War I in which a million young men had their first view beyond the home horizon, the years since are thickly dotted with songs about faraway places. The following range over the States and beyond, including in some cases the traveler's intent or desire to return. Many more are in the Tops in Their Times, the reminder list for short memories when the urge to sing or play is frustrated by inability to recall titles.

Avalon
Yona from Arizona *
Alabamy Bound
Anywhere I Wander
Allegheny Moon
In the Land of the Buffalo
Somewhere on Broadway
Broadway Rose
Back Back Back to Baltimore
Bali Ha'i
Beyond the Sea
Come to the Land of Bohemia
Night Time down in Burgundy
Bimini Bay
Nightingale Sang in Berkeley Square
Put Me Off at Buffalo
Down in Bombay
Bay of Biscay, O!
California, Here I Come
Moonlight on the Colorado
Isle of Capri
I Want to Be in Chicago Town
Chicago That Toddlin' Town
Riding down the Canyon
Carolina in the Morning
Cryin' for the Carolines
White Cliffs of Dover
Duna
All Aboard for Dixie Land
When It's Night Time in Dixie Land
I'm on My Way to Dublin Bay
On the Rocky Road to Dublin
East of the Sun and West of the Moon
Ebb Tide
Far Away Places
Don't Fence Me In
Two Tickets to Georgia
Everything is Peaches Down in Georgia
Georgia
Georgia on My Mind
In Dear Old Georgia
Galway Bay
Moonlight on the Ganges
In the Valley of the Hudson
Hindustan
Tulip Time in Holland
There's a Girl in Havana
Homing
When You're a Long Long Way from Home

* Not the same as "Anona" discussed on page 61.

Song of India
My Idaho
Indiana
In a Little Red Barn on a Farm in Indiana
Can't Get Indiana Off My Mind
Ioway
Jersey Bounce
Over on the Jersey Side
Blue Juniata
Killarney and You
Kansas City Kitty
I've Got a Gal in Kalamazoo
Lazy Lou'siana Moon
Limehouse Blues
Moon of Manakoora
By the Waters of Minnetonka
Down Mexico Way
On Miami Shore
Memphis Blues
Mississippi
At a Mississippi Cabaret
In My Castle on the Nile
Along the Navajo Trail
Streets of New York
In Old Oklahoma
Pride of the Prairie
April in Paris
Last Time I Saw Paris
Rolling Down to Rio
Rio Rita
Where the River Shannon Flows
By the River Saint Marie
Away Down South in Heaven
San Antonio
Sierra Sue
A Lane in Spain
Spain
In a Little Spanish Town
The River Seine
South Sea Island Magic
Shanghai
There's a Place That I Know Where the Sweet Tulips Grow
Take Me to that Swanee Shore
I'm Going South
Sioux City Sue
Tripoli
Trade Winds
Timbuctoo
In Sunny Tennessee
Back Home in Tennessee
Deep in the Heart of Texas
Tuxedo Junction
Vienna Dreams
On the Beach at Waikiki
There's a Home in Wyoming
In Zanzibar

APPENDIX B

"The Missouri Waltz" is cited in James J. Fuld's *American Popular Music—Reference Book 1875–1950,* supplement page five. "The music has been variously claimed to have been composed by, in addition to the two mentioned above [John Valentine Eppel—copyrighted under the name of Frederick Knight Logan 1914] Dab Hannah or Henry Clay Cooper, or even to have been a traditional Negro melody." He refers also to the *Missouri Historical Review,* Vol. 40 (1946), pp. 443–44 and to a story by Justin L. Faherty, "Mystery of the Missouri Waltz," St. Louis *Globe Democrat,* October 21, 1945.

On June 26, 1959, I wrote Fuld that I had noted his comment, that I had not seen the *Review* reference or the Faherty story "but I doubt that it contained this." Letter to Fuld:

"In 1911 or 1912 John Eppel, orchestra leader, Boone, Iowa, introduced a new waltz while playing for a dance at the Sigma Alpha Epsilon house (Ames, Iowa). It brought encores and more.... As part of freshman stunt night, 1912, Jack Porterfield (now of Mountain Home, Arkansas) and George H. Lewis, then of Los Angeles, wrote topical words to the new waltz that everyone was humming or whistling or trying to:

Sigma Alpha Epsilon, to you we'll all be true
Sigma Alpha Epsilon, for you a lot we'll do
You bring back fond mem'ries of good fellows met
Of the good times we've had that we'll never forget
(Repeat first two lines.)
So smoke up your pipes, boys, and let's have a song
To bring back the dear days now gone.

"The upshot—John always played it for the ΣAE dances, the ΣAEs sang the words to it, the girls liked it so much that, when John played his 'Missouri Waltz' at the other frat houses, the girls who had learned the ΣAE words would sing them, to the discomfiture of their escorts." That ends the letter to Fuld.

APPENDIX C

About this time, Samuel Hopkins Adams wrote a series of magazine articles which exposed many of the fraudulent claims in the patent-medicine industry. These exposures of what the medical profession knew, and many in the public suspected, led to the passage of the Pure Food and Drug Act of 1906. About Peruna, Hopkins had reported that it was banned on Indian reservations because it was intoxicating.

APPENDIX D

The Louisiana Purchase Exposition was held in St. Louis in 1904. On April 30, 1803, the purchase, acquired by treaty with France and about $15,000,000, comprised the territory west of the Mississippi that it now divided among thirteen states. The purchase was ratified by Congress on October 21, 1803.

The Lewis and Clark expedition to explore the lands known only to a few hunters and trappers started from St. Louis, Missouri, on May 14, 1804. After reaching the mouth of the Columbia River on the West Coast, the expedition returned to St. Louis on September 23, 1806.

About the exploratory trip, the *Patrick Gass Journal* of 1807 carries this note by the publishers:

It will not be forgotten that an immense sum of treasure has been expended in the purchase of this country, and that it is now considered as belonging to the United States. Here at no distant period settlements may be formed, and in a much shorter term than has elapsed since the first were made in America, from which hath arisen a great, powerful and independent nation, the posterity of the present inhabitants of the Union may unfurl the standard of independence on the plains of the Missouri and Columbia.

As evidence of the youthfulness of that great, powerful, and independent nation, President Jefferson was still living when my grandfather, James Gooch, was born to be one of those who unfurled the standard near, if not precisely on, the plains of the Missouri.

APPENDIX E

Two limericks are quoted here, the first one to show that the Thring melody can fit either ta-tum (iamb) or ta-ta tum (anapest) rhythms found in limericks. The first is the oldest limerick of my acquaintance:

There was a fair girl from Nantucket
Had a bustle as big as a bucket
She filled it with oats
And some mean billy goats
Came right up behind her 'n tuck it

Both ta-tum and ta-ta tum rhythms are in that one.

The other I like particularly because it recalls so many pleasant memories of Ted Robinson, lexicographer and versifier who wrote a poem, most of them gems, five days a week for about thirty years to head his "Philosopher of Folly" column in Cleveland's *Plain Dealer*.

Latin

In Creta est virgo est nata
Munditia tam celebrata
Ut, lecto aggressa,
Stet capite Cressa
Ne pedibus sit maculata

American

There was a young lady from Crete
Who was so exceedingly neat
That, rising from bed,
She would stand on her head
Lest she should be soiled on her feet.

APPENDIX F

Depending upon one's interests, the following can be helpful when delving into old sheet music.

Dichter, Harry. Catalogues and pamphlets. Harry Dichter, 7332 Brentwood Ave., Philadelphia, Pa., 19151.
Catalogues and pamphlets include dates of publishing, composers, and frequently prices of old popular songs as far back as Colonial times. Mr. Dichter also offers reprints of songs by subject matter and composers.

Fuld, James J. *American Popular Music*. Harry Dichter, 7332 Brentwood Ave., Philadelphia, Pa. 19151, 1956. 103 pp.
A reference book of first printings of songs from 1875 into the 1950's. Excellent as far as it goes but "too thin," as I told the author when it came out.

Fuld, James J. *The Book of World Famous Music*. New York, Crown Publishers, Inc., 1966. 564 pp.
"Information about almost 1,000 songs and other compositions including the first lines of the music and words"—popular, folk, and classical, including a wealth of information about classical instrumental music, much about composers and lyricists when facts exist. Lore and speculation are identified as such. Already in its third printing a year after publication. A book for professional and amateur musicians and for those on the periphery of music.

McNamara, Daniel I. *ASCAP Biographical Dictionary of Composers, Authors and Publishers.* New York, Thomas Y. Crowell Co., 1952. 636 pp.
Alphabetically arranged by composers' names, contains their birthplace, vital statistics, brief biographical notes, and principal compositions, including lyricists' names.

Mattfeld, Julius. *Variety Music Cavalcade,* rev. ed. Englewood Cliffs, N. J., Prentice-Hall, Inc., 1964. 713 pp.
Lists selected popular songs by years, composers, lyricists, and publishers. Splendid summation of historical events, Colonial times into the 1960's, by Abel Green, editor of *Variety.*

Soneck, Oscar George Theodore. *A Bibliography of Early Secular American Music.* Revised by William Treat Upton. Washington, D.C., Library of Congress Music Division, 1945. 517 pp.
Covers period before the 1800's.

Spaeth, Sigmund. *A History of Popular Music in America.* New York, Random House, 1948. 729 pp.
Selected songs chronologically from Colonial times with comments on many of them, their writers or performers. Also a chronological list without comment. The Foreword alone is worth the price to those who point with pride to much of our popular music.

APPENDIX G

About *Casey Jones* and *Ingineer Joe*—In the January 1957 issue of *Music Journal,* I commented upon "Casey Jones," 1909, the song that commemorates John L. Jones, the railroad engineer whose monument in Jackson, Mississippi, carries these words: "To the memory of the locomotive engineer whose name as Casey Jones became part of folklore and the American language." * Some have believed that the lyrics' theme came from a Negro who worked with Jones and who reshaped an older, folk-type song.

In the *Journal* article, I set down the words of "Ingineer Joe" which could be "Casey's" prototype, though there is no assurance. It was sung in France by a Negro labor battalion during World War I. Clevelander Charles E. Bailey wrote it down as sung by a group as a work song. It may be a variant from "Casey" just as "Night Shades Are Falling," in the chapter about Negro songs, evolved from an unknown ditty, perhaps several. Here are the four verses that were in *Music Journal.*

* Sigmund Spaeth, *History of Popular Music in America.*

In-gen-eer Joe was a good in-gen-eer. He told his fire-man
he need-n't fear. All that he need-ed was a -wood and coal.

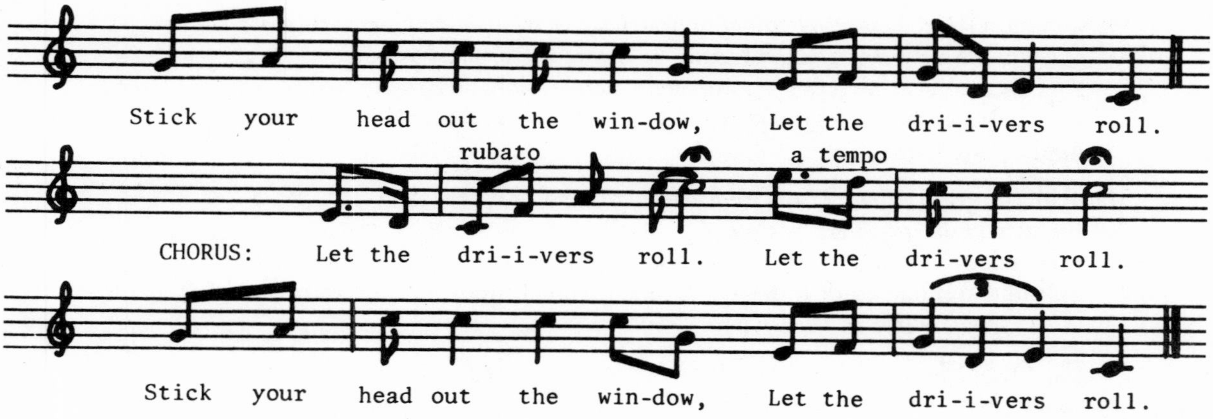

The change of Joe to Richard is characteristic of old folk ballads. The reference to Jay Gould, 1836–92, whose financial manipulations triggered the "Black Friday" panic of September 24, 1869, gives some credence to the possibility that "Joe" was already old when "Casey" was written in 1909.

APPENDIX H

Unlike much society lore, the birth date of the Woodshed idea is on record in a note to Secretary Adams, January 17, 1949: "King [President O. H. King Cole] doesn't know it but he has an unappointed . . . committee without portfolio working toward making one phase of Buffalo [site of the June 1949 convention] a joyous one. . . . The committee was born at breakfast yesterday [at the Board's winter meeting in Toledo] and consists of Charlie Merrill [Charles M., then immediate past president, now a judge of the United States Circuit Court, San Francisco] and me, who are going to devote the next five months to providing for the individual member who wants to sing but doesn't attend Buffalo as part of an organized quartet . . . your committee suggests that a room at a convenient point, such as one on the mezzanine [in Buffalo Statler] be designated by a big sign "THE WOODSHED—No Organized Quartets Need Apply."

Adams and Cole endorsed the idea. The former wrote me that it coincided with a general suggestion he'd had from Harold Gray of the Traverse City, Michigan, chapter. On January 20 I suggested to Adams that President Cole appoint Merrill, Gray, and me to prepare the Woodshed at Buffalo.

APPENDIX I

Champion quartets by year, location of contest, name of quartet and chapter represented:

YEAR	AT	NAME OF QUARTET AND CHAPTER	PRESIDENT	RESIDENCE
1939	Tulsa	Bartlesville Barflies Bartlesville, Okla.	Rupert I. Hall	Tulsa, Okla.
1940	New York City	Flat Foot Four Oklahoma City, Okla.	Rupert I. Hall	Tulsa, Okla.
1941	St. Louis	Chord Busters Tulsa, Okla.	Dr. Norman F. Rathert	St. Louis, Mo.
1942	Grand Rapids	Elastic Four Chicago, Ill.	Carroll P. Adams	Detroit, Mich.
1943	Chicago	Four Harmonizers Chicago, Ill.	Harold B. Staab	Northampton, Mass.
1944	Detroit	Harmony Halls Grand Rapids, Mich.	Harold B. Staab	Northampton, Mass.
1945	Detroit	Misfits Chicago, Ill.	Phil W. Embury	Warsaw, N. Y.
1946	Cleveland	Garden State Quartet Jersey City, N. J.	Phil W. Embury	Warsaw, N. Y.
1947	Milwaukee	Doctors of Harmony Elkhart, Ind.	Frank H. Thorne	Chicago, Ill.
1948	Oklahoma City	Pittsburghers Pittsburgh, Pa.	Charles M. Merrill	Reno, Nev.
1949	Buffalo	Mid-States Four Chicago, Ill.	O. H. King Cole	Sheboygan, Wis.
1950	Omaha	Buffalo Bills Buffalo, N. Y.	O. H. King Cole	Sheboygan, Wis.
1951	Toledo	Schmitt Brothers Manitowoc, Wis.	Jerry D. Beeler	Evansville, Ind.
1952	Kansas City	Four Teens Scott Air Force Base, Ill.	James F. Knipe	Cleveland, Ohio
1953	Detroit	Vikings Rock Island, Ill.	Edwin S. Smith	Wayne, Mich.
1954	Washington	Orphans Wichita, Kan.	John Z. Means	Manitowoc, Wis.
1955	Miami	Four Hearsemen Amarillo, Tex.	Berney Simner	St. Louis, Mo.
1956	Minneapolis	The Confederates Memphis, Tenn.	Arthur A. Merrill	Schenectady, N. Y.
1957	Los Angeles	Lads of Enchantment Albuquerque, N. M.	Rowland F. Davis	New York, N. Y.
1958	Columbus	Gay Notes Tulsa, Okla.	Joseph E. Lewis	Dallas, Tex.

YEAR	AT	NAME OF QUARTET AND CHAPTER	PRESIDENT	RESIDENCE
1959	Chicago	Pitchikers Springfield, Mo.	Joseph E. Lewis	Dallas, Tex.
1960	Dallas	Evans Quartet Salt Lake City, Utah	Clarence F. Jalving	Holland, Mich.
1961	Philadelphia	Sun Tones Miami, Fla.	John B. Cullen	Washington, D. C.
1962	Kansas City	Gala Lads Alhambra, Calif.	Louis Laurel	El Paso, Tex.
1963	Toronto	Town & Country Four Pittsburgh, Pa.	S. Wayne Foor	Rochester, N. Y.
1964	San Antonio	The Sidewinders Riverside, Calif.	Dan Waselchuk	Green Bay, Wis.
1965	Boston	Four Renegades Chicago, Ill. & Gary, Ind.	Albert L. Smith, Jr.	Fort Worth, Tex.
1966	Chicago	Auto Towners Dearborn, Mich.	R. A. Wright	Altadena, Calif.
1967	Los Angeles	Four Statesmen	James Steedman	Kenmore, N. Y.
1968	Cincinnati	Western Continentals	Wesley R. Meier	San Diego, Calif.
1969	St. Louis	Mark IV	Robert D. Gall	Independence, Mo.
1970	Atlantic City	(Competition held after this book was printed)	Wilbur D. Sparks	Alexandria, Va.

APPENDIX J

Ring Lardner's Addiction to Harmony * Midwesterners read Ring Lardner in Chicago's *Inter-Ocean* and later his "Wake of the News" in the *Tribune* before he deserted sports writing for book writing. Few know his attainments in the field of informal music for fun. What he contributed musically was pure amateur. What he wrote about amateur harmonists was the work of a skilled pro.

He had the ear for off-the-cuff singing and a bass voice that rumbled. Somehow it was in keeping with his gauntness. When the moon came over the mountain in sufficient proof and quantity, he and three others might continue to search for the lost chord until dawn.

Dr. Sigmund Spaeth asked Lardner to write the Foreword to *Barber Shop Ballads* (1925—out of print) in which Spaeth set down the first arrangements and recordings ever made of barbershop quartets Americanus, with Spaeth singing baritone.

Lardner referred to the writer of the lyrics of "Honey—bless your heart" as a man of few words. Regarding "Mandy Lee," another catch-as-catch-can favorite, he dwelt upon the disharmony that often erupts on next-to-the-last Lee, and stated: "Only once in my radiant career have I been in an unpre-

* Adapted from *The Harmonizer,* July–August 1963.

meditated quartet in which everybody was right on those two songs." That was with three members of the Cornell (New York) Glee Club. "How I happened to be singing with them will remain my secret and theirs." He added that singing "Honey" was "like corn liquor and co-educational poker games. It generally ends in a brawl."

Had Lardner thought to do it, he'd have pointed out that eruptions in singing "Honey" break out, almost invariably, at the end of the line: "I've done been true, my gal, TO YOU." That is because uneducated or obstinate leads sing the melody of "to you" as a descent from "do" to "sol." The insipid pale and anemic major chord that results shatters the morale, as well as tempers, of three others who had been anticipating a blend of tenor, bari, and bass into a melody rise from "la" to "do" in a soul-satisfying seventh chord so rich that they'd have repeated it four times had it jelled. Eventually it does, repeatedly.

Lardner recommended severe punishment for a lead who says he knows a song when he doesn't. He reserved special scorn for the "man who thinks bass is just a lead, two, three, or six octaves lower than melody." Sportswriter Ring Lardner could hold down second bass with any pennant-winning four-part team today.

Index

Index

Index

Index

Index